READINGS OF *THE WRECK*

Essays in Commemoration of
the Centenary of G.M. Hopkins'
The Wreck of the Deutschland

Edited by Peter Milward, S.J.
assisted by Raymond Schoder, S.J.

LOYOLA UNIVERSITY PRESS

1976

LIBRARY OF CONGRESS
CATALOGING IN PUBLICATION DATA

Readings of "The Wreck"

Includes bibliographical references.
1. Hopkins, Gerard Manley, 1844-1889. *The Wreck of the Deutschland.*   I. Milward, Peter, 1925-   II. Schoder, Raymond V., 1916-

PR4803. H44W78   821'.8 [B]   76-29714

ISBN 0-8294-0249-7

Cover by Deborah Brown Callahan

About this book

Readings of "The Wreck" was set by Black Dot Typographers, Inc. The text is 10/12 Souvenir Light; the reduced matter, 9/11; and the notes, 8/10.

It was printed by Photopress, Inc., on Warren Olde Style 60-pound paper and bound by The Engdahl Company.

The reduced price of this book was made possible by a generous grant from the Condon Fund.

CONTENTS

Preface

We live in an age of centenaries—especially literary ones. The occasions commemorated are usually the births and deaths of great writers, such as Shakespeare (1964) and Milton (1974); and commemorative volumes are not infrequently produced, as is only appropriate. It is, however, less common to commemorate the centenary of an individual masterpiece—and still less in the form of a published symposium. Yet this is just what is being done (I almost said "perpetrated") in the present volume, which celebrates neither the birth nor the death of Gerard Manley Hopkins (1844-1889), but his unique poem *The Wreck of the Deutschland*. (The wreck itself, that is, the first striking of the sandbank, occurred about 5:00 A.M. on Monday, December 6, 1875; and the disaster to human lives, including those of the five nuns commemorated in the poem, the following morning, December 7. The actual composition of the poem must have preoccupied Hopkins during his subsequent leisure moments, especially in the Christmas vacation of that year and the Easter vacation of the following year. The date of its completion is uncertain; but an appropriate date would be April 16, 1876, the feast of Easter, which is recalled in the concluding stanzas of the poem.)

There is, however, ample justification (I venture to maintain) for a volume of this kind, in view of the immense amount of literary and other interest shown both in the poet and in his poem during the past fifty years or so—since it was first published to the world, not by his fellow Jesuits, but by his agnostic friend Robert Bridges in 1918. At that time Bridges referred to it as "a great dragon folded in the gate to forbid all entrance," standing as it did at the head of his "Poems 1876-1889." All the same, the "dragon" has since shown a strange power no less of fascinating than of repelling prospective readers, a *mysterium fascinans et tremendum*. The more it is studied by preceding generations, the more (it seems) is left to be studied by generations to come, till it proves, like the plays of Shakespeare himself, to be well-nigh inexhaustible in its variety and profundity of implication—like a great dragon folded in coil upon coil.

It was only a few years ago that Hopkins studies received a further impetus (if further was needed) by the foundation of the Hopkins Society in England—and (I might add) by the foundation of a similar, though independent, society about the same time on the opposite side of the globe in Japan. Each society has since been producing its regular annual publications; and, more recently, a *Hopkins Quarterly* has been inaugurated in America. In such a situation it was natural for some Hopkins scholars to conceive the plan of a symposium of essays to commemorate the approaching centenary of *The Wreck of the Deutschland*; and it was equally natural for them to entrust the task of editorship to the editor of the fourth edition of Hopkins' *Poems*, Professor Norman MacKenzie, of Queen's University in Canada.

This task, indeed, he undertook for a time; and he had already contacted several contributors (including myself), when he found that increasing pressure of academic duties would not allow him to continue. In fact, at that point, early in 1973, it seemed that the project would have to be abandoned—with no immediate likelihood of a publisher. Those few who had already submitted their contributions (including myself) were advised to look for publication elsewhere—in the newly established *Hopkins Quarterly,* for instance. That summer, however, I happened to be passing through America on my way to England, on sabbatical leave from Japan. I took the opportunity of visiting Professor MacKenzie at his home in Kingston, Ontario; and there we had much to discuss both on Hopkins in general and on this wrecked project in particular—whether it could not be salvaged even at this late hour. Then I went on to England, where I also had the opportunity of discussing the matter with the secretary of the Hopkins Society, Father Alfred Thomas, S.J. It was he who, at the suggestion of Professor MacKenzie, invited me to take over the task of editing the volume. After some hesitation, considering the remoteness of Japan from the academic and publishing worlds of England and America, I accepted—somewhat in the spirit of fools who "step in where angels fear to tread," or of blind men who (as we say in Japan) "have no fear of treading on a snake."

From Professor MacKenzie and Father Thomas I received a useful list of names and addresses of likely contributors, most of them authors of recognized works on Hopkins, as well as the names of one or two possible publishers. But my first problem was to devise some comprehensive plan for the symposium which I might present to the contributors in soliciting their contributions. Otherwise the result would be something too chaotic for any publisher, especially in these troubled times, even to consider. It seemed to me important for the unity of the symposium that each writer should write his or her part with some notion of the whole work in mind. At first, I played with the idea of getting each to take one or two stanzas of the poem, at least as a starting point for a more general approach. This would, I thought, have the advantage of providing a unified framework for the inevitably diversified contributions. On the other hand, it had the obvious disadvantage of savoring too much of Procrusteanism; and so I abandoned it.

Then it occurred to me to invite contributions of a less academic, more personal nature, considering (with Newman) that the true appreciation of literature is subjective rather than objective. I reflected that Hopkins scholars, in particular, should welcome such an approach to a symposium on *The Wreck of the Deutschland,* partly because Hopkins' own approach to poetry was so intensely personal and partly because Hopkins studies today seem to have become rather too impersonal. On a more practical level, I thought such a plan would attract a wider circle of readers, and thereby many a prospective publisher with his eye on the prospective market. I therefore sent out a circular letter to the proposed contributors, explaining my plan; and I was most gratified by their favorable response. Only a few, while undertaking to contribute, expressed some reservations about the subjective approach; and a few others, while welcoming the approach, expressed their regret at being unable for various reasons to contribute. Those who accepted also submitted (as requested) the particular approach they proposed to take, with a provisional title—in many cases borrowing it from the words of the poet himself.

It was now my task to put these proposals together in the form of a provisional list of contents; and I accordingly arranged them under four main headings, representing the different approaches to (or readings of) *The Wreck* I discerned in them: 1) Theological Readings; 2) Structural Readings; 3) Semantic Readings; and 4) Biographical Readings—with three or four contributions neatly grouped in each division. This further suggested the general title for the symposium, *Readings of The Wreck,* which had (for me, at least) the additional advantage of alliteration, and which alone (in the general wreck of this second plan) I have retained. Not that even then was I altogether content with so schematic an arrangement, which again savored of Procrusteanism. But it at least provided me with a plan which I could propose to the contributors and within which they could proceed with the composing of their contributions. It was also a convenient plan I could propose to prospective publishers, since it was no less important to obtain their interest than that of my contributors—and this was by no means so easy a task. For scholars are notoriously more ready to write books and articles than publishers are to publish them.

After several fruitless attempts to find a publisher, in the midst of the economic crisis of 1974, I received invaluable assistance from Father Raymond Schoder, S.J., of Loyola University of Chicago—one of the promised contributors to this volume, who was already collaborating with me on another Hopkinsian volume to be published in the same year under the title *Landscape and Inscape*. With the help of a timely subsidy, he introduced the project to Father Vincent Horrigan, S.J., director of Loyola University Press, and elicited a favorable reply.

When the actual contributions began coming in, however, I soon realized that I must abandon even the lingering remnants of my Procrusteanism. No matter what the editor proposes, it is the contributors after all who dispose; and it is a part of wisdom to accept their disposition with good grace, and to admit the inadequacy of the original proposal. Considering the manuscripts all together (apart from one or two stragglers), I found it impossible to arrange them in any such neat order as I had envisaged. Yet they must (I still insisted) be arranged somehow: there must be some reason for placing one here and another there. Only, as I cannot display them in a schematic order in the table of contents, it must be the function of this preface (as I conceive it) to explain not only the genesis of the book, but also the disposition of its contents. And this, at least, I propose to do schematically.

In the first place belongs, without any doubt, the introductory article of Professor MacKenzie—partly because he was the original inspirer of this volume and partly because the article itself originated in my request at least (allowing for his pressure of work) of an introduction. This subsequently developed (in his generosity) into the present article which still bears some of the characteristics of an introduction.

This article, moreover, sets the pace (as it were) for those that follow—those I had originally set aside under the heading of "Biographical Readings" for the final section. Thus have the last become, in a truly Christian manner, the first. These include Canon Philip Martin's researches into the background of the drowned nuns and their drowning and Professor Paul Mariani's imaginative but informed reconstruction of the scene as a whole.

The above contributions are by no means limited to a merely factual account of the wreck itself; but they look beyond its details with the eyes of the poet and suggest various interpretations of his poem. In the next contribution, however, Mr. Francis Lees looks from the wreck to the Victorian background of the poem and presents a significant contrast between the scientific fatalism of the day, shared by many contemporary poets, and the religious inspiration of Hopkins, which he shared with the nuns and in which he looked through the fact of death to its ultimate meaning.

This leads the way to what may be termed (though it had not been in my original plan) a series of "religious readings": with Father Raymond Schoder's assessment of the Ignatian quality of Hopkins' mind as exposed in the poem; my own study of the poem as an Ignatian meditation, with a triple composition of place; and Dr. James Cotter's unified interpretation of the poem in terms of its pervading Christology, from the viewpoint of the early church fathers whose writings Hopkins was then studying at St. Beuno's College.

The next two essays deal with the poem itself from the viewpoint of the poet himself. Sister Marcella Holloway presents an interpretation of the poem in the light of Hopkins' own critical opinions and explanations, as set forth in his different prose writings; while Father Robert Boyle proposes a very different kind of interpretation in the light of Hopkins' later poems, particularly *The Shepherd's Brow*—and, it should be added, of his current preoccupation with the writings of James Joyce.

Two more essays turn from the Christian to the classical tradition in which Hopkins was also educated and which entered into his composition of the poem. Dr. Alison Sulloway draws attention to his use of myth in the tradition of Greek tragedy; and Dr. Warren Anderson estimates the extent of his indebtedness to the example of Pindar.

Passing now from the content to the form of the poem—to some extent already considered by Dr. Anderson—we have two other essays: one by a young Japanese scholar, Mr. Kunio Shimane, on the acoustic qualities of the poem, which the poet himself regarded as of the utmost importance; and another by the late Father John Keating (for which I have to thank Dr. Sulloway for her good offices), on the stanzaic pattern of the poem and its structural parallelism, which owes as much to Hebraic as to Hellenic influence.

Last but not least, I have placed the more personal essay of Mrs. Ruth Seelhammer as a tribute to two Hopkins associates, Father Keating himself and Father Charles Keenan; while in and through them she looks to that living inspiration which the poet found in the deaths of the five nuns. This essay, in fact, while being the least scholarly of all the contributions, is the one which (if I may say so, without offending the other contributors) most nearly fulfills my original aim of a symposium of personal appreciations. That, I am afraid, was not to be. Yet it seems to me that if they all serve to lead forward from Professor Mac-Kenzie's severely objective account of the wreck in his opening paragraphs to Mrs. Seelhammer's moving tribute to her two priest "heroes," then my aim is more than realized—in a kind of updating of the very event Hopkins celebrated just a hundred years ago. As the French say, "Plus ça change, plus c'est la même chose." There may have been only one *Deutschland* wrecked on the Kentish Knock with those five nuns on board. But death and disaster under various forms, as the poet observes in his eleventh stanza, are ever-present realities; and through them we can look now, as he did then, to the divine truth which "heeds but hides, bodes but abides" beyond.

The above account of the genesis and arrangement of this volume may suffice to show that the task of editing was no easy one—even when all the contributions had come in, to the last of the latecomers. It was not only a problem of arrangement that I faced, but also one of presentation: how to reduce the various contributions at least to an outward show of conformity—at least in the matter of annotation, references, and typography. Among other things, I have taken it upon myself as editor to remove all footnotes (considering that some contributors provided me with elaborate annotation and others with none at all), by incorporating them into the text. I have also followed a policy of italicizing all titles of poems, for the sake of clarity, instead of following the usual convention of books on literature. The apparent conformity of the titles in the list of contents is, moreover, to some extent, an effect of my editing—by extending to all what I found observed by many: the main title in words of Hopkins, with a subtitle explaining the contents in a more direct, less cryptic manner. To this extent, at least, I have retained something of my original idea of following the stanzas of *The Wreck* two by two.

This apparent conformity is, however, deceptive. A careful reading of the essays themselves will at once dispel such an impression, not only by reason of their variety of approach to the poem, but also by reason of their often contradictory interpretations. What is confidently affirmed by one author will be found (all unconsciously) no less confidently negated by another. It may well be an interesting pastime for future generations of Hopkins scholars—not to mention present generations of literary reviewers—to disentangle the underlying contradictions assembled in these pages. For myself, as editor, so far from wringing my hands over these discrepancies, I rather welcome them—in much the same spirit (I must admit) as the mischievous Puck: "This their jangling I esteem a sport." Not that I rejoice (like Puck) in mere confusion or error; but I think that much may be gained by the airing of different, even discordant, opinions as to the interpretation of a poet like Hopkins, who was (it seems to me) second only to Shakespeare in the ambiguity no less than in the richness of his language. Thus, so far from claiming to be the last word on *The Wreck* (except in a merely temporal, and therefore temporary, sense), it is my hope that this volume may only stimulate further discussion—and further discrepancy—on what the poet himself had in mind when he undertook the composition of his poem a hundred years ago.

Sophia University, Tokyo

Peter Milward, S.J.

July 1975

Readings of *The Wreck*

The Wreck of the
Deutschland

*To the
happy memory of five Franciscan nuns
exiles by the Falck Laws
drowned between midnight and morning of
Dec. 7th, 1875*

PART I

1

THOU mastering me
God! giver of breath and bread;
World's strand, sway of the sea;
Lord of living and dead;
Thou hast bound bones and veins in me, fastened me flesh,
And after it almost unmade, what with dread,
Thy doing: and dost thou touch me afresh?
Over again I feel thy finger and find thee.

2

I did say yes
O at lightning and lashed rod;
Thou heardst me truer than tongue confess
Thy terror, O Christ, O God;
Thou knowest the walls, altar and hour and night:
The swoon of a heart that the sweep and the hurl of thee
trod
Hard down with a horror of height:
And the midriff astrain with leaning of, laced with fire of stress.

3

The frown of his face
Before me, the hurtle of hell
Behind, where, where was a, where was a place?
I whirled out wings that spell
And fled with a fling of the heart to the heart of the Host.
My heart, but you were dovewinged, I can tell,
Carrier-witted, I am bold to boast,
To flash from the flame to the flame then, tower from the grace
to the grace.

4

I am soft sift
In an hourglass—at the wall
Fast, but mined with a motion, a drift,
And it crowds and it combs to the fall;
I steady as a water in a well, to a poise, to a pane,
But roped with, always, all the way down from the tall
Fells or flanks of the voel, a vein
Of the gospel proffer, a pressure, a principle, Christ's gift.

5

I kiss my hand
To the stars, lovely-asunder
Starlight, wafting him out of it; and
Glow, glory in thunder;
Kiss my hand to the dappled-with-damson west:
Since, tho' he is under the world's splendour and wonder,
His mystery must be instressed, stressed;
For I greet him the days I meet him, and bless when I under-
stand.

6

Not out of his bliss
Springs the stress felt
Nor first from heaven (and few know this)
Swings the stroke dealt—
Stroke and a stress that stars and storms deliver,
That guilt is hushed by, hearts are flushed by and melt—
But it rides time like riding a river
(And here the faithful waver, the faithless fable and miss).

7

It dates from day
Of his going in Galilee;
Warm-laid grave of a womb-life grey;
Manger, maiden's knee;
The dense and the driven Passion, and frightful sweat:
Thence the discharge of it, there its swelling to be,
Though felt before, though in high flood yet—
What none would have known of it, only the heart, being hard
at bay,

8

Is out with it! Oh,
We lash with the best or worst
Word last! How a lush-kept plush-capped sloe
Will, mouthed to flesh-burst,
Gush!—flush the man, the being with it, sour or sweet,
Brim, in a flash, full!—Hither then, last or first,
To hero of Calvary, Christ's feet—
Never ask if meaning it, wanting it, warned of it—men go.

9

Be adored among men,
God, three-numberèd form;
Wring thy rebel, dogged in den,
Man's malice, with wrecking and storm.
Beyond saying sweet, past telling of tongue,
Thou art lightning and love, I found it, a winter and warm;
Father and fondler of heart thou hast wrung:
Hast thy dark descending and most art merciful then.

10

With an anvil-ding
And with fire in him forge thy will
Or rather, rather then, stealing as Spring
Through him, melt him but master him still:
Whether at once, as once at a crash Paul,
Or as Austin, a lingering-out swéet skill,
Make mercy in all of us, out of us all
Mastery, but be adored, but be adored King.

PART II

11

'Some find me a sword; some
The flange and the rail; flame,
Fang, or flood' goes Death on drum,
And storms bugle his fame.
But wé dream we are rooted in earth—Dust!
Flesh falls within sight of us, we, though our flower the
same,
Wave with the meadow, forget that there must
The sour scythe cringe, and the blear share come.

12

On Saturday sailed from Bremen,
American-outward-bound,
Take settler and seamen, tell men with women,
Two hundred souls in the round—
O Father, not under thy feathers nor ever as guessing
The goal was a shoal, of a fourth the doom to be drowned;
Yet did the dark side of the bay of thy blessing
Not vault them, the million of rounds of thy mercy not reeve
even them in?

13

Into the snows she sweeps,
Hurling the haven behind,
The Deutschland, on Sunday; and so the sky keeps,
For the infinite air is unkind,
And the sea flint-flake, black-backed in the regular blow,
Sitting Eastnortheast, in cursed quarter, the wind;
Wiry and white-fiery and whirlwind-swivellèd snow
Spins to the widow-making unchilding unfathering deeps.

14

She drove in the dark to leeward,
She struck—not a reef or a rock
But the combs of a smother of sand: night drew her
Dead to the Kentish Knock;
And she beat the bank down with her bows and the ride
of her keel:
The breakers rolled on her beam with ruinous shock;
And canvas and compass, the whorl and the wheel
Idle for ever to waft her or wind her with, these she endured.

15

Hope had grown grey hairs,
Hope had mourning on,
Trenched with tears, carved with cares,
Hope was twelve hours gone;
And frightful a nightfall folded rueful a day
Nor rescue, only rocket and lightship, shone,
And lives at last were washing away:
To the shrouds they took,—they shook in the hurling and
horrible airs.

16

One stirred from the rigging to save
The wild woman-kind below,
With a rope's end round the man, handy and brave—
He was pitched to his death at a blow,
For all his dreadnought breast and braids of thew:
They could tell him for hours, dandled the to and fro
Through the cobbled foam-fleece. What could he do
With the burl of the fountains of air, buck and the flood of the
wave?

17

They fought with God's cold—
And they could not and fell to the deck
(Crushed them) or water (and drowned them) or
rolled
With the sea-romp over the wreck.
Night roared, with the heart-break hearing a heart-broke
rabble,
The woman's wailing, the crying of child without check—
Till a lioness arose breasting the babble,
A prophetess towered in the tumult, a virginal tongue told.

18

Ah, touched in your bower of bone,
Are you! turned for an exquisite smart,
Have you! make words break from me here all alone,
Do you!—mother of being in me, heart.
O unteachably after evil, but uttering truth,
Why, tears! is it? tears; such a melting, a madrigal start!
Never-eldering revel and river of youth,
What can it be, this glee? the good you have there of your own?

19

Sister, a sister calling
A master, her master and mine!—
And the inboard seas run swirling and hawling;
The rash smart sloggering brine
Blinds her; but she that weather sees one thing, one;
Has one fetch in her: she rears herself to divine
Ears, and the call of the tall nun
To the men in the tops and the tackle rode over the storm's
brawling.

20

She was first of a five and came
Of a coifèd sisterhood.
(O Deutschland, double a desperate name!
O world wide of its good!
But Gertrude, lily, and Luther, are two of a town,
Christ's lily and beast of the waste wood:
From life's dawn it is drawn down,
Abel is Cain's brother and breasts they have sucked the same.)

21

Loathed for a love men knew in them,
Banned by the land of their birth,
Rhine refused them, Thames would ruin them;
Surf, snow, river and earth
Gnashed: but thou art above, thou Orion of light;
Thy unchancelling poising palms were weighing the worth,
Thou martyr-master: in thy sight
Storm flakes were scroll-leaved flowers, lily showers—sweet
heaven was astrew in them.

22

Five! the finding and sake
And cipher of suffering Christ.
Mark, the mark is of man's make
And the word of it Sacrificed.
But he scores it in scarlet himself on his own bespoken,
Before-time-taken, dearest prizèd and priced—
Stigma, signal, cinquefoil token
For lettering of the lamb's fleece, ruddying of the rose-flake.

23

Joy fall to thee, father Francis,
　　Drawn to the Life that died;
With the gnarls of the nails in thee, niche of the lance, his
　　Lovescape crucified
And seal of his seraph-arrival! and these thy daughters
And five-livèd and leavèd favour and pride,
　　Are sisterly sealed in wild waters,
To bathe in his fall-gold mercies, to breathe in his all-fire glances.

24

Away in the loveable west,
　　On a pastoral forehead of Wales,
I was under a roof here, I was at rest,
　　And they the prey of the gales;
She to the black-about air, to the breaker, the thickly
Falling flakes, to the throng that catches and quails
　　Was calling 'O Christ, Christ, come quickly':
The cross to her she calls Christ to her, christens her wild-worst Best.

25

The majesty! what did she mean?
　　Breathe, arch and original Breath.
Is it love in her of the being as her lover had been?
　　Breathe, body of lovely Death.
They were else-minded then, altogether, the men
Woke thee with a *We are perishing* in the weather of Gennesareth.
　　Or is it that she cried for the crown then,
The keener to come at the comfort for feeling the combating keen?

26

For how to the heart's cheering
The down-dugged ground-hugged grey
Hovers off, the jay-blue heavens appearing
Of pied and peeled May!
Blue-beating and hoary-glow height; or night, still higher,
With belled fire and the moth-soft Milky Way,
What by your measure is the heaven of desire,
The treasure never eyesight got, nor was ever guessed what for
the hearing?

27

No, but it was not these.
The jading and jar of the cart,
Time's tasking, it is fathers that asking for ease
Of the sodden-with-its-sorrowing heart,
Not danger, electrical horror; then further it finds
The appealing of the Passion is tenderer in prayer apart:
Other, I gather, in measure her mind's
Burden, in wind's burly and beat of endragonèd seas.

28

But how shall I . . . make me room there:
Reach me a . . . Fancy, come faster—
Strike you the sight of it? look at it loom there,
Thing that she . . . There then! the Master,
Ipse, the only one, Christ, King, Head:
He was to cure the extremity where he had cast her;
Do, deal, lord it with living and dead;
Let him ride, her pride, in his triumph, despatch and have done
with his doom there.

29

Ah! there was a heart right!
There was single eye!
Read the unshapeable shock night
And knew the who and the why;
Wording it how but by him that present and past,
Heaven and earth are word of, worded by?—
The Simon Peter of a soul! to the blast
Tarpeïan-fast, but a blown beacon of light.

30

Jesu, heart's light,
Jesu, maid's son,
What was the feast followed the night
Thou hadst glory of this nun?—
Feast of the one woman without stain.
For so conceivèd, so to conceive thee is done;
But here was heart-throe, birth of a brain,
Word, that heard and kept thee and uttered thee outright.

31

Well, she has thee for the pain, for the
Patience; but pity of the rest of them!
Heart, go and bleed at a bitterer vein for the
Comfortless unconfessed of them—
No not uncomforted: lovely-felicitous Providence
Finger of a tender of, O of a feathery delicacy, the breast of the
Maiden could obey so, be a bell to, ring of it, and
Startle the poor sheep back! is the shipwrack then a harvest,
does tempest carry the grain for thee?

32

I admire thee, master of the tides,
Of the Yore-flood, of the year's fall;
The recurb and the recovery of the gulf's sides,
The girth of it and the wharf of it and the wall;
Stanching, quenching ocean of a motionable mind;
Ground of being, and granite of it: past all
Grasp God, throned behind
Death with a sovereignty that heeds but hides, bodes but abides;

33

With a mercy that outrides
The all of water, an ark
For the listener; for the lingerer with a love glides
Lower than death and the dark;
A vein for the visiting of the past-prayer, pent in prison,
The-last-breath penitent spirits—the uttermost mark
Our passion-plungèd giant risen,
The Christ of the Father compassionate, fetched in the storm
of his strides.

34

Now burn, new born to the world,
Double-naturèd name,
The heaven-flung, heart-fleshed, maiden-furled
Miracle-in-Mary-of-flame,
Mid-numberèd he in three of the thunder-throne!
Not a dooms-day dazzle in his coming nor dark as he
came;
Kind, but royally reclaiming his own;
A released shower, let flash to the shire, not a lightning of fire
hard-hurled.

35

Dame, at our door
Drowned, and among our shoals,
Remember us in the roads, the heaven-haven of the
reward:
Our King back, Oh, upon English souls!
Let him easter in us, be a dayspring to the dimness of us,
be a crimson-cresseted east,
More brightening her, rare-dear Britain, as his reign rolls,
Pride, rose, prince, hero of us, high-priest,
Our hearts' charity's hearth's fire, our thoughts' chivalry's
throng's Lord.

Chapter I

"Thy Dark Descending"

Light and Darkness in *The Wreck*

by Norman H. MacKenzie

A hundred years ago, in the stormy winter of 1875-1876, a German passenger liner set sail from Bremen for Southampton, en route to New York. Trade between Europe and America had been so depressed—recessions are no prerogative of the present—that the ship had been laid up for many months at Bremerhaven, and on this, her final and fatal voyage, she was fortunately carrying only a small fraction of the seven hundred and fifty passengers who could in more properous times have crowded into her steerage and saloon accommodation. She was, moreover, short of her full cargo by some six hundred to seven hundred tons of merchandise.

In command of the *Deutschland* was an experienced sea captain, five further officers all with master's certificates, two German river pilots, and an English pilot who had crossed the North Sea a hundred and twenty times before, though technically his sole function on board was to assist in guiding the ship in Southampton waters. Despite this impressive array of experience, the *Deutschland,* steered by dead reckoning because of the impenetrable vault of swirling snow cloud, was piloted in the darkness onto the sandbanks which lie in wait to the north of the Thames estuary.

At the inquiry into the disaster held by the Board of Trade, even those most familiar with the North Sea confessed that they did not understand all the complexities of its currents; but from their evidence it was clear that the ship must have been running with the tide for some seven hours before she struck, being borne surreptitiously forward beyond her officers' calculations, and finally edged to the west as the flood tide set strongly over the sandbanks. Since the captain admitted that he had made no allowance for the tides in charting his position and course, the inquiry concluded that the loss of over sixty lives and the vessel herself was due to "disregard by the master of the force and direction of the tide."

That then is the underlying significance of stanza 32, where Hopkins ends his narrative of the wreck at the crux of greatest physical danger and highest spiritual hope, and turns to the Creator of these global powers against which men pit their limited understanding.

> **I admire thee, master of the tides,**
> **Of the Yore-flood, of the year's fall;**
> **The recurb and the recovery of the gulf's sides,**
> **The girth of it and the wharf of it and the wall;**
> **Stanching, quenching ocean of a motionable mind;**
> **Ground of being, and granite of it: past all**
> **Grasp God . . .**

Our centenary volume, however, is not in commemoration of an historical event. The *Deutschland* was only one of four hundred and twenty-five vessels of all sizes totally lost round the shores of Great Britain between July 1, 1875, and June 30 of the following year. It is true that her wreck occupied more prominence in the public mind than any similar calamity, but it would have been long since forgotten if the striking newspaper reports of the prayer of the tall nun (who was among those drowned) had not produced a passionate ode from a Jesuit of genius, then studying theology in the sheltered beauty of Wales, a poet in whom the uncertain winds of inspiration had for seven years been at a lull.

This is a literary centenary. It is not a wreck we are celebrating, nor the tales of neglect or heroism which circulated after it, but the vision which came to Hopkins through a Christian's cry to her Master, built by him into a memorable and major poem. Considering that the ode, though completed in 1876, was not published until 1918, its effect upon the imagination of readers has been phenomenal.

It is as a devotional ode that we approach it, not a versified *Lloyd's Shipping Intelligence* (cf. L I, pp. 51-52). We must not, of course, forget how carefully Hopkins, scrupulous in everything, used all the limited reports he could obtain in an effort to recapture the authentic atmosphere of the calamity. So too Milton, whose writings Hopkins continually drew upon, prepared himself through years of laborious study for the composition of *Paradise Lost* and *Samson Agonistes*. No one imagines that when Milton hazards the motives of his biblical actors, venturing beyond his learned or sacred sources, he is infallibly inspired. We turn to his magnificent poems because they express general truths about human nature, in moving reaches of verse such as one which influenced *Binsey Poplars* as well as *The Wreck*, beginning

> O dark, dark, dark, amid the blaze of noon,
> Irrecoverably dark, total eclipse
> Without all hope of day!
> O first-created beam, and thou great Word,
> "Let there be light," and light was over all.

The test of a work of art is not how neatly it squares with historical fact—Shakespeare would be sternly condemned by that inappropriate inquisition—but whether it rings true to the receptive reader. Judgments will inevitably differ according to the critic's capacity for empathy and his personal convictions, but *The Wreck of the Deutschland*, provided we do not make the wrong demands of it, should shine among the triumphs of English literature through succeeding centuries.

The tall nun is the central human figure in Part II. Unless the poet's bone-embowered heart had been wakened by the *Times* report of her cry "O Christ, Christ, come quickly!" there would have been no ode. She is given a central role which might have astonished the learned assessors at the inquiry. With great artistry Hopkins allows her to tower above everyone else on board, contrasted with the self-abasing poet himself in stanzas 18 and 24. The nun's fellow passengers (who may have been largely Protestant) afterwards commented more admiringly on the conduct of the stewardess than on the leader of the nuns, whose cries they found disturbing. That should be no surprise: straying sheep do not normally welcome the warning voice of the shepherd.

Hopkins can surely have learned very few authentic facts about his heroine beyond the accounts of her prayer. As far as we know he met no survivors from the wreck. Into the numerous stanzas about the Franciscan sister, therefore, the poet must have poured the meditations of many years, his reading of the lives of the saints and mystics, crowned by his personal knowledge as to how a pure soul reacts under drastic challenge.

During artistic creation the most widely flung material may be coalesced into a masterful unity. Major contributions were made by the Douay version of Job and the prophets, and by the psalms as he had sung them from the Book of Common Prayer. But minor influences were also at work. We may speculate, for example, that Hopkins had read that overintense religious novel by the Reverend Edward Monro, *The Dark Mountains* (London, 1858), on which so many Victorian children were brought up. Stanza 28 may contain a reminiscence of one reference to Christ the King: "'Sir, have you seen Him?' said the boy, eagerly addressing Cyril. . . . 'seen whom?' said Cyril. . . . 'Whom?' said the other, 'why the only One.' 'You mean the King,' said Cyril colouring" (p. 98).

The same prayerful imagination welded into the poem his convincing descriptions of the attacking winds and seas. Hopkins had himself never undergone a prolonged rough winter voyage. His exposure to the sea was virtually confined to a few channel crossings to Europe or to the Isle of Man, with such other events as a three-mile ferry trip across the Firth of Clyde in a fierce gale. But some of the phrases used in *The Wreck of the Deutschland* can be traced to his holiday journals after he had scrutinized the wayward moods of the water from the safety of the cliffs (cf. J, pp.148, 214, 235). Yet the huge waves which leap the deck of the defeated *Deutschland* are so tellingly presented that they seem the wording of a survivor. To match in prose the persuasive magnificence of his storm, created by a few virile lines which sweep into stanzas here and there throughout the poem, we might turn to the novels of Joseph Conrad.

By a curious and little-noticed coincidence, as the *Deutschland* steamed toward the English Channel from the northeast, a small French brig, the *Mont-Blanc,* with Conrad on board, was caught by gale-force winds as she battled toward the channel from the southwest. Conrad had signed on as an apprentice for that unlucky passage, and his eighteenth birthday, which fell on the day before the *Deutschland* left the safety of Bremen, was spent on his homeward voyage from Martinique, made miserable by weeks of Atlantic storms. The brig's jibboom was smashed, bringing down the topgallant mast and rigging, and endangering the vessel as the boom swung like a battering ram against the bows with her every plunge. When at last she had faltered her way up the channel to Le Havre she had to undergo month-long repairs.

Conrad never directly described that nightmare ordeal, but there is no doubt in my mind that he infused some of those experiences as a lowly member of the f'c'sle into his novel *The Nigger of the "Narcissus."* It is well-known that Conrad had actually served as an officer on board the *Narcissus* for six months in 1884, and that the gales and mountainous rollers which almost foundered that ship off the Cape of Good Hope also made extensive refitting necessary at the end of her voyage. Conrad was a creative artist, however, not a reporter, and in conversation with his biographer, Gérard Jean-Aubry, he insisted upon his right to dismantle and reassemble incidents from the past. "As you know, I do not write history, but fiction, and I am therefore entitled to choose as I please what is most suitable in regard to characters and particulars to help me in the general impression I wish to produce" (*The Sea-Dreamer*, p. 104). Accordingly, among events suggested by his spell in the *Narcissus* he has mingled elements from other ships—the dramatic embarkation of the crew, the name of the mysterious Negro, the personalities of the Scandinavians, the final landfall.

The preface to the novel shows how close Conrad came to Hopkins' theory of inscape:

> Art itself may be defined as a single-minded attempt to render the highest kind of justice to the visible universe, by bringing to light the truth, manifold and one, underlying its every aspect. It is an attempt to find in its forms, in its colours, in its light, in its shadows . . . what of each is fundamental, what is enduring and essential—. . . the very truth of their existence.

Conrad found darkness and light as fascinating as did Hopkins himself.

In *The Wreck of the Deutschland* Hopkins accentuates the perils of the voyage from Bremen by means of forebodings, a device familiar in great literature of all ages, from the times of the Hebrew prophets and the Greek dramatists. In the assessors' view, however, so far from the tragedy being caused by the overwhelming physical forces pitted against the *Deutschland*, it had come from too great a sense of security on the bridge. To the captain the east-northeast wind was in no "cursed quarter" since it was driving him on his way. In fact, an analysis of the circumstances in which over eighteen thousand vessels had been wrecked around Britain between 1866 and 1876 showed that, of winds from all sixteen points of the compass, those from the east-northeast and east-southeast were the least liable to cause disaster.

But the priest's mind was full of the biblical associations between the east wind and destruction, familiar in more than a dozen places, such as the forty-eighth psalm: "Thou shalt break the ships of the sea: through the east wind." Moreover in England, as the Oxford English Dictionary reminds us, the east wind has proverbially bleak and injurious overtones. And finally we must concede that once the ship was actually on the sandbank, the east wind would raise the greatest seas around her, a fact which evidence at the inquiry revealed.

What historical fanatic would want to tame the verb *struck* into *touched* in the superb fourteenth stanza, to please the literalists?

> **She drove in the dark to leeward,**
> **She struck—not a reef or a rock**
> **But the combs of a smother of sand . . .**

It may be true that the chief officer described the first contact with the sandbank as "a slight touch," and that the chief engineer estimated that the ship was doing about two knots only when he felt "a slight touching, as if the ship struck a heavy sea from the head." But the shocks very soon became frequent and violent, as the vessel broached sideways, and was lifted, only to be flung down again on the bank, by each successive wave.

The emotional and spiritual truth of *The Wreck of the Deutschland* is the vital question. There lay the greatest danger, the temptation toward "pious insincerity," which T. S. Eliot diagnosed as the commonest explanation for the failure of so much religious verse to "reach the highest levels of poetry." "People who write devotional verse," said Eliot, "are usually writing as they want to feel, rather than as they do feel" (*After Strange Gods,* pp. 28-29). Victorian religious magazines often filled their interstices with mediocre poems in which both the piety and the imagination seem suspect; but Hopkins was able to assure Bridges that "what refers to myself in the poem is all strictly and literally true and did all occur; nothing is added for poetical padding" (L I, p. 47).

This important guarantee of spiritual sincerity must nevertheless not be extended beyond its sphere, or construed into a claim for literal precision in the narrative itself. Hopkins had neither the time nor the facilities for such an historical investigation. As happens in all traumatic accidents, eyewitnesses from the *Deutschland* contradicted each other in their subsequent narratives, and every newspaper account of the wreck I have seen contains both palpable and probable errors. His ode, dedicated to the restoration of Christ as England's real monarch, represents his imaginative and consecrated reconstruction of the story around a five-word prayer. It is, we might say, his "Vision of the Tall Nun."

The difference between the pre-Catholic and the mature poetry of Hopkins might be described in terms of instress, largely absent from his early verse, and triumphantly present in the best of his later pieces. We can illustrate the difference dramatically by comparing his allusions to the light of the setting sun in two poems about the sea, his high-school *A Vision of the Mermaids* (about which so little has been written) and

The Wreck of the Deutschland, an intensely serious adult vision.

A Vision of the Mermaids is a remarkable poem for so young a writer. While reminiscent of Keats and Tennyson in a general way, it is full of verbal inventiveness, of unique terms in thought and phrase. What impresses me most is the early age at which Hopkins became aware of the importance of the "underthought" as a source of unity. His theory about the "undercurrent of thought governing the choice of images used" was not expounded until January 1883, but it most effectively interlaces *The Wreck* stanzas, and is laboriously attempted even in the poem about the mermaids (L III, pp. 252-53).

An example occurs at the outset of the earlier poem, where the roseate light of sunset is painstakingly pictured in water imagery to harmonize with the main story. The pale green of the sky becomes "beryl lakes" on which the brilliant cloudlets float as water lilies; the splendor is seen as "swimming" until it is "ebb'd back" when the light cools. The sunset, phase by phase, is visualized in twenty packed lines. Moreover, it is not left as an ornamental arch but is structurally related to the action and mood of the whole piece.

The mature Hopkins, however, is a man remade. When we turn to *The Wreck of the Deutschland,* stanzas 5 or 26, with their sunlight and starlight, we cannot help contrasting the swift strength with which he can now reach sublime heights.

> **I kiss my hand**
>   **To the stars, lovely-asunder**
> **Starlight, wafting him out of it; and**
>   **Glow, glory in thunder;**
> **Kiss my hand to the dappled-with-damson west:**
> **Since, tho' he is under the world's splendour and wonder,**
>   **His mystery must be instressed, stressed . . .**

The "swimming splendour" of *A Vision of the Mermaids* may be decked out in a museum case of precious stones—turquoise, sapphire, onyx, garnet, lapis lazuli, rubies, and amethyst—but there is no God under "its splendour and wonder," and the "keen glimpses of the inner firmament" reveal no inner truths.

In *The Wreck of the Deutschland,* on the other hand, the onset of night and the coming of dawn are not simply occasions for poetic display. Darkness and light take on a gradually deepening symbolism.

The poet's self-surrender before the altar in stanza 2 is at night, and in consequence the dove imagery of the following stanza suggests to me the awful spectacle of the dark lit up by a forest fire, from which the dove flees in terror to the bright beacon on the hilltop. The opening passage in Part II lets in the late summer sunlight for a brief space as the flowering meadow grass sways in the breeze, blind to the approaching scythe. But the winter clouds quickly muster to death's drum, and under their oppressive canopy the waves of the North Sea are *black-backed* as they roll the ship on her way.

The second night of the voyage wedges the *Deutschland* on the Knock, and after a day made bitter by hope deferred, "frightful a night-fall folded rueful a day." From this point until stanza 31 the survivors have around them (expressive Greek phrase) the "black-about air." "Night roared"—like the roar of a lion which seems to reverberate from all sides, confusing its prey into running, "dead," toward the danger they most nervously wish to avoid. With dramatic propriety, Hopkins transforms the darkness into an active agent.

Only once is the violent obscurity relieved—in the beautiful reminiscence of stanza 26 (one of my favorite sections). The scene is no longer the wind-raked North Sea, but a sheltered valley enfolding the moist drooping clouds. As these lift slowly aloft, like a great bird, a patch of bright blue sky, as on a jay's wings, fills us with the exhilaration of Maytime:

> **Blue-beating and hoary-glow height; or night, still higher,**
> **With belled fire and the moth-soft Milky Way.**

But the respite is momentary. The ordeals of numbing cold and slamming breakers are intensified for the sufferers by the "unshapeable shock night," a darkness that can be felt but not understood. The behavior of the elements makes it appear as though across the original writing of creation ("And God saw all the things that he had made, and they were very good") has been superimposed at right angles a palimpsest of disorder and disaster, making the divine words indecipherable. But Hopkins sees the nun as able to "read" the apparent confusion, to hear the voice of Christ behind death's stormy bugle call, above the wind's brawl and the haunting wails of the bereaved.

Light (though not that of dawn) begins to glimmer in stanza 21, but it is visible only to the interior eye. From the "Orion of light" a spiritual fire descends on the Franciscan sisters in "fall-gold mercies" and "all-fire glances." Hopkins projects himself imaginatively into the conjectural state of mind in the tall nun: so far from being afraid of the "electrical horror" of the lightning, she seems to catch an inner fire herself. She serves as a warning signal flame to her fellow sufferers, a "blown beacon of light" fanned by the rush of the air into higher brilliance. From the light in her heart, by a metaphysical image which Father Milward aptly compares with the "burning babe" in Southwell's poem, Christ seems to be reborn on the Kentish Knock (Milward, p. 152).

Not till the final stanza does the dawn seem to break, as it did at last for the miserable survivors huddled in the shrouds of the water-logged *Deutschland*. Here the poet has a wistful vision of Christ, the "Sun of righteousness," rising over England in spectacular recoronation splendor and majesty.

Another poet, also deeply versed in the half-revelations of the mystics, once wrote

I said to my soul, be still, and let the dark come upon you
Which shall be the darkness of God (T. S. Eliot, *East Coker* III).

If the nun read the "unshapeable shock night" as the darkness of God what might it have symbolized for her? There has been much speculation as to whether Hopkins had a specific theological or biblical reference in mind at the close of stanza 9: "[Thou] Hast thy dark descending and most art merciful then."

One possible answer is that this darkness of mercy may allude to the "darkness over all the land" at the time of his supreme love displayed in the crucifixion. Hopkins in an early sermon described to his simple Leigh parishioners the ostensible shipwreck of Christ's human career: "Then the clouds gathered, the hour of storm, the power of darkness came, the sun got bloody red, Christ was crucified; and his enemies that loved darkness better than light triumphed that he was gone. On Easter Day this same sun had another rising . . . " (S, p. 40). By ending his narrative of the nun's sacrificial testimony in the stormy night with a resurrection prayer, "Let him easter in us," Hopkins suggests to me that he may have felt some parallel between the darkness over Calvary and the night when the tall nun made the sacrifice of herself to Christ.

This concept involves us in Hopkins' own individual theory as to the reason for the creation of man. He concluded that because Christ was our example and (as the Good Shepherd) had laid down his life, so he ought to be followed by the elect, his lambs, the flower of the flock, ceding over their lives in symbolic or real sacrifice: "the world, man, should after its own manner give God being in return for the being he has given it or should give him back that being he has given. This is done by the great sacrifice. To contribute then to that sacrifice is the end for which man was made" (S, p. 129).

If the poet could measure the nun's faith only by the five reiterated words of her cry, to him she seemed to have triumphantly fulfilled the purpose of her creation. Finding herself in "an extremity where [God] had cast her," in a darkness which had suddenly blazed with light, she surrendered herself utterly to him.

It is to her, "Dame, at our door/Drowned," that his prayer is directed in the great crescendo of the concluding stanza: how luminous with happiness "rare-dear Britain" would be if the story of the nun's certainty in the face of death could so move her people that there would be no more need for those desperate weapons of the divine arsenal— storm and darkness and calamity. Then Christ might become the all-admired King of the British Isles, the warmth of a Christian hearth fire would replace the gale-blown warning beacon fire, the throng that now "catches and quails" for fear would feel the presence of a Lord of love, and the "black-about" night of infidelity would disappear into the ever-strengthening brightness of a new Easter Day.

Notes

a   In this article I have drawn on all the surviving reports of the wreck which I have been able to find, but particularly the inquiry held by the Board of Trade. The reports of its evidence and findings, carried by the London *Times,* were too extensive for inclusion in *Immortal Diamond,* edited by Norman Weyand, S.J., and Raymond V. Schoder, S.J. (London, 1949), Appendix. Much exploration of North Sea currents has taken place recently, but how much remains to be determined can be seen from *North Sea Science,* edited by E. D. Goldberg (London, 1973). See also *Abstracts . . . of Wrecks, Casualties, and Collisions Which Occurred On and Near the Coasts of the United Kingdom, from the 1st July 1875 to the 30th June 1876* (London, 1876), p. xiv.

b   The log kept by the neighboring lightship describes the weather at 9:00 P.M. on Monday as "blue sky and cloudy," though a moderate gale was still blowing. By 3:00 A.M., the wind was slightly milder, the sky was "overcast and distant objects visible" (*Times,* December 24, 1875). Stars could be seen from time to time. Hopkins exaggerates the effect of darkness, and assumes that the snow was still falling thickly (stanza 24), though the snowstorm had in fact cleared about 9:30 A.M. on Monday. Whether these changes were made consciously or unconsciously, they provide the right contrast for the shining spiritual light of stanzas 29 and 30.

Chapter II

"Christens Her Wild-Worst Best"

The Experience of the Nuns and the
General Significance of *The Wreck*

by Philip Martin

The five exiled nuns on board the *Deutschland* are regarded by many commentators as types of martyrdom; I would suggest that Hopkins presents them rather as types of a less exalted and more general vocation—that of the ordinary Christian: that is to say, of the vocation to be a person whose life is fused with Christ's life, and in and through whom Christ is reborn, to save and redeem the world. Of the "tall nun" Hopkins writes

> . . . here was heart-throe, birth of a brain,
> Word, that heard and kept thee and uttered thee outright.

The "uttered word" is the Word of God born again in and through the nun, so that at the end of the poem the poet can speak of Christ as being "new born to the world." The tall nun is singled out from her companions as their representative, but she stands for every Christian who is fulfilling the purpose for which he was created and redeemed; consequently what is said in the poem of her has a significance for every Christian soul.

Quite apart from its central position in the poem, the fate of the nuns is more fully documented than that of any other persons involved in the disaster, and particular reference was made to them in the secular as well as the religious press. The five Tertiaries Regular of the Franciscan Order were booked as second-class passengers on the *Deutschland,* bound for New York on their way to Canada. In the passenger lists their names are given as Mothers Barbara Hultenschmidt, Norbeta Reinkober, Aurea Badziura, Brigitta Damhorst, and Henrica Fassbaender; in Captain Brickenstein's list of missing persons they are described as "Sisters of Mercy." There is no evidence that any other religious, or priests, were on board, and for this reason alone the nuns must have been conspicuous among the passengers.

But it is their conduct at the height of the disaster, early on the Tuesday morning, which was specially remarked in most reports of the wreck. In his first account the *Times* correspondent wrote from Harwich: "Five German nuns, whose bodies are now in the deadhouse here, clasped hands and were drowned together, the chief sister, a gaunt woman 6 ft. high, calling loudly and often, 'O Christ, come quickly!' till the end came" (December 11, 1875). From the *East Kent Mercury* we learn that "five nuns and other women refused to leave the saloon and were drowned as the water rose" (December 18, 1875); and in a later dispatch to the *Times* it is reported that the nun "noted for her extreme tallness is the lady who at midnight on Monday, by standing on a table in the saloon, was able to thrust her body through the skylight and kept exclaiming, in a voice heard by those in the rigging above the roar of the storm, 'My God, my God, make haste, make haste!' " (December 13, 1875).

> . . . the inboard seas run swirling and hawling;
>   The rash smart sloggering brine
> Blinds her; but she that weather sees one thing, one;
> Has one fetch in her: she rears herself to divine
>   Ears, and the call of the tall nun
> To the men in the tops and the tackle rode over the storm's brawling.

The stories told by some of the survivors of the wreck when they eventually arrived in New York add further detail to the British press reports already quoted—although the tale grew in the telling. William Leick of Cleveland, Ohio, spoke of the moment when the order was given for all those below to come up on deck. "Most of us went out," he said, "but some persisted in remaining in the cabins and main saloon, among them the five nuns. The Stewardess at last induced the Sisters to come up to the entrance of the companion, but she was herself struck by a sea and washed across the deck and back again. The nuns fled back terrified into the saloon . . . One of them, a very large woman, with a voice like a man's, got halfway up through the skylight, and kept shrieking in a dreadful way, 'Mein Gott! mach es schnell mit uns! Give us our death quickly!' All five were drowned in the saloon, and the Stewardess told me that from her place on the seat of the skylight when she looked down she could see their bodies washing about." The next morning, when it was safe to descend from the rigging, Mr. Leick went down into the saloon to look for his luggage; "the five nuns and other bodies were lying about the floor. One of the nuns had been washed into my stateroom and her arm was lying across my valise" (*New York Herald*, December 27, 1875). A member of the crew of a smack who subsequently boarded the wreck told how "huddled together in the saloon were seen the bodies of those who had sought asylum there; how the rising tide had forced them farther and farther aft as it filled the saloon, till they were hemmed in and perished; how the women, for the most part, had shawls tied over their heads, 'so that they shouldn't see their deaths'" ("Garboard Streyke" [F. A. Smythies], *The River, the Sea and the Creek*, p.11). George Frederick, of Albany, reported that when the bodies of the drowned nuns were found in the saloon "it was discovered that they had been despoiled of gold rings and crosses" (*New York Herald*, January 3, 1876).

As soon as news of the nuns' death was received, Father Francis, father guardian of the Franciscan Friary at Stratford, went to Harwich, sought out the German vice-consul, and arranged for the coffins to be brought by rail to Stratford, where they arrived on the evening of Friday, the tenth of December. They were taken into what was then the schoolroom (now the hall) beneath St. Francis' Church, and the bodies were prepared for burial by the Sisters of the Sacred Hearts of Jesus and Mary, who until two years before had had a convent in Stratford and who still undertook pastoral work in the area served by the Friary. On Monday, the thirteenth of December, a solemn requiem Mass was offered *coram archiepiscopo* (Cardinal Manning) before the burial in St. Patrick's Cemetery at Leytonstone. The Mass was sung by Father Francis; the deacon was an exiled German friar, Father Gabriel, and the subdeacon Father Hogan, of Spanish Place. In his sermon the cardinal spoke of the nursing and teaching work of the nuns in Germany, of their exile, and of the wreck. "Compelled to embark without delay, they were obliged to face the perils of the sea in a cold season . . . Since five o'clock in the morning of that fateful Monday until Wednesday (*sic*) evening, the unfortunate passengers watched vessels passing in the distance, unable to come to their aid . . . And these holy souls were so resigned in the tranquillity of their confidence in God, that they showed not the slightest sign of agitation or fear. They remained quietly in their cabins, and when at length they were asked to mount the rigging, as a last chance of safety, they refused—they were already prepared for the great journey of eternity—life and death were the same to them. When at length a means of escape was at hand they allowed others to take their places and to save themselves. . . . We can confidently hope that the calm resignation and peaceful joy of these holy women served as an example for those who shared their dangers in those long hours of agony" (*Franciscan Monthly,* March 1897). The burial was recorded in the cemetery register as of "four females names unknown." (They were buried in Plot A13, Grave 373.) It is surprising that in spite of the information about the identity of the nuns which was available in Harwich soon after the disaster the nuns should have been buried, on the thirteenth of December, as of "names unknown." The inscription on the gravestone gives the names of four of the nuns; the name of the fifth (Henrica Fassbaender) whose body was never recovered, does not appear, either because it was never inscribed on the stone or because it has since been obliterated by exposure to the weather. The latter is probably the case, as the inscription ends with the words: ". . . four of whom were interred here, Dec. 13th."

It is of course easy to mock at the cardinal's eloquence, for his description of the nuns' last hours is directly contrary to eyewitness accounts and is largely the product of devout imagination. One turns with relief from that maudlin sentimentality to the strength and profundity of Hopkins' understanding of the same scene. The general impression given in the sermon is one of passivity, of resignation; Hopkins, with a more discerning eye and a deeper spiritual intuition, sees not passive resignation, but (even within the natural fear) positive and creative acceptance; not the resigned bearing of a cross, but the redemptive embracing of one.

> **She to the black-about air, to the breaker, the thickly**
> **Falling flakes, to the throng that catches and quails**
> **Was calling 'O Christ, Christ, come quickly':**
> **The cross to her she calls Christ to her, christens her wild-worst Best.**

Gardner's note on the last line may be considered not to go far enough. It reads: "'(crucifix) held tightly to her breast,' and/or 'she identifies her own suffering (*cross*) with that of Christ'" (*Poems* 4, p. 261). But this was, I believe, more than an identifying of her own suffering with Christ's suffering; rather was it a uniting of herself with him in and through the suffering shared. To her the cross, the suffering, meant Christ himself; she therefore accepted it (him) devotedly and joyfully; because she knew that Christ was present, behind and within her own agony, the nun positively accepted her "wild-worst" and "christened it Best." She "named" or "called" her last agony "Best": the use of the capital letter signifies the Lord himself; the cross is embraced as if it were he who died upon it. I suggest that this line can be understood more adequately if it is interpreted in the context of the concluding lines of the previous stanza:

> **. . . these thy daughters . . .**
> **Are sisterly sealed in wild waters,**
> **To bathe in his fall-gold mercies, to breathe in his all-fire glances.**

and also in association with the references in stanzas 32 and 33 to "the Yore-flood" and "the all of water." For by the device of using the word "christen" (rather than "name" or "call") in such a context Hopkins relates the nun's extremity to the experience of baptism in such a way that a number of different symbols and images are intertwined—in particular, those of water, the seal, and the sign of the cross.

Water is one of the universal pre-Christian archetypes of rebirth—witness the alchemical formula recalled by Jung, "Water which kills and makes alive" (*Psychologie der Übertragung,* p. 130)—and one constant element in the ritual and symbolism of Christian baptism, through which the individual is incorporated into Christ so that he becomes a new creature, has from the earliest times been the symbolic "drowning" of the candidate by immersion in water. The "Yore-flood" (Noah's flood, which is paralleled in the folklore of many nations besides the Hebrews) at once destroys and renews life; as Father Beirnaert writes, "the deluge reabsorbs the world and humanity into water (instituting a new epoch)" (*The Mythic Dimension in Christian Sacramentalism*). In the New Testament (for example, 1 Peter 3:20 ff.) the deluge is seen as an image of this ambivalence of water in baptism: souls were saved by means of the very water which destroyed the world; "the like figure whereunto even baptism doth also now save us." The ancient formula for the blessing of the baptismal water in the Easter Vigil contains the

words: ". . . who by the outpouring of the deluge didst signify the sacrament of rebirth . . . make this water fruitful for the rebirth of mankind." Water is "at once the object of a sacred terror because one fears
to drown there and of a passionate attraction because in the bosom of
the waters lie concealed youth and immortality" (Mircéa Eliade, *Traité
d'Histoire des Religions*, p. 182). Thus it is of destroying and life-giving
water that the Christian fathers write in relation to baptism. "At one and
the same time," writes St. Cyril of Jerusalem, "you died and were born;
the saving water became both your grave and your mother" (*Cat.* 20
[*Myst.* 2] 3). The apparently hostile waters of the Red Sea are seen to be
the means of the "saving of the nations" (*De Bapt.* 9). "We little fish,"
writes Tertullian, "are born in the water, and only by remaining in the
water can we be saved" (*De Bapt.* 1); "the soul is transformed by a
second birth from water" (*De Anima* 41). Firmicus Maternus speaks of
the "water by which men are reborn and made new" (*Prof. Rel. Err.* 2,
5). Indeed, the very word "water" is frequently used as a synonym for
baptism: "O happy water!" (Tertullian, *De Bapt.* 15). For the nun in the
shipwreck the symbol became the reality; what the world saw as her
drowning was f her incorporation into Christ. Like Marina (in both
Shakespeare and Eliot) she was "born at sea"; her "wild-worst" was in
truth her "christening."

In this stanza it is the tall nun who represents her companions in this
sacramental drowning, this "second birth from water." In the previous
stanza Hopkins uses another image and symbol of the same experience
of union with Christ: the five "daughters" of St. Francis

> **Are sisterly sealed in wild waters,**
> **To bathe in his fall-gold mercies, to breathe in his all-fire glances.**

Here their extremity is related to the experience of St. Francis on Mount
Alverno; but their transformation into the express image of Christ was
"sealed" not with stigmata (as was that of their "father" St. Francis) but
"in wild waters." The stigmata in his flesh were the proof and confirmation of his vision, "the seal of his seraph-arrival." But a shipwreck can
serve God's saving purposes as well as a seraph; because in the nuns, as
in St. Francis, Christ has triumphed, they also are "sealed"—in "wild
waters." But in a baptismal context the word "seal" means more than
"proof" or "confirmation"; it has also a technical significance. To be
"sealed in (wild) waters" is a way of describing baptism which is fully
consistent with patristic terminology, and is an expression which brings
together two symbols of baptism which more commonly occur separately. Just as in the fathers the word "water" by itself is often used as a
synonym for baptism, so is the word "seal" by itself. "Baptism," writes
Professor G. W. Lampe, "is itself described as the seal . . . Constantine
spoke of his baptism as a sealing" (*The Seal of the Spirit*, p. 239).
Hermas does indeed bring the two words together when he writes, "the

seal is the water" (9, 16. 3). In the story of Thecla's self-baptism, the reply to her request to St. Paul, "Only give me the seal in Christ, and trial shall not touch me," is, "Be patient, and you shall receive the *water*" (*Acta Pauli et Theclae,* 32). The nuns were "sealed"—in "wild waters"; drowning was the means of their incorporation into Christ.

In stanza 23 this baptismal "sealing" is related both to Christ's "lovescape crucified" and to the nun's calling "the cross to her . . . Christ." In his vision St. Francis learned that he "must needs be transformed into the express image of Christ crucified"; and this is the calling of every Christian. Christ referred to his coming passion as a baptism: "I have a baptism to be baptized with" (Luke 12:50); and it is into his passion and death that the Christian disciple is baptized. He is incorporated into Christ, his life is united to Christ's life, through sharing in Christ's passion, death, and resurrection, so that he emerges a new man. "As many of us as were baptized into Jesus Christ were baptized into his death . . . we have been planted together in the likeness of his death; we shall be also in the likeness of his resurrection" (Romans 6:3, 5). For this reason the signing with the sign of the cross has from earliest times figured in the ceremonies of baptism. "Even so early as the latter years of the 2nd century the commonest meaning of *sphragis* (seal) is 'the sign of the cross'" (Lampe, p. 263). Baptism is both a death by drowning and a death by crucifixion, which every Christian is called to share with Christ, in order to find newness of life. In the tall nun this experience was fully achieved. Like Thecla in the arena the nun in the shipwreck so to speak baptized herself anew into Christ's death— signing herself with the saving sign of the cross, receiving the seal, and immersing herself in "wild waters"; some might also even perceive in the phrase "breathe in his all-fire glances" an association with the *sufflatio* of the baptismal ritual. She was not simply resigned to martyr- dom, but positively offered herself to be incorporated into and united with Christ, using for the sacrament of baptism the materials which came to hand; and this is precisely the calling of every Christian.

To respond to the daily call to offer his pains for the sins of others unites a man most closely and most deeply with Christ. He begins to know "the fellowship of his sufferings" and to share in the passion out of which the power of saving love is so abundantly released.

> **The dense and the driven Passion, and frightful sweat;**
> **Thence the discharge of it . . .**

in and through the Christian as with his Master. Christianity does not claim to explain suffering; it tells men what to do with it. Christians are to offer their small pains in union with Christ's passion, on behalf of man- kind for whom he offered his own life; each one is to "christen his wild-worst." "Where souls err," writes Archbishop Leen, "is in not recognizing suffering when it presents itself. They cannot trace, in the ugly, ragged, harsh, uncouth, and shapeless thing that actually offers itself to experience, the fair and dignified creation of their imaginings" (*By Jacob's Well*, p. 115). The nun on board the *Deutschland*

> **Read the unshapeable shock night**
> **And knew the who and the why.**

She saw, beneath and behind the horror of storm and imminent death, the Lord, the Lover; she saw "shape" in what seemed "unshapeable"; she knew that Christ was present—within speaking distance—and therefore accepted with joy the situation which held him close. She used her suffering properly and therefore entered into the redeeming work of God.

This is the crux of the whole poem. The world's sorrows are understandable only in the light of Christ's cross, and Christ's cross can be understood only in the light of the world's sorrows. Only the redeeming passion of Christ makes sense of an otherwise "unshapeable" human existence; the only way to discern reason and purpose in the seeming illogicality and injustice of life's sufferings and frustrations is to look upon them all *sub specie crucis,* in the light of the cross. The Christian answer to the problem of innocent suffering is to regard it all in relation to the pain of God himself, the crucifixion of the Word. Commenting on the *Spiritual Exercises* Hopkins wrote: "Suppose God shewed us in a vision the whole world enclosed first in a drop of water, allowing everything to be seen in its native colours; then the same in a drop of Christ's blood, by which everything whatever was turned to scarlet, keeping nevertheless, mounted in the scarlet, its own colour too." (S, p. 194). Christ's passion does not remove, or change, events or suffering; but, if men enter into the passion and take it to themselves, the events and the suffering "keep their own colour," but are also "mounted in the scarlet." Suffering, while still continuing to be suffering, is at the same time transformed.

Michel Quoist writes in most practical terms of this creative transformation and use of human suffering: "If you are to suffer to some purpose (your sufferings) must be united to those of Jesus on the cross. Through Jesus Christ the Redeemer, useless, meaningless, intolerable suffering becomes the raw material of our redemption. It's not the suffering itself which is redemptive, but the love of Jesus which gives inner meaning to the gift of suffering." The sufferings of each of us, he goes on, afford an opportunity "of giving yourself and of saving both yourself and others . . . In each experience of suffering you can encounter your Saviour; through suffering he invites you to save the world in union with him. So bear your burden of suffering generously in union with him, and generously offer it in union with him" (*The Christian Response*, p. 132). The nun on board the *Deutschland*—the type of a true Christian—in her experience of suffering encountered her Savior, and accepted his invitation to save the world in union with him. Even if we accept the greater part of the eyewitness evidence of the nuns' conduct, we may yet believe that, beneath their natural terror as death approached, their habit of recollection issued in contrition and intercession, and that in intention they "generously offered" their sufferings in union with Christ.

Hopkins believed passionately in the love of God, and was convinced that God desires all men to be saved; but how could God be at work in the wreck? How was his saving love to be reconciled with what the poet was bound to believe must be the fate of those drowned in a state of sin? Was the power of Christ's redemption operative even there and then? The answer which the poem seems to give is that the redemptive power of God in Christ was effective through the self-offering of the nuns, for their salvation and for that of their fellow passengers.

> **. . . did the dark side of the bay of thy blessing**
> **Not vault them, the millions of rounds of thy mercy not reeve**
> **even them in?**

John Keating is of the opinion that this question is asked "doubtfully yet hopefully" (Keating, p. 25); but the plain significance of the words poses a question which expects an affirmative answer. The salvation of God was accomplished in the tall nun, and through her in the "comfortless unconfessed of them."

Here is, I believe, an even deeper mystery than the mysterious power of intercession by which the love of one Christian can through Christ's prayers open another soul to the redeeming power of God. In his retreat notes Hopkins writes of Christ's accomplishing the redemption of all men through "the great sacrifice"; and he speaks of those who "take part in the sacrifice," those who, themselves redeemed by Christ, participate in his redeeming sacrifice; and he says that God "for the sake of one ear or grape" would accept "the whole sheaf or cluster" (S, p. 197). The paradox of God's mastery and mercy, of his justice and love, exemplified in the shipwreck, the dilemma (in Newman's phrase "to dizzy and appal") of how his saving will could have been accomplished in the "comfortless unconfessed" of the passengers who were lost, was resolved by the nun's entering into the passion by her "taking part in the sacrifice," by her "christening of her wild-worst." She was united to Christ not only in her sufferings, but also in what she did with them.

In an unpublished sermon preached in the University Church in Oxford in 1965 Canon David Anderson spoke of the significance of the Old Testament sin-offering and of the concept of Jesus on the cross being the reality of that type. He went on to speak of those missionaries in the Congo (as it then was) who "preferred to stay and share in the evil of the times, an evil which only in a very remote sense they had

helped to create, rather than to contract out and withdraw to safety."
Their terrible suffering was a "deliberate, freely accepted suffering.
What is achieved by this deliberate sharing in the evil of others? All
depends on what kind of sharing it is. Whenever we seek to share with
others in the evil of their condition, bringing with us not a nerveless pity
but the hope and inspiration of an implacable love, then we are sharing
in the reproach of Jesus outside the camp, and he is acting through *us*"
(preached on Sunday, January 24). It was thus, the poem suggests, that
in the wreck of the *Deutschland* Christ achieved his work, his strange
work, of redemption. Then and there the world's judgments were over-
turned: what the world saw as loss was gain; what the world saw as
sheer destruction was creative; that which destroyed bodies wrought the
salvation of souls; the shipwreck was a harvest.

It was because the nun "christened her wild-worst Best" that the
poet's prayer came to be answered:

> **Make mercy in all of us, out of us all**
> **Mastery, but be adored, but be adored King.**

The shipwreck was a peculiar and extreme disaster, but the truth is there
for all men to take to their own comfort and inspiration: in every pain
and desolation a Christian may meet in his life, however great or small,
there lie the materials of the heavenward road, the opportunity of sharing in the redeeming sacrifice of Christ. "Even your headache," writes
Michel Quoist, "your exhaustion, your physical pain, the difficulties of
your work, your disappointments, your hurt feelings, your failures, your
humiliations . . . Christ has already experienced all of your sufferings
and has already offered them all to his Father—and the Father has
already accepted them from the hands of his Son . . . In virtue of the
love of Jesus Christ they have already redeemed the world" (*The Christian Response*, p. 132). This is the "christening," the redemptive sharing, to which every Christian is called, and which is within the reach
of all.

Chapter III

"O Christ, Christ, Come Quickly!"

Lexical Plenitude and Primal Cry
at the Heart of *The Wreck*

by Paul L. Mariani

W hen the tug *Liverpool* churned through the heavy, slogging seas that Tuesday morning in early December 1875 chuffing out from the Harwich rescue station and out into the slate gray North Atlantic, twenty and more miles southeast toward the Kentish Knock, what was it that its rescue crew and these reporters for papers like the London *Times* and the *Illustrated London News* saw? They would have seen, of course, the bow of the large (328 feet) North German steamer, the *Deutschland,* wedged into those treacherous shallows, the stern still lifting and falling like some giant toy, its screw propellers useless, sheared off in that desperate last-minute attempt to clear the shoals. And too they would have seen the fishing smacks hovering near the crippled ship's sides, their crews out early for the day's take, stripping the ship's dead, those bobbing bodies, of their purses, wallets, wedding rings, whatever. And they would have seen some of the sixty and more corpses themselves, either on the ship or floating on the rough icy waters, dancing with the waves, and one, the corpse of a sailor, his head gone, swinging with the lilt of the ship's pitch, still attached by his waist to a rope tied taut to the rigging, as though the just-past storm had mocked his valiant, vain efforts to rescue some now-dead woman or child who had cried out from the deck for help. Once aboard, they would have seen those corpses afloat or sunk in the flooded compartments, and—a rare sight—the bodies of four nuns, one six foot if she were an inch, their blue hands clenched, swaying in the swamped saloon. (A fifth had been pulled loose from that closed circle and sucked, swept, pulled out into that vast sea sometime before dawn.) Later, after all the bodies that had been recovered had been brought into the deadhouse at Harwich and photographed for identification purposes, some of the survivors would remember that, at the height of the storm, as the black tides rose over twenty feet, the tall nun, the one who was evidently the superior, had cried out over and over again in German, "O Christ, Christ, come quickly!" until the sea stopped her mouth. What had she meant? Was it terror? hallucination? a cry to have the ordeal over and done with, as with that body they'd found behind the wheelhouse, its wrists roughly slit?

Sometime the following morning—December 8, the solemn feast of the Immaculate Conception—a young (thirty-one) second-year theology student at St. Beuno's College in North Wales heard and, it being a holiday, probably read the first news dispatches in the *Times* of the wreck of the *Deutschland.* Mr. Gerard Hopkins, S.J., had seen and felt the snowstorm that had covered Wales and caused that ship to sail thirty miles off course and into that smother of sand, had in fact slept soundly at the very time people were dropping exhausted from the freezing rigging down onto the deck or into the raging seas. Shipwrecks had always interested him (he liked reading of violent action, he once told his brother Everard); and all this week and the next and the next after that he would scan the published reports of the disaster, would read the demands for official inquiries into the conduct of the Harwich rescue station which had failed all through that Monday storm to respond to the *Deutschland's* distress signals, and would no doubt shake his head at the reprehensible conduct of his countrymen who had been more intent on plundering than on rescuing the survivors. That Christmas Eve he thanked his mother for sending along the news clippings of the wreck. (In her enthusiasm she had even sent along some duplicates.) And sometime, probably during the week of the disaster itself, Hopkins had even been told by his rector, Father James Jones, S.J., an Irishman in his mid-forties, that perhaps someone could, even should, write something about the special circumstances of this disaster, which had seen these five German nuns, a cloistered community of Franciscans from Westphalia, exiled by the virulently anti-Catholic Falck Laws and forced to emigrate to a sister house in Canada, all drowned instead off the English coast. There had been a solemn funeral Mass for the dead sisters at Stratford-le-Bow, at which Cardinal Manning himself had delivered the address, and the four nuns whose bodies had been recovered had been put to rest at Leytonstone, very near Hopkins' own home in Hampstead. The whole incident had, as Hopkins wrote his mother that Christmas Eve, "made a deep impression on me, more than any other wreck or accident I ever read of" (L III, p. 135).

Father Jones, who appears to have understood the special needs of his sensitive theology student, seems to have realized that indeed it might be good to have someone write something about the disaster, and even to have suggested—or at least given permission—to Hopkins to go ahead and do some verses. After all, Hopkins had in the past done a few occasional pieces, including, very recently, an Englishing of a hymn (wrongly) attributed to St. Francis Xavier for the Jesuit saint's feast day on December 3. And Hopkins—in the flush of his learning Welsh—had even tried his hand at a version in that difficult tongue of the same hymn and for the same august occasion, though few if any of his fellow Jesuits could have said if that attempt had succeeded or failed.

So here was a man who for seven years now had kept his muse silent, considering his priestly vocation to be at odds with his poetic one, who had done only such occasional verse as his superiors had requested, and who now in the winter of 1875 had received what he interpreted as permission to do something on a much-publicized disaster. Consider that for those seven years of silence his closest and most constant companions had been his fellow Jesuits: novices, philosophy students, theology students, figures like Father Henry Coleridge, S.J., and Mr. Francis Bacon, S.J.; that his daily studies and readings at meals consisted of, among others, Suarez and Molina, Rodriguez, Augustine's *Confessions,* Francis Xavier, Ignatius Loyola, Newman and Patrignani, Segneri and Salazar. Consider the fact that when Robert Bridges wrote, asking him what he had read of Hegel, Hopkins wrote back that he had little time for any reading other than his theological studies and that, in any event, he would have preferred Duns Scotus to a—*pace tua*—dozen Hegels. Suarez and Scotus have never constituted the average literary staple of British readers and seldom have they served as muses for British poets. They might, some of them, rightly belong to the vast, forbidding shelves of required reading for all those generations of English divines, themselves no longer read, but relatively little of all that has found its way into our English texts and anthologies.

And *what* was Hopkins to write, and what form to use? We have little hard information to reconstruct a psychogenetic reading of *The Wreck* poem, but we do know that Hopkins began, by his own telling, with the present twelfth stanza, began, that is, in a narrative mode, to describe the actual events of the disaster as he had learned them from the papers—"On Saturday sailed from Bremen,/American-outward-bound,/Take settler and seamen, tell men with women,/Two hundred souls in the round"—and that he soon enveloped that narrative in the larger modality of the Pindaric ode, as the disaster became a cause for celebration, a victory over death itself. Hopkins knew well that English was not rich in ode literature, but he clearly wanted that form for its formal freedoms and its celebratory tradition. For what had happened out there in those dark waters was tragic only if viewed from its dark underside and in the short view. What he wanted, rather, was to correct that partial vision, to stress upon his readers that indeed what had happened might well be cause for rejoicing.

There is in *The Wreck* ode a religious intensity, an emotional force which is comparatively rare in the English language. Hopkins' poetry, as he himself admitted, must be prepared for, takes some getting used to. Otherwise it will seem forced, strange, indeed even repellent. *The Wreck of the Deutschland* in particular generates the reaction one associates with the kind of intense, subjective religious response one might make in the midst of a long and serious spiritual retreat. Its priorities and sense of reality belong, finally, to that order of experience which to anyone with even a taste for Plato may well be the "truer" order, its news truer even than the truth of the *Times.* Hopkins himself offered the poem only to *The Month,* the literary organ of the Jesuits of the English Province, offered it in fact to Father Coleridge, his "oldest friend in the Society." And when, after holding on to the poem for several months, the editor finally rejected it in September 1875, Hopkins considered the matter of publication closed. If the Jesuits found it too idiosyncratic, then what would others think? If Hopkins thought of an audience beyond his own Lord, it was those Catholic readers who might, one would have thought, have given the poem at least a sympathetic reading.

Midway through the ode, literally at the heart or "midriff" of the poem, Hopkins, "here all alone" in his room at St. Beuno's, in the very process of discovering his own response to the wreck, finds himself weeping at those events as they stress themselves upon him. But these, he sees, are tears of joy, joy at the realization of the wondrous ways in which God works even in times of great storm and stress. By a long and intense meditation in the Ignatian mode on those words the tall nun had uttered, her counterstress to the "unshapeable shock night" of the storm, words which had in fact been published all over England, Hopkins comes to see by degrees their inner significance, their unerring aim, their true inscape. From personal experience and personal witness, he is able to tell not only what that cry meant but, indeed, what the probable effect of the nun's response has been on the others, including the "comfortless unconfessed" of them. What she had felt so intensely there in her last extremity had been the foredrawing of her whole being toward her Lord and Master, as her whole self, now on the brink of dissolution, like some "lush-kept plush-capped sloe," had answered with a *yes* to Christ's stress straining against her midriff. That, then, was the meaning of her cry, the real presence of her Lord comforting her and her sisters, with the storm and its attendant figure, death, transfigured for them in recognizing and accepting God's will for them. In a flash, the storm king has become the solicitous bridegroom.

Hopkins could, of course, respond to the sister's cry because he had already said his *yes* to the stress of Christ's terrifying and terrible presence. At some point, somewhere, before some altar in the depths of some nameless night, he too had felt his inescapable presence and had confessed him "truer" than even his tongue could have confessed. So now Hopkins, again pressed to it, can utter in the lexical plenitude of his magnificent ode something of that primal cry. Now, as God's finger touches him anew, Hopkins knows it is the same source of inspiration that had touched the nun that night. And that stress sets lexical flecks flashing off from that arch, original cry, that *yes,* that first, best word. As with the original act of preaeonian creation, it is in the selving, the stress of proclaiming one's self, in which the Utterer begets the Uttered, the Word, Christ, *Ipse,* the Sacrificed, that the dapple, stipple, dazzling multifoliate plenitude of the entire creation is likewise struck off. "It is," as Hopkins wrote in his notebook during the Long Retreat of his Tertianship in the fall of 1881, "as if the blissful agony or stress of selving in God had forced out drops of sweat or blood, which drops were the world . . . [creating] one 'cleave' out of the world of possible creatures" (S, p. 197).

So too with the act of creating the utterance which is the poem, moving by necessity beyond the original instress, the unnameable name of Christ, the Sacrificed, the *Yes.* So too the direction that Hopkins' poetic response will take must also, of necessity, come to "one 'cleave' out of the world of possible creatures." There is, of course, at the heart of this ode, and the reeving or roping in its two parts, the original *yes* of the sacrificed Christ on the cross to which Hopkins had responded with his own *yes* and to which the nun had likewise responded with hers in that storm. In turn, her response had triggered a fresh response in Hopkins, and may well have triggered all those possible other *yeses* of the other shipwrecked souls, and finally, by an extension outward, the possible *yes* of every reader of Hopkins' publication of her good news. So there is the explicit petition at the conclusion to Part I:

> **Make mercy in all of us, out of us all**
> **Mastery, but be adored, but be adored King**

and the doubling of that petition at the end of Part II:

> **Let him easter in us, be a dayspring to the dimness of us,**
> **be a crimson-cresseted east,**
> **More brightening her, rare-dear Britain, as his reign rolls,**
> **Pride, rose, prince, hero of us, high-priest,**
> **Our hearts' charity's hearth's fire, our thoughts' chivalry's**
> **throng's Lord.**

One notices other mathematical proportions between the parts of the poem (as one would expect from the poet who fretted over the inner nature of the parts of the sonnet and could see in a tree its sonnetlike inscape), as with the play between threes and fives, numbers echoing the eternal trinity and the aeonian lovescape of the crucified Christ, doubled in the stigmata of St. Francis of Assisi as well as in the sealing in death of these five Franciscan nuns, as sign begets sign. So, if one considers the stress patterns of each stanza in Part I (Part II contains an extra stress in the first line of each of its stanzas), we get the following count: 2-3-4-3-5-5-4-6, which splits down the middle into a 12:20 or 3:5 ratio. And the middle of each stanza divides around that same stress count. This can hardly be accidental, especially when one considers such lines as "Be adored among men,/God, three-numbered form," or, in the corresponding antepenultimate stanza of Part II, the line, "Mid-numbered he in three of the thunder-throne!" And there are these lines as well:

> **Five! the finding and sake**
> **And cipher of suffering Christ,**
> **Mark, the mark is of man's make**
> **And the word of it Sacrificed.**

We ought not be surprised, though, to find such structural chimings of these sacred numbers repeating themselves in the very placement of stresses in the poem. As with Providence itself, Hopkins' poem leaves little to randomness, to the chance happening. And so, if we continue to look along the line of this 3:5 ratio, we see that one of the structural turning points of the ode occurs in the very center of the twenty-first stanza, three-fifths of the way into the poem itself. There, the plight of the nun reaches its uttermost pitch, as the elements conspire to destroy these "loathed" and "banned" exiles. But, even as it reaches that crescendo, the temporal gives way to the eternal, and the "storm flakes" become "scroll-leaved flowers, lily showers" in Christ's—and now our—eyes, as once again the Word calms the endragoned seas.

So the number five, read aright for (and as) Christ's sake, rings out its inner significance for Hopkins. And the day too that he came to those sisters? Had that been random, without meaning? They had been sealed into their *martyrdom*—for those Falck Laws had killed these cloistered nuns as much as anything—sometime before December 7 had dawned. December 7: the eve of the Immaculate Conception, the "Feast of the one woman without stain." And that fact likewise rings with significance for Hopkins alone in his room in that dark Advent season. For Mary, herself conceived without sin, without the blight man had been born to and which had twisted the heart to lean "unteachably after evil," had been able to likewise conceive Christ without stain.

But there is that other conception, Hopkins sees, when heart and mind, feeling the keen instress of God's grace, utter as one that Word/word "outright," that is, right out, but also correctly. And so too the nun's utterance, her own conceiving of the ordeal she is undergoing, her reading aright "the unshapeable shock night," brings the bridegroom to this virginal maid and chimes with Mary's own *yes*, her *fiat*. And that primal cry and first stress, echoing the stress of the crucified Christ, once proclaimed, ripples outward across the foundering wreck in the dark, as word begets word, chiming likewise perhaps—for it is a question Hopkins poses and poises here in stanza 31, and not a certitude—in those other poor souls. Did they too, some of them at least, as their numbed hands clawed against the cold rigging before they dropped heavily into the black waters, did they confess that name somewhere deep within themselves? For Christ, that enormous lover, that compassionate giant, harrowing hell with his man-marked wounds, sweeps down even after the drowned for "The-last-breath-penitent," after any sign of a counterresponse in his beloved, to take him or her home with him.

"You understand of course," Hopkins wrote his agnostic friend, Bridges, in mid-January 1879—and when Bridges bridled, Hopkins explained his intentions and then dropped the subject for good—

> You understand . . . that I desire to see you a Catholic or, if not that, a Christian or, if not that, at least a believer in the true God (for you told me something of your views about the deity, which were not as they should be). Now you no doubt take for granted that your already being or your ever coming to be any of these things turns on the working of your own mind, influenced or uninfluenced by the minds and reasonings of others as the case may be, and on that only (L I, p. 60).

But the kind of assent Hopkins was speaking of did not rest alone or even primarily on intellectual arguments (as Hopkins well knew, even if he did not say so to Bridges). It depended, rather, on responding—at whatever the personal cost—to the stress of Christ's own love for men in spending himself on the cross. If Bridges could, then, bring himself to put himself out for others, as, for example, by giving alms to those in need at one of the hospitals where he served as a staff physician, then Hopkins was convinced that Christ would not be behindhand in his own counterresponse. Bridges, one gathers, answered something testily about not being interested in donning hairshirts or that sort of thing. Pushed to it, he had retreated from Hopkins' suggestion, as many naturally would, to give until there was some "sensible inconvenience," as Hopkins had put it, to give, that is, till the giving hurt.

It was no idle advice Hopkins offered, for that had been precisely what he himself had done again and again, responding to his Lord's emptying of himself (which was what the *kenosis* Paul had spoken of in his letters came to) with his own emptying of himself. Where was it Hopkins had first confessed the Lord's terrifying yet consoling presence? Had it been his conversion experience at the small country church at Horsham that summer of 1866, while he was studying for his examinations with Alfred Garrett and taking those long, quiet country walks? "It was this night I believe but possibly the next," Hopkins wrote in his *Journal* for July 17 of that year, "that I saw clearly the impossibility of staying in the Church of England, but resolved to say nothing to anyone till three months are over" (J, p. 146). Was it sometime during the first week of that Long Retreat two years later at the Jesuit novitiate at Roehampton? Or was it another time? We do not know and Hopkins' ode does not say, though it celebrates from its first word to its last, and in all the extraordinary verbal pyrotechnics in between, the mastery of Christ over his creation.

And what a dapple of language it is, with its rich *cynganhedd*, words chiming against words, all foregrounding the inner radical significations of those lexical echoes. In stanza 8, for example consider the incrementation of *lash, last, lush, plush, flesh, gush, flush, flash, last, first, feet*, as those words move (one would think) inevitably foredrawn toward the feet of Christ, toward the Sacrificed Word, as tongue utters now "the best or worst/Word last!" Consider too how these chimings foredraw toward their inevitable lexical complementation, *lash* and *last* and *lush* and *plush* and *flesh* all brought hovering about that guessed-at *yes,* the *fiat* of Hopkins, the surrender of the nun. And yet, in another of those Christian paradoxes, for all the poem's incredibly rich language, its images of a "dappled-with-damson west," its sea "flint-flake, black-backed in the regular blow," its "rash smart sloggering brine," its May season with "Blue-beating and hoary-glow height," for all this incredibly varied wording and compounding of words, Christ remains "Beyond saying sweet, past telling of tongue."

Until very near the end of his relatively short life, Hopkins would continue to oscillate between lexical plenitude and lexical spareness, counterpointing the starkness of some of his dark sonnets against the verbal richness of such pieces as *The Leaden Echo and the Golden Echo* or his unfinished *Epithalamion.* That oscillation, one comes to see, reflects Hopkins' consciously failing attempts to utter what can, finally, only be imperfectly uttered no matter how rich the verbal lode one has at one's command. The opposite tack *in extremis,* one sees, would be to elect silence, and we know that Hopkins tried that way as well, and more than once. One of the things that *The Wreck* ode says, and says so well, is that the poem's inscape, its central significance and "uttermost mark," is the simple *yes* paid out to Christ, to the first word, the alpha of the creation and of this other poetic creation echoing that, to the *Thou* which sits at the head of the ode, as well as to the poem's and creation's last, best word, that signature of apocalyptic closure, the omega word, *Lord.* And so the extraordinary baroque uncoiling of those two hundred and eighty lines in between this first and last word loops out in its own unreeving to fold back, in an imitation of the great procession of all creation out and back to God, to the primal utterance, that sign, that cipher, that Word.

When the tug *Liverpool* churned through the heavy, slogging, rash smart seas on the eve of the feast celebrating the Immaculate Conception, chuffing out from the Harwich rescue station and into the still restless, flint-flaked slate gray North Atlantic, out toward the sand smother named the Kentish Knock, what was it one saw? And who could say for certain that the phosphorescence coming off some of those bobbing bodies, dancing here in these foam-flecked waters, was not indeed a sign of the transfigured *soma,* signifying a sea-change now into something rich and strange? Who could say for sure that this tempest-tossed shipwreck had not indeed become a harvest and that these selves, these souls, were not home safe now, these waters become, in a flash, in a trumpet crash, truly the "heaven-haven of the reward"?

Notes

a   I should like to modify here what I wrote in my *Commentary* concerning the mode in which Hopkins means us to understand how it was that the nun "fetched" Christ. Except for a few very minor points, I would still stand by my reading of *The Wreck* presented there. But I no longer maintain—nor have I for several years—that Hopkins meant his readers to believe that Christ had literally walked the waters of the Thames that December night and that the nun's cry was in fact attesting to that kind of miracle. At the time I wrote that chapter, I had recently read Professor

Elisabeth Schneider's *The Dragon in the Gate* and had been impressed by her arguments supporting such a reading. Now, six years later, I believe that when Hopkins spoke of "real fetching, presentment, or 'adduction,'" of a real presence as opposed to "mere vision," that such fetching does not have to take the form of a ghostly presence; the presence Hopkins is speaking of is, rather, one felt so certainly in the very center of the heart that the heart becomes in its turn so instressed that it must respond with its own counterstress, its own utterance. Hopkins clearly believed in miracles and signs, and made no secret of it, but, as James Finn Cotter has said in his impressive study, *Inscape: The Christology and Poetry of Gerard Manley Hopkins,* Hopkins "would hardly invent one where eyewitness reports gave no grounds for its occurrence." The real center of Hopkins' ode is much more firmly rooted in the Christian experience than Professor Schneider's reading suggests.

b There is, both in this poem and elsewhere in Hopkins' poetry, a kind of daring play with Christ's/God's name, especially when the poet is under extreme emotional stress. So, for example, I believe that Hopkins was well aware that many readers, reading the nun's words, "O Christ, Christ, come quickly," might be tempted to read them as an empty expletive, Christ's name evoked the way most of us do from time to time when the hammer finds the thumb instead of the nail, for example. Under extreme stress, we might evoke that name as a sign to which the whole self is foredrawn, or we might use it as an empty cipher. So, it is "for Christ's sake" or "for God's sake" or "O Christ, Christ," and we "lash," then, "with the best or worst/Word last."

Chapter IV

"The Strong Spur, Live and Lancing"

The Motive of Martyrdom in *The Wreck*

by Francis Noel Lees

I n his book *Hopkins the Jesuit,* Father Alfred Thomas observes that the wreck of the *Deutschland* was not the only nautical disaster to take place in the early seventies of the nineteenth century. A ship called the *Captain* sank in 1870 and Hopkins noted the fact in his diary. On November 4, 1875, about a month before the *Deutschland* ran aground, a steamship coming from Vancouver, the *Pacific,* foundered. In both cases the loss of life was greater, in the first case very much greater, than in that of the *Deutschland.* There was also—to move away from the sea—a coal-mining disaster of magnitude on the very same day as the *Deutschland* calamity. "One would like to know," says Father Thomas, "why this particular shipwreck should have given rise to the poem" (Thomas, p. 168).

We could make a great deal of that question, we could easily make too much of it, one feels, and yet the question does remain; and Hopkins does not precisely answer it. He does say, of course, to his mother in 1875, "it made a deep impression on me, more than any other wreck or accident I ever read of" (L III, p. 135); and to Canon Dixon, "when in the winter of '75 the Deutschland was wrecked in the mouth of the Thames and five Franciscan nuns, exiles from Germany by the Falck Laws, aboard of her were drowned I was affected by the account . . ." (L II, p. 14). These observations do not take us very far—far enough, I suppose, for our general need as readers of poetry but not far enough for our particular curiosity as priers into inner, spiritual biography. *Why* did it make so deep an impression? *Why* did it so sharply affect him?

We may obviously take it that it was the presence on board of the five nuns, the loss then of their lives and the most notable behavior of one of them that made for Hopkins the appeal of this particular shipwreck. The nuns had been exiled from their native land for being Catholic religious, but it was not merely that they were coreligionists that fired Hopkins' mind. It is very unlikely that no one else on board was a Catholic. Hopkins, indeed, speaks of other passengers as "the comfortless, unconfessed of them," not, therefore, it would seem, infidels; but he speaks of them in passing only. Nor was it, I think, because they were fellow religious. It was, rather, because being Catholic religious they were on shipboard by duress and through this it was that they lost their lives. They were, it may be maintained, martyrs, or as good as, and for Hopkins, as for very many Catholics and others, the appeal of the martyr was very deep. There, at any rate, used to be a stiffening of the sinews, a summoning-up of the blood, in English Catholics as they sang the hymn to the martyrs, "Faith of Our Fathers," and imitated in mind and aspiration their persecuted forebears who had been so courageous in act. "Our Lord Jesus Christ . . . is the supreme object of our love, gratitude and reverence. Next to Him, we honour the noble army of martyrs," wrote John Henry Newman in a collection published in 1870 of some of his Anglican writings. Of the saints who are subjects of poems by Hopkins all but one (St. Alphonsus) are officially martyrs of the Church: St. Thecla, St. Dorothea, St. Winifred, and the recently canonized Margaret Clitheroe. There, I suggest, lies an answer to Father Thomas' question. Not the closest answer, perhaps, but at any rate a closer one.

In the pages of the *National Reformer*, a secularist periodical founded by Charles Bradlaugh, there appeared in 1874 the poem *The City of Dreadful Night* by James Thomson. The authoritative figure in "the mighty fane" of Section XIV, a figure with "two eyes which burned as never eyes burned yet" and with a "voice of solemn stress" proclaims this message:

And now at last authentic word I bring,
Witnessed by every dead and living thing;
    Good tidings of great joy for you, for all:
There is no God; no fiend with names divine
Made us and tortures us; if we must pine,
    It is to satiate no Being's gall.

It was the dark delusion of a dream,
That living Person conscious and supreme,
    Whom we must curse for cursing us with life;
Whom we must curse because the life He gave
Could not be buried in the quiet grave,
    Could not be killed by poison or by knife . . .

I find no hint throughout the Universe
Of good or ill, of blessing or of curse;
    I find alone Necessity Supreme;
With infinite Mystery, abysmal, dark,
Unlighted ever by the faintest spark
    For us the flitting shadows of a dream.

And the "I" of the poem, a listener with others to this "great sad voice" continues a little later:

How the moon triumphs through the endless nights!
    How the stars throb and glitter as they wheel
Their thick processions of supernal lights
    Around the blue vault obdurate as steel!
And men regard with passionate awe and yearning
The mighty marching and the golden burning,
    And think the heavens respond to what they feel . . .

With such a living light these dead eyes shine,
    These eyes of sightless heaven, that as we gaze
We read a pity, tremulous, divine,
    Or cold, majestic scorn in their pure rays:
Fond man! they are not haughty, are not tender;
There is no heart or mind in all their splendour,
    They thread mere puppets all their marvellous maze.

If we could near them with the flight unflown,
    We should but find them worlds as sad as this,
Or suns all self-consuming like our own
    Enringed by planet worlds as much amiss:
They wax and wane through fusion and confusion;
The spheres eternal are a grand illusion,
    The empyréan is a void abyss.

Yet here in *The Wreck of the Deutschland* we have Hopkins expressing his faith in God, a living, personal God, an almighty God, yet a caring God, with immense confidence:

Thou mastering me
    God! giver of breath and bread;
World's strand, sway of the sea;
    Lord of living and dead;
Thou hast bound bones and veins in me, fastened me flesh,
And after it almost unmade, what with dread,
    Thy doing: and dost thou touch me afresh?
Over again I feel thy finger and find thee.

And here he is telling his joy in a nature which images forth its Creator in its "splendour and wonder":

I kiss my hand
    To the stars, lovely-asunder
Starlight, wafting him out of it; and
    Glow, glory in thunder;
Kiss my hand to the dappled-with-damson west:
Since, tho' he is under the world's splendour and wonder,
    His mystery must be instressed, stressed;
For I greet him the days I meet him, and bless when I understand.

In 1872 a history of the world grimly entitled *The Martyrdom of Man* was published. It was by Winwood Reade, elder brother of the novelist Charles Reade. Reade proceeds further along the way which the Tennyson of *In Memoriam* in 1850 had been dismayed to see seeming to lie before him. Tennyson had written as follows:

Are God and Nature then at strife,
    That Nature lends such evil dreams?
    So careful of the type she seems,
So careless of the single life . . .

> . . . And he, shall he, . . .

Who trusted God was love indeed
  And love Creation's final law—
  Tho' Nature, red in tooth and claw
With ravine, shriek'd against his creed . . .

As Reade draws to his conclusion he writes: "Pain, grief, disease and death, are these the inventions of a loving God? . . . It is useless to say that pain has its benevolence, that massacre has its mercy. Why is it so ordained that bad should be the raw material of good?" And again: "Those who believe in a God of Love must close their eyes to the phenomena of life, or garble the Universe to suit their theory." He concludes:

> Not only the Syrian [that is, Christian] superstition must be attacked, but also the belief in a personal God, which engenders a slavish and oriental condition of the mind; and the belief in a posthumous reward which engenders a selfish and solitary condition of the heart . . . The supreme and mysterious Power by whom the universe has been created . . . , that awful One to whom it is profanity to pray, of whom it is idle and irreverent to argue and debate, of whom we should never presume to think save with humility and awe; that Unknown God has ordained that mankind should be elevated by misfortune and that happiness should grow out of misery and pain. I give to universal history a strange but true title—*The Martyrdom of Man* . . .

Reade's notion of a "supreme and mysterious Power" is Herbert Spencer's "Unknowable." We are firmly on the road of that rationalistic freethinking which was increasing its adherents and going beyond the strict letter of agnosticism into this hypostatization of something which on its own terms was simply not known. (T. H. Huxley, coiner of the word "agnostic" in 1869 or thereabouts, was himself to say in his essay "Agnosticism and Christianity" that he did "not very much care to speak of anything as 'unknowable'," adding later, "I confess that, long ago, I once or twice made this mistake; even to the waste of a capital 'U'.") Yet there is a superficial resemblance between Reade's grasp of things and Hopkins'. Hopkins, in *The Wreck*, says these things:

> **They fought with God's cold—**
> **And they could not and fell to the deck**
> **(Crushed them) or water (and drowned them) . . .**

>   **. . . past all**
> **Grasp God, throned behind**
> **Death with a sovereignty that heeds but hides, bodes but abides . . .**

>   **. . . with fire in him forge thy will . . .**

> Thou art lightning and love, I found it, a winter and warm;
> Father and fondler of heart thou hast wrung:
> Hast thy dark descending and most art merciful then.

> Well, she has thee for the pain, for the
> Patience . . .

There is, in fact, a common recognition that in life there is pain, suffering, calamity; that we can speak of life in the words of the antiphon *Salve Regina*, as "in hac lacrymarum valle, in this vale of tears." But after this Hopkins diverges into an almost tangible, palpable belief in a personal God. It is very plain that Reade's assertion, "it is ordained that bad should be the raw material of good," bears no real resemblance to Hopkins' ideas. For Hopkins his personal God is constantly "heeding," "boding." His purposes are mysterious but not arbitrary; and the benefits emergent from suffering which are certainly envisaged are benefits for the sufferer himself—and spiritual ones, benefits only to be conceived by a literal believer in that place of "posthumous reward," heaven. There is no stream of bad and good moving along heedless of the individual person, the individual soul.

A vivid embodiment of a dramatically sardonic development of the Reade views is to be found in Thomas Hardy's poem on the loss of the *Titanic, The Convergence of the Twain.* This was written much later, in 1914: it may nonetheless be properly referred to here. The poem ends:

> And as the smart ship grew
> In stature, grace, and hue,
> In shadowy silent distance grew the Iceberg too.

> Alien they seemed to be:
> No mortal eye could see
> The intimate welding of their later history.

> Or sign that they were bent
> By paths coincident
> On being anon twin halves of one august event.

> Till the Spinner of the Years
> Said 'Now!' And each one hears,
> And consummation comes, and jars two hemispheres.

But it is Leslie Stephen, in his *An Agnostic's Apology* (1893) who comes very close to giving an irreligionist's criticism of *The Wreck of the Deutschland,* ignorant of its very existence though he must have been. He comments scornfully on those who think they "know that God is good and just." Such people are "marked by a certain tinge of mysticism"—and "mysticism" was very much a word of scorn in the rationalist vocabulary—"they feel rather than know":

> The awe with which they regard the universe, the tender glow of reverence and love with which the bare sight of nature affects them is to them the ultimate guarantee of their beliefs. Happy those who feel such emotions! Only, when they try to extract definite statements of fact from these impalpable sentiments, they should beware how far such statements are apt to come into terrible collision with reality. And, meanwhile, those who have been disabused with Candide, who have felt the weariness and pain of all "this unintelligible world," and have not been able to escape into any mystic rapture, have as much to say for their own version of the facts. When, rapt in the security of a happy life, we cannot even conceive that our happiness will fail, we are practical optimists. When some random blow out of the dark crushes the pillars round which our life has been entwined as recklessly as a boy sweeps away a cobweb, when at a single step we plunge through the flimsy crust of happiness into the deep gulfs beneath we are tempted to turn to Pessimism. Who shall decide and how?

To be exact, Hopkins' "reverence and love" at the sight of "the world's splendour and wonder" were not the guarantee of his beliefs. Stephen, however, would thus have described those beliefs.

I have, I suppose, merely shown that Hopkins was a Catholic, and a most fervent one, standing out in decisive contrast to the strong flow of rationalizing, despiritualizing agnosticism, and even atheism of the latter part of the nineteenth century: which, of course, followed upon the new findings of the scientific mind in geology and biology, in German biblical criticism, all of which cut away, or seemed to, the grounds of traditional orthodox belief. This can hardly be thought news; but the reason for my wishing to bring out the differences between Hopkins' beliefs in the poem and those of the dominant new thinking of the period is in order to demonstrate that there is nothing in the poem that could be felt to be allied with any class of rationalist heterodoxy. This is because of a passage in a letter to Bridges of May 1878 where Hopkins writes: "I must tell you that I am sorry that you never read the Deutschland again. Granted that it needs study and is obscure, for indeed I was not over-desirous that the meaning of all should be quite clear, at least unmistakable . . ." (L I, p. 50). This seems a strange thing for him to have said unless there were involved some idea or sentiment of an unorthodox kind, yet it seems clear to me from the comparisons I have made that nothing in the direction of free thought, at any rate, could be alleged. The poem is deeply, challengingly Catholic (I should perhaps say "Romanist") in both intrinsic thinking and incidental expression.

Perhaps, then, we should look for some item of incautious, overbold devotionalism; but though there are several examples of devotional boldness of idea—the emblematic development of the number five, for instance, or the analogy drawn between the nun and the Blessed Virgin as mother in "But here was heart-throe, birth of a brain,/Word, that heard and kept thee and uttered thee outright"—these may be criticized as poetry for being merely fanciful, they cannot be thought matters which the poet would be doctrinally wary about disclosing. They are, in any case, not covert; they are, for all their difficulty of language, quite explicit. It is true that Hopkins' strong feeling for Christ as King was doctrinally advanced. On this point that most expert of commentators Father Christopher Devlin has said, "the whole tendency of modern devotion is moving in a direction which Hopkins seems to have anticipated"—and the church feast of Christ the King was instituted by Pius XI in 1925. The matter, however, is clearly not one to have required reticence and it is, after all, writ large and bold in the poem. Elisabeth Schneider and Alison Sulloway have both thought Hopkins claimed that Christ actually appears to the nun in the poem, and this would indeed have been an assertion theoretically open to official formal correction and therefore conceivably for the poet to be reserved about. Such a view depends on stanza 28 with its excited premonitory syntax:

> **Strike you the sight of it? Look at it loom there,**
> **Thing that she . . . there then! the Master,**
> *Ipse,* **the only one, Christ, King, Head:**
> **He was to cure the extremity where he had cast her . . .**

The interpretation may rest on thinking that "the sight of it," "Look at it loom there," and "Thing that she . . ." refer to Christ appearing; but "it" and "thing" are not acceptable ways of speaking of Christ. They are proper words, however, for referring to what the poet realizes, which is the nun's response to the situation, her grasp of it. The urgent, interrupted syntax only communicates the gradual dawning on the poet of the "mind's burden" of the nun, her "all-comprehending inscape of Christ" as Lord and Master (as the late John Keating put it), of her implicit trust in him, her total surrender. If the interpretation does not rest on this but simply on "there then! the Master, *Ipse* . . . ", there would then be a most unacceptable shift of referent from that of the preceding phrases. In either case I do not understand why Hopkins would applaud the nun with "Ah! there was a heart right! There was single eye!" for having Christ appear to her. There is really no apparition, or even vision, in the poem, behind or below the poem.

It seems to me that we may turn again to the point I have tried to make about the appeal of this virtual martyrdom. While a young schoolboy, Hopkins showed his willingness to inflict distress upon himself by abstaining from liquids for a week, and he finally collapsed. This incident seems to be representative of an inclination to be drawn to the ascetic, to suffering—as, I should think, a way of testing the will. There is his surprising comment on a flogging described by R. H. Dana in *Two*

Years Before the Mast—"*and it happened*—oh, that is the charm and the main point"; and there are allusions to bloodshed in some of his imagery. I cannot see the pathological in any of these, but I can think that they show a fascination with occasions of pain and with the power of enduring it, so much so as to lead to a strong desire to suffer—for Christ, that is—himself. Part I of the poem is centered in Hopkins' own experience of consolations gained through suffering, and it ends with the lines:

> **Make mercy in all of us, out of us all**
> **Mastery, but be adored, but be adored King.**

Certainly close to a wish to be oppressed for "the Kingdom of Heaven's sake" (his phrase in letter of 1888 to Bridges: L I, p. 270)! I think that in the first place Hopkins' reticence in *The Wreck* concerns a deep wish to suffer martyrdom—not all that unusual in young Catholics—and that the reticence is due to a natural shyness about in any way proclaiming such a desire. Hopkins was a gentleman: it would not have been gentlemanly to wear his heart thus upon his sleeve—but, then, for most, or many, it still wouldn't be. Secondly, I suggest that Hopkins felt that England as a whole, including himself, needed the shock of suffering, that some calamity was required to bring this complacent, materialistic, "very rich nation" (as he describes it in 1871 to Bridges) back to God: "England has grown hugely wealthy but this wealth has not reached the working classes; I expect it has made their condition worse . . . The more I look the more black and deservedly black the future looks . . ." And in 1888, explaining his poem *Tom's Garland* to Bridges, he comments thus: "But presently I remember that this is all very well for those who are in, however low in, the Commonwealth and share in any way the common weal; but that the curse of our times is that many do not share it, that they are outcasts from it and have neither security nor splendour . . ." (L I, pp. 273–74). That poem, incidentally, is significantly linked with *Coriolanus*, Shakespeare's similarly slanted play, by its use of the well-known body/society analogy of Menenius' belly fable, by elements of diction and by its central idea of the laborer's garland—implicitly (perhaps unconsciously) contrasted with "Coriolanus, crown'd with an oaken garland." It is, as Hopkins says it is, a "very pregnant," deeply felt poem, and its drift matches well the lines in *The Wreck*.

> **Wring thy rebel, dogged in den,**
> **Man's malice, with wrecking and storm.**

It is an incidental prayer, hope or half-hope in the poem that England, "whose honour O all my heart woos," be "dealt" the "stroke" of suffering so that Christ the King might come back "upon English souls"; and this is obviously not a wish the poet could have been very

frank about. And primary feelings of an urge toward martyrdom provided, I am inclined to think, what Hopkins speaks of in the sonnet *To
R. B.* as the "strong spur, live and lancing like the blowpipe flame,"
which left his mind the "mother" of *The Wreck of the Deutschland.*

Chapter V

The "Carrier-Witted" Heart

The Ignatian Quality of *The Wreck*

by Raymond V. Schoder, S. J.

To understand Hopkins it is essential to realize three qualities of his mind—he is very individual, very British, and very Jesuit.

His individualism, fostered by his love of Scotist philosophy, led to that remarkable originality and pioneering boldness which distinguished him from nearly all his contemporaries in so many ways, and indeed from almost all other generations too. It made him less liked and understood among most of his associates but all the more admired now. We can be grateful for this example of "pied beauty" among personalities —"counter, original, spare, strange," which makes Hopkins endlessly fascinating and his poetry charged with a unique tang and vibrancy.

His unabashed Englishness earned him sometimes painful teasing among his colleagues at University College in Dublin, but that did not daunt him in his enthusiasm for "rare-dear Britain," and the climax of this poem shows how strong, and how religiously motivated, this loyalty was in his heart.

The Jesuit quality of Hopkins' outlook and ideals is no less clear and central, though somewhat more difficult to define. Fellow Jesuits perceive it readily as an overall tonality behind Hopkins' whole thinking and allegiance. My endeavor here will be to bring this aspect of his thought into more explicit focus and appreciation.

The Jesuit viewpoint is of course basically Christian and Catholic; but it is distinctively so in various ways. This is due to the extraordinary traits of the founder, St. Ignatius Loyola, whose personality and special emphases were stamped on the Order. Any adequate biography of Ignatius will bring these features to the fore. His own *Autobiography* is precious for understanding him. His *Spiritual Exercises* mirror his distinctive qualities most clearly, and these are again visible in the *Constitutions* of the Order which Ignatius so carefully drew up. All this was intimately familiar to Hopkins in a way much more profound than a mere reading and study of books ordinarily achieves. It was his very life and love.

Hopkins was totally committed to the Jesuit ideal and spirit, dynamically convinced of its high merits in itself and for him, vitally motivated, formed, and guided by it in his whole personal life. At first, when soon after his conversion to the Catholic Church he contemplated becoming a Jesuit, he was apprehensive over the reputed demands and austerity, but was encouraged by his spiritual mentor Newman, who wrote him: "Don't call 'the Jesuit discipline hard', it will bring you to Heaven" (L III, p. 408). He learned the truth of this from experience and wrote "this life here, though it is hard, is God's will for me as I most intimately know, which is more than violets knee-deep" (L III, p. 235). He reasserted this time and again: "It is enough to say that the sanctity has not departed from the Jesuit order, to have a reason for joining it. Since I made up my mind to this I have enjoyed the first complete peace of mind I have ever had" (L III, p. 51). And to the Anglican canon Dixon:

"I have not only made my vows publicly some two and twenty times but I make them to myself every day . . . my mind is here more at peace than it has ever been and I would gladly live all my life, if it were so to be, in as great or a greater seclusion from the world and be busied only with God" (L II, p. 76). And later: "My vocation puts before me a standard so high that a higher can be found nowhere else" (L II, p. 88). Details of Hopkins' life in the Society are fully provided in Alfred Thomas, S. J., *Hopkins the Jesuit,* and Martin C. Carroll, S. J., "Gerard Manley Hopkins and the Society of Jesus," in *Immortal Diamond.*

The Wreck of the Deutschland as it exists was possible only from this Jesuit background. A great chasm separates this magnificently rich and powerful ode from the much lighter early poems of his Oxford period. Hopkins' whole life had changed and immeasurably deepened. Unquestionably the profoundest impact had been his conversion to Catholicism, which gave him a new certainty and joyous sense of calling and of purpose within the secure framework of God's truth. His vocation to the Jesuits, as a close follower of Christ the crusading King, was also deeply transforming. The spiritual training in the Order was uniquely penetrating and uplifting and he clearly conformed to it gladly. Most searchingly renovative was his Long Retreat in the novitiate, in September 1868. This was a month-long complete experience of the *Spiritual Exercises* of St. Ignatius under expert guidance, a very intense period of prayer and growing self-knowledge. Its primary aim was twofold in St. Ignatius' intention: a) "To conquer oneself and put one's life in order so that one never acts out of any misdirected attachment to creatures," and b) "To gain an interior knowledge of our Lord, who for me was made Man, in order that I may love him better and follow him more closely." The goal of the *Exercises* is a radical remaking of one's life into a truly Christlike pattern: generous, noble, innocent, totally dedicated to God's truth and love and service and rising above the values and pursuits of the merely natural and human world. The Long Retreat is an incomparably energizing experience of all-out Christian motivation and ideals. Hopkins emerged from it a new man.

There followed daily deepening in prayer, mostly on the life and example of Christ, and intense study of church history and doctrine, culminating in the full-time concentration on theology which Hopkins was still engaged in when he wrote *The Wreck.* He was later to make the Long Retreat again, during tertianship in 1881–1882—at which time he composed his illuminating comments on the *Spiritual Exercises.*

All this theology and Ignatian vision lies behind the powerful thought of *The Wreck,* where it is poured out with enthusiasm and constitutes the chief substance of this great ode on God's mastery and mercy, the mystery of divine providence leading men through suffering to purification and spiritual peace, and the benevolent kingship of Christ. As Pick says, this poem "is the very epitome of the *Spiritual Exercises*" (Pick, p.

41), which Milward reaffirms: "the spirit of St. Ignatius' *Exercises* is also the prevailing spirit of this poem" (Milward, p. 157). In it, Hopkins sees all things in God, and God in all things, in truly Ignatian fashion, and with apostolic intent like a good Jesuit he seeks to help the reader see things this way also.

It will help toward understanding this Ignatian quality of the poem to trace in it echoes or applications of specific elements of the *Spiritual Exercises*.

In a preliminary Annotation, St. Ignatius remarks that "the Creator and Lord communicates Himself to the soul devoted to Him, embracing it in His love and praise, and disposing it in the manner whereby it can best serve Him thereafter." This is the theological context for the exclamation in the poem:

> **Thou art lightning and love, I found it, a winter and warm;**
> **Father and fondler of heart thou hast wrung:**
> **Hast thy dark descending and most art merciful then.**

This is behind the description of Christ as "kind, but royally reclaiming his own; a released shower, let flash to the shire," and it explains the nun's divinely guided insight:

> **Ah! there was a heart right!**
> **There was single eye!**
> **Read the unshapeable shock night**
> **And knew the who and the why . . .**

A famous element of the *Exercises* is the initial Principle and Foundation, a severely logical basis for actually governing one's whole life by the realities of man's dependence on God as his origin and goal and the necessity of choosing only those alternatives which effectively lead one to that goal. It starts out with the statement: "Man was created to praise, reverence, and serve God our Lord and by this to save his soul." Hopkins elaborated on this in his Commentary:

> God has a purpose, an end, a meaning in his work. He meant the world to give him praise, reverence, and service; to give him glory. . . . He does not need it. . . . nevertheless he takes it: he wishes it, asks it, he commands it, he inforces it, he gets it (S, pp. 238–39).

God as supreme and total Creator dominates the opening and whole mood of the poem:

> **God! giver of breath and bread;**
> **World's strand, sway of the sea;**
> **Lord of living and dead;**
> **Thou hast bound bones and veins in me, fastened me flesh . . .**

That God achieves glory and praise from his faithful is brought out in the case of the nun who through service of God even at the cost of life attained to the "heaven-haven of the reward" and led many to find God's love in their anguish ("be a bell to, ring of it, and startle the poor sheep back!"), so that "Thou hadst glory of this nun."

The Foundation ends with the crucial principle: "We should always solely desire and choose that which best leads us toward the goal for which we were created." That goal is the "heaven of desire," the "heaven-haven of the reward," where the saved "bathe in his fall-gold mercies, breathe in his all-fire glances."

A notable device of Ignatius' shrewd psychology of prayer is the Composition of Place, which he describes precisely in the *Exercises:*

> This means to see with the sight of the imagination the physical place where is found that which I wish to contemplate.
>
> (E.g., at the start of the Call of Christ the King, Ignatius says:)
>
> See with the gaze of the imagination the synagogues, towns, and villages where Christ our Lord went about preaching.
>
> (And at the start of the Nativity meditation:)
>
> See with the gaze of the imagination the road from Nazareth to Bethlehem. Consider its length, its breadth, whether it is a level road or whether it goes through valleys or over hills. In the same way look at the cave of the Nativity: was it big or small, or low or high? And how was it furnished and arranged?

By this effective procedure, St. Ignatius wants the exercitant to use pictures to visualize what is otherwise beyond all imagining, to "feel the divine" and be an empathetic part of the mystery being contemplated. Hopkins knew this prayer aid well, and during his theology course read a paper on it, on April 28, 1877: "The Composition of Place in the Spiritual Exercises." His point was to insist that it is always a real place which St. Ignatius means, not a fictitious one; and the true purpose of the Composition is to make one present in spirit at the scenes, with the persons, and so forth, so that they may really act on him and he on them (cf. Thomas, p. 178). Already a few weeks before giving that paper Hopkins had in a 'Dominical' sermon at St. Beuno's developed the device: "Go in mind to that time and in spirit to that place; admire what Christ says as if we hear it, and what he does as if we saw it, until the heart perhaps may swell with pride for Jesus Christ the king of glory" (S, p. 225).

The dominant, central theme of the *Exercises,* and of all Ignatian spirituality, is Christ the King. This Hopkins adopted with delight as the key and focus of his life. How it applies to his greatest poem is studied at length by Sister Mary Adorita Hart in *The Christocentric Theme of G. M. Hopkins' Wreck of the Deutschland* and in James F. Cotter's *Inscape: The Christology and Poetry of Gerard Manley Hopkins.* For the Ignatian background there is the admirable study by Hugo Rahner, S. J., "The Christology of the Spiritual Exercises," in his brilliant *Ignatius the Theologian.*

In the *Exercises,* the great meditation on Christ the King presents him for our admiration and following, in his noble crusade to win all men from evil, sin, and death to humility, decency, and a life worthy of God's approval and blessing. This theme permeates the whole poem and is given many a notable expression. As Father Milward says, Hopkins "delights to view Christ under the title of King, according to the spirit of St. Ignatius' *Exercises*" (Milward, p. 157).

> ... but be adored, but be adored King.
> *Ipse,* the only one, Christ, King, Head ...
> Our King back, Oh, upon English souls!

Christ is the "hero of us," "hero of Calvary," "our passion-plungèd giant." Similarly in *The Loss of the Eurydice,* "Holiest, loveliest, bravest, / Save my hero, O Hero savest." And in his most successful sermon, Hopkins excitedly extols Christ:

> Our Lord Jesus Christ, my brethren, is our hero, a hero all the world wants. You know how books of tales are written, that put one man before the reader and shew him off handsome and brave and call him My Hero or Our Hero. . . . But Christ, he is *the* hero. . . . He is a warrior and a conqueror; of whom it is written he went forth conquering and to conquer. He is a king, Jesus of Nazareth king of the Jews, though when he came to his own kingdom his own did not receive him. . . . And those even that do not follow him, yet they look wistfully after him, own him a hero, and wish they dared answer to his call (S, pp. 34–35).

St. Ignatius has us pray for an interior knowledge of our Lord Jesus Christ that will lead to loving him better and following him more closely. So Hopkins prays:

> With an anvil-ding
> And with fire in him forge thy will
> Or rather, rather then, stealing as Spring
> Through him, melt him but master him still. . . .
> Make mercy in all of us, out of us all
> Mastery, but be adored, but be adored King.

In following her divine King, the nun has led others to him, and for her pain and patience has Christ as her reward. This King, "The Christ of the Father compassionate," even descended into limbo to lead out the souls languishing there.

One of the major meditations in the Second Week of the *Exercises* is on the incarnation. Hopkins followed Duns Scotus' doctrine on that mystery, holding that the Son of God became man, not as a necessary means to redeem mankind from sin but as a supreme expression of divine love, in order to share creaturehood and reap a harvest of loving souls as a tribute to his Father. (This is echoed in: "Is the shipwreck then a harvest, / does tempest carry the grain for thee?") The mystery of God's new life among men is strikingly captured in the paradox: "Warm-laid grave of a womb-life grey."

The companion meditation on the nativity of Christ is alluded to in "Manger, maiden's knee." It becomes the analogue to Christ's spiritual birth in the soul through faith and grace: "here was heart-throe, birth of a brain." It is doubtful if a more splendid characterization of this mystery has ever been phrased than Hopkins'.

> Now burn, new born to the world,
> Double-naturèd name,
> The heaven-flung, heart-fleshed, maiden-furled
> Miracle-in-Mary-of-flame . . .

A pivotal meditation in the Second Week is on the Two Standards—the symbols of Lucifer and of Christ as military leaders calling men to their service. In it, Christ calls on his followers to scorn riches, honor, and pride, and to seek to excel in poverty of spirit and humility and help lead other men to that ideal. His loving followers respond by eagerly petitioning to be accepted into such service under so noble a leader, and they ask the intercession of Mary, our Lady, to obtain such a privilege. In the poem, Christ is set forth as the model to be imitated: the "suffering Christ . . . and the word of it Sacrificed." This theme he develops at length in his Commentary on the *Exercises* (S, pp. 196–202).

Following such a heroic example is painful, but glorious, as the nun proved:

> . . . she cried for the crown then,
> The keener to come at the comfort for feeling the combating keen?

She is praised as an outstanding follower of Christ, an example of the *insignis* that Ignatius challenges us to be:

> The Simon Peter of a soul! to the blast
> Tarpeian-fast, but a blown beacon of light.

As mentioned above, the whole intent of this dynamic ode is apostolic, Hopkins' effort to inspire the reader to trust, love, and imitate Christ and find in him alone the meaning and goal of life. As Elisabeth Schneider remarks, this poem is all about *conversion*—Hopkins' own conversion to the Catholic Church and the hoped-for conversion of all England, with which the poem ends (Schneider, p. 14).

In his reflections on the Three Degrees of Humility, St. Ignatius urges the exercitant to strive for the Third Mode, which consists in preferring and seeking out actual poverty, suffering, humiliations, low esteem by the world in order to be more like Christ and to enjoy the strength of his love. The five nuns had experienced this: "Loathed for a love men knew in them, / Banned by the land of their birth." And when the chief nun prays exultingly for death, the poet marvels: "Is it love in her of the being as her lover had been?"

The psychological focal point of the *Exercises* is the Election, in which after much prayer, self-examination, and meditation on the life and example of Christ the exercitant carefully makes, with the help of God's illumining grace, a brave choice of a way of life to follow henceforth as a more authentic Christian. Elaborate rules are given to guide to the right procedure and leave proper scope for God's decisive grace. The nun chooses wisely when she calls out:

> ... **"O Christ, Christ, come quickly":**
> **The cross to her she calls Christ to her, christens her wild-worst Best.**

Hopkins refers to two types of God's calling to an election of courageous dedication to him:

> **Whether at once, as once at a crash Paul,**
> **Or as Austin, a lingering-out sweet skill ...**

This is a poetic way of saying what St. Ignatius does about the two times of an Election:

> The first is when God our Lord so moves and attracts the will that it neither doubts nor is able to doubt, but follows what it has been shown—as did St. Paul and St. Matthew in following Christ our Lord. The second is when clear knowledge is obtained through the experience of successive consolations and desolations.

The Election is meant to be a lifetime choice, a decisive determination of how one will serve God henceforth as he is understood to want. It is clear how the nun elects to stay lovingly loyal to God in the face of fear, suffering, and death, when she calls the cross, and therefore Christ, to her and "christens her wild-worst Best." It is also clear that there is reference in Part I of the poem to Hopkins' own decisive Election, but there is disagreement among commentators on how to identify and interpret this. The profound personal experience so dramatically described in stanzas 1-4 is surely not what McChesney thinks—a nightmare which Hopkins records experiencing on September 18, 1873 (J, p. 238, McChesney, p. 37). This is wholly inadequate to the description. Devlin (S, p. 12) and Gardner (*Poems* 3, p. 221) are convinced that the poet is referring to a deep prayer-experience and generous acceptance of God's call, made during his novitiate Long Retreat in 1868. This is plausible, but I think not right. Keating argues that Hopkins is not talking about a single experience but a series, a recurrent crisis: the agony of facing up to the distressing paradoxes of God's benvolence yet severity, of the world's beauty yet cruelty, of man's insignificance yet intrinsic worth (Keating, pp. 21–29, 57).

I agree rather with Fathers Boyle and Milward, that the spirit-shaking event was Hopkins' conversion to the Catholic Church in 1866 (in Weyand, pp. 333–50; Milward, p. 23). My main argument is that during

the deliberation Hopkins is terrified by "the hurtle of hell behind"—
which would apply to the fateful choice for or against God's truth and
Church, but not to a mere choice of religious vocation, which is a
counsel, not necessary for salvation. Hopkins affirms that the experience was personal and real, assuring Bridges that "what refers to myself
in the poem is all strictly and literally true and did all occur; nothing is
added for poetical padding" (L I, p. 47). He also explicitly states that
"My conversion when it came was all in a minute" (L III, p. 27).

Clearly Hopkins had had his own shipwreck and tossing by storm,
and had been saved by Christ when he trusted him and "carrier-
witted . . . fled with a fling of the heart to the heart of the Host." This
had occurred during silent depth-stirring prayer in a chapel before the
blessed sacrament. (Hopkins is reticent about details of the intimate
experience.) His dove-winged heart had then, he is proud to boast,
flashed from the flames of damnation to the brighter flame of God's
love, towered upward from that grace of conversion to the higher grace
of intense and lasting supernatural life, buoyed by the vein of the
gospel-proffer, Christ's gift, grace. It was an encounter fraught with
terror at God's grandeur and unrelenting demand and the fearsome
horror of the height where he stood, with God far above and hell a
yawning chasm below. He had cowered in the presence of infinite
power and authority ("lightning and lashed rod"—the latter meaning, I
think, *fasces,* the rods lashed together which were the symbol of Roman
official authority). The crucial factor is that he had, by God's mercy and
grace, accepted this challenge and thrown himself with total trust into his
Father's arms, "Father and fondler of the heart thou has wrung": "I did
say yes."

He certainly reaffirmed this decision for God when during his first
Long Retreat he generously accepted the call of Christ the King and
offered himself in lifelong service as a member of the Society of
Jesus—which he later made publicly and officially permanent by his
vows. It is this life-changing *yes* to God and to his vocation as a Jesuit
which Hopkins recalls, with mixed trembling and joy, when he sees the
parallel to it in the nun's choice of the cross and the self-immolating
Christ, christening her wild-worst her Best, her goal, her all. This shows
once again how profoundly Ignatian this poem is.

The Third Week of the *Exercises* is devoted to Christ's passion and
death, as supreme expression of his infinite love and as the key to his
solving and amelioration of man's own sufferings and failures. *The
Wreck* is steeped in Hopkins' very Ignatian tenderness and awe in the
face of Christ's passion and what it means to us. Philip Martin well says:
"The man who wrote 'The Wreck of the Deutschland' was not only a
poet but also a religious; he had himself meditated long upon the Passion and the Resurrection of the Lord" (Martin, p. 29).

We read of "the dense and the driven Passion, and frightful sweat," and of the five wounds, "cipher of suffering Christ." We are told that "The appealing of the Passion is tenderer in prayer apart," when "the sodden-with-its-sorrowing heart" is "drawn to the Life that died" and finds there a strength and a solace which the world cannot give. Hopkins is resonant to that part of St. Ignatius' favorite prayer, the Anima Christi: *"Passio Christi conforta me."*

The meaning which Hopkins sees, in the light of Christ's example and love, in the suffering inherent in human life, is that suffering forces man to God; our tears cleanse the soul's eyes to see deeper truths. (Aeschylus, whom Hopkins loved to read, had already understood this: "Zeus, who has put men on the way to wisdom by confirming the law that by suffering comes understanding": *tôi pathei mathos thenta kyriôs echein* [*Agamemnon*, pp. 174–78].)

> Wring thy rebel, dogged in den,
> Man's malice, with wrecking and storm. . . .
> Father and fondler of heart thou hast wrung:
> Hast thy dark descending and most art merciful then.

> With an anvil-ding
> And with fire in him forge thy will. . . .
> Make mercy in all of us, out of us all
> Mastery. . . .

> Thou martyr-master.

> The cross to her she calls Christ to her . . .

> The majesty! what did she mean?

> . . . is the shipwrack then a harvest, does tempest
> carry the grain for thee?

This is that "mystery [which] must be instressed, stressed," which "rides time like riding a river," that "hearts are flushed by and melt," regarding which "the faithful waver, the faithless fable and miss." Because of his faith and his Ignatian formation, Hopkins *did* understand this basic mystery of life, and in this great poem helps us understand it too. That is a very apostolic, very Jesuit purpose and endeavor.

The culminating meditation of the *Exercises* is the remarkable Contemplation for Attaining to Love, by which Ignatius, one of the great mystics, teaches how to live in constant awareness of God's gifts, of his ceaseless self-giving, and how he is ever present in his creatures and works in them for our good. It made a deep impression on the sensitive, spiritual Hopkins, and is clearly echoed often in this poem.

God is seen as "giver of breath and bread; / World's strand, sway of the sea; / Lord of living and dead." Hopkins developed this idea in his Commentary: "God is lord of life and death . . . as a providence concerned with our health, food, generation, and pleasures" (S, p. 166).

We are reminded how God dwells in the creatures he has made:

> **I kiss my hand**
> **To the stars, lovely-asunder**
> **Starlight, wafting him out of it; and**
> **Glow, glory in thunder;**
> **Kiss my hand to the dappled-with-damson west:**
> **Since . . . he is under the world's splendour and wonder.**

Hopkins frequently expands on this idea in his Commentary: he explains that the four themes of the Contemplation for Attaining to Love are 1) "all God gives us or does for us He gives and does *in love*, 2) God's being in things by His Presence, 3) by His Power, 4) by His Essence" (S, p. 194). Again, "Suppose God shewed us in a vision the whole world inclosed . . . in a drop of Christ's blood, by which everything whatever was turned scarlet, keeping nevertheless mounted in the scarlet its own colour too" (S, p. 194). Once more: "All things therefore are charged with love, are charged with God and if we know how to touch them give off sparks and take fire, yield drops and flow, ring and tell of him" (S, p. 195)—a clear recollection of his 1877 poem *God's Grandeur*.

God works in his creatures for our spiritual growth and good:

> **. . . stealing as Spring**
> **Through him, melt him but master him still.**

He uses many means of death to bring men finally to himself: sword, flange and rail, flame, fang, flood, storms which bugle his fame. As Hopkins notes in his Commentary, "It is by communication of his power that God operates the likeness of himself in things" (S, p. 195), "his power, that is the display of His hand or finger working in the world" (S, p. 175).

The man of faith takes delight in all this, in finding God everywhere about him, "beyond saying sweet, past telling of tongue."

Besides these discernible echoes of the *Exercises*, there are a number of other distinctively Ignatian attitudes behind *The Wreck's* structure and message. From the *Constitutions* and from his numerous letters many aspects of Ignatius the man and the saint are readily seen. One of the most characteristic is his ability to "find God in all things." Hopkins learned this well, and the poem is charged with it. He saw the world as an expression of God, its purpose being to bring us to praise and love him. This is only another facet of the Ignatian vision behind the Contemplation for Attaining to Love, with a slightly broader scope.

Hopkins himself exercised it:

> I kiss my hand
> To the stars, lovely-asunder
> Starlight, wafting him out of it . . .
> Kiss my hand to the dappled-with-damson west . . .
> For I greet him the days I meet him, and bless when I understand.

This is the same paramystical experience which he records in his *Journal* for August 17, 1874: "As we drove home the stars came out thick; I leant back to look at them and my heart opening more than usual praised Our Lord to whom and in whom all that beauty comes home" (J, p. 254). The basic theme of the poem, capsulized in stanza 5, is that "mystery [which] must be instressed, stressed" that all events in life, even ruinous ones, are *external graces* for man's spiritual good, if only man will see and accept them as such, in union with Christ. Even the killing cold which brought death to many on the ship is "God's cold." And in the tragic disaster of the nuns Hopkins sees God at work reminding him once more of his mysterious ways: "Over again I feel thy finger and find thee."

The nun too recognizes her Best, her loved one, in her wild-worst ruin, and

> Read the unshapeable shock night
> And knew the who and the why . . .

Perhaps the most strikingly special characteristic of St. Ignatius was his overwhelming reverent awe at the grandeur and majesty of God our Lord. Hopkins readily resonated to this in his own spiritual outlook:

> Thou mastering me
> God! . . .
> Lord of living and dead . . .
>
> I admire thee, master of the tides,
> Of the Yore-flood, of the year's fall;
> The recurb and the recovery of the gulf's sides,
> The girth of it and the wharf of it and the wall;
> Stanching, quenching ocean of a motionable mind;
> Ground of being, and granite of it: past all
> Grasp God, throned behind
> Death with a sovereignty that heeds but hides, bodes but abides.
>
> Be adored among men,
> God, three-numberèd form . . .

(On which the best commentary is the brilliantly skillful wording in *Margaret Clitheroe*: ". . . those Three, / the Immortals of the eternal ring, / the Utterer, Utterèd, Uttering.") God's infinite power is admiringly recognized:

> **. . . in him [man] forge thy will . . .**
> **. . . melt him but master him still. . . .**
> **Make mercy in all of us, out of us all**
> **Mastery, but be adored, but be adored King.**

We hear the "sister calling / A master, her master and mine!"

A great reverence and love of our Lady, the Virgin Mary, was another notable trait of Ignatius, and therefore of Hopkins—whose marvelous *The Blessed Virgin Compared to the Air We Breathe* is uniquely beautiful and apt Marian theology. Hopkins rated Mary second only to Jesus Christ, but with clear awareness of her mere creaturehood: "The first intention of God outside himself . . . outwards, the first outstress of God's power, was Christ; and we must believe that the next was the Blessed Virgin. . . . [she] was beyond all others redeemed, because it was her more than all other creatures that Christ meant to win from nothingness and it was her that he meant to raise the highest" (S, p. 197). The poem speaks of Mary as "the one woman without stain," as he was to repeat at the end of *Duns Scotus's Oxford:* "Mary without spot." Her greatest glory is her divine motherhood: "Jesu, Maid's son," which Hopkins subtly understands as another form of Christ's *kenosis,* humbling himself from divine status to human also: "Warm-laid grave of a womb-life grey"—which he later explained: "In her then as well as on the cross Christ died and was at once buried, her body his temple becoming his sepulchre" (S, p. 190).

Ignatius saw every man as important, because created in God's image and redeemed by Christ's all-embracing sacrifice of love. Similarly, Hopkins is concerned for all, since as he beautifully wrote: "I think the trivialness of life is . . . done away with by the Incarnation" (L III, p. 9). Though the ode is primarily about the nuns, especially their tall leader, he is deeply concerned over the eternal destiny of the others too:

> **Yet did the dark side of the bay of thy blessing**
> **Not vault them, the millions of rounds of thy mercy not reeve**
> **even them in?**

> **. . . but pity of the rest of them!**
> **Heart, go and bleed at a bitterer vein for the**
> **Comfortless unconfessed of them.**

Dread of sin, as defiant offense against the majesty of God; and of hell, sin's wages, is a deep Ignatian instinct which this poem reflects: "Wring thy rebel . . . Man's malice"—which his Commentary elaborates: "a resistance to God's will . . . the rebellion or revolt made against God's precept and expressed will, the resistance of will to will which is in man malice or uncharity" (S, p. 135), and again: "here the inordination, ugliness of sin . . . the preposterousness, rebellion" (S, p. 133).

But by God's mercy can come that delivering grace "that guilt is hushed by, hearts are flushed by and melt"—that repentance which St. Ignatius has the exercitant pray for earnestly: "contrition and tears for my sins." It is this which will save sinful man from "the hurtle of hell."

Ignatius' great trust in divine grace was thoroughly germane to Hopkins' theological sense. He was convinced that God guides us, with a benevolent providence, by his supernatural grace—that illumination of the mind and stimulus to the will that gently but often firmly leads us to our true good, whether we recognize it as such or not. As he explains, "grace lifts the receiver from one cleave of being to another" (S, p. 158). It is "truly God's finger touching the vein of personality, which nothing else can reach" (S, p. 158), as he experienced again in reflecting on the *Deutschland's* disaster: "Over again I feel thy finger and find thee."

Grace is a loving means of God's guidance and influence in our lives: "God exercises his mastery and dominion over his creatures' wills in two ways—over the affective will by simply determining it so or so (as it is said, the heart of the king is in the Lord's hand to turn it which way he will); over the *arbitrium* or power of pitch by shifting the creature from one pitch contrary to God's will to another which is according to it, or from the less to the more so" (S, p. 151). When man humbly accepts God's grace, the very correspondence and acceptance is "a grace, and even the grace of graces. . . . being a momentary shift from a worse, ungracious / to a better, a gracious self. [This] is a grace, a favour . . . in the strict sense of that word" (S, p. 154). This is how God can "Make mercy in all of us, out of us all / Mastery." It is a "gospel-proffer, a pressure, a principle, Christ's gift," "That guilt is hushed by, hearts are flushed by and melt," a "Stroke and a stress that stars and storms deliver." It is because of such grace that "To hero of Calvary, Christ's feet— / Never ask if meaning it, wanting it, warned of it—men go." But the spiritually sensitive soul will follow the impulse of grace instinctively, "carrier-witted . . . To flash from the flame to the flame then, tower from the grace to the grace."

God's fatherly providence "is under the world's splendour and wonder" and "rides time like riding a river." It is a "lovely-felicitous Providence/Finger of a tender of, O of a feathery delicacy," a "mercy that outrides/The all of water, an ark/For the listener." It is God lovingly at work in our lives.

The Society of Jesus came into being as an instrument of the Catholic Church to combat the Lutheran and other Protestant revolt in the sixteenth century. St. Ignatius was fiercely loyal to the Holy See and the hierarchical Church while fully recognizing the deficiencies and sins of many of its human representatives. Hopkins reflects this loyalty in his meditation on the paradox of St. Gertrude the mystic and Luther being both born at Eisleben:

> O Deutschland, double a desperate name!
>   O world wide of its good!
> But Gertrude, lily, and Luther, are two of a town,
> Christ's lily and beast of the waste wood. . .

This is not a very "ecumenical" attitude; but it flows directly and honestly out of Hopkins' very deep, very Ignatian, love of the Church as Christ's sacred body among men. It is worthy of St. Paul, and of the first great Ignatius, the martyr bishop.

Perhaps the most truly Ignatian attitude of all, certainly a central and decisive one, is an adoring acceptance of Christ as the focus, the substance, the meaning of all things. Cotter aptly remarks: "The narrative [element in *The Wreck*] dramatizes the ode's intent as a hymn of praise to Christ, the God-Man, shaper and rescuer of the world. The *Deutschland* is a Pindaric song of triumph in Christ's victory over chaos and death" (Cotter, p. 152). Further, "Of all his writings, the *Deutschland* contains the most complete statement of that gnosis or living knowledge of the Lord Jesus which was Hopkins' constant aim of perfection" (Cotter, p. 145). This "intimate knowledge of Our Lord Christ" which St. Ignatius urges praying for is what St. Paul so graphically characterized: ". . . the supreme profit of knowing my Lord Jesus Christ . . . so that Christ may be my wealth. . . . This will bring me to know Christ and the power flowing from his resurrection and how to share in his sufferings by being formed into the pattern of his death, in the hope that thus I may also arrive at the resurrection from the dead" (Philippians 3:8–11). As Milward stresses, "It is a fundamental principle in Hopkins' poetic thought that God is present in his creatures not only as Creator, but also as Redeemer; not only as the Word in the beginning whereby all things were made, but also as the Word Incarnate in the mysteries of His life, death, and resurrection" (Milward, p. 37). This is what Hopkins means by:

> Wording it how but by him that present and past,
> Heaven and earth are word of, worded by?

For Hopkins, Christ is "Jesu, heart's light"; for the dying nun he is "her pride." For all believers, Christ is "hero of Calvary," whose self-sacrifice is a triumphant victory over evil and the powers of death.

In his sermons, Hopkins frequently emphasizes this loving admiration of Christ: "Go in mind to that time and in spirit to that place, admire what Christ says as if we heard it, and what he does as if we saw it, until the heart perhaps may swell with pride for Jesus Christ the king of glory" (S, p. 225). "This man, whose picture I have tried to draw for you, brethren, is your God. He was your maker in time past hereafter he will be your judge. Make him your hero now" (S, p. 38). "But we, brethren, *we will*, if you please, crown Christ king; He is and shall be king, lord, master of mind, heart, and will" (S, p. 232). His very terror is really his love, leading all to himself.

In his Dublin Meditation Points for February 1884, Hopkins extolled Christ, his great love: "Crown him king over yourself, of your heart. Wish to crown him King of England, of English hearts and of Ireland and all Christendom and all the world" (S, p. 254–55). That culminating principle of Hopkins' Ignatian-rooted theology finds its noblest expression in the extraordinary ending of the poem:

> **Our King back, Oh, upon English souls!**
> **Let him easter in us, be a dayspring to the dimness of us,**
> **be a crimson-cresseted east,**
> **More brightening her, rare-dear Britain, as his reign rolls,**
> **Pride, rose, prince, hero of us, high-priest,**
> **Our hearts' charity's hearth's fire, our thoughts' chivalry's throng's**
> **Lord.**

The deeply Ignatian quality of Hopkins' mind is abundantly clear, drawn from his admiring study of the sources. It comes out, "like shining from shook foil" in all his poetry and prose. Our study of it here in the great ode which inaugurated his new and higher poetic achievement should be sample enough to demonstrate this.

The Wreck of the Deutschland is a phenomenon, one of the great human literary triumphs. Into it Hopkins poured his pent-up religious enthusiasm and newfound insights, producing what is surely the greatest ode since Pindar, a bursting splendour of thought and feeling and beauty and power like a great symphony of Beethoven. "The achieve of, the mastery of the thing!"

Note

Major sources on the Ignation mind, spirituality, and heritage are:

St Ignatius' Own Story (the *Autobiography*), translated by William J. Young, S. J., (Chicago, Regnery, 1956)

The Spiritual Exercises of St. Ignatius, translated by Thomas Corbishley, S. J., (New York, J. P. Kenedy, 1963)—also in other translations

St. Ignatius Loyola: The Constitutions of the Society of Jesus, translated by George Ganss, S. J., (Chicago, Loyola University Press, 1969)

Hugo Rahner, S. J., *Ignatius the Theologian* (London, Herder and Herder, 1968)

Finding God in All Things: Essays in Ignatian Spirituality from Christus, translated by William J. Young, S. J., (Chicago, Regnery, 1958)

Hugo Rahner, S. J., *The Spirituality of St. Ignatius* (Baltimore, Newman, 1953)

Joseph de Guibert, S. J., *The Jesuits: Their Spiritual Doctrine and Practice*, translated by William J. Young, S. J., (Chicago, Loyola University Press, 1964)

Chapter VI

"On a Pastoral Forehead in Wales"

The Composition of Place of *The Wreck*

by Peter Milward, S. J.

The place of composition of *The Wreck of the Deutschland* was, as we all know, St. Beuno's College, near the village of Tremeirchion in North Wales. Gerard Manley Hopkins was then in the second year of his theological studies, preparing for his ordination as priest in the Society of Jesus. Consequent on the event of the shipwreck which occurred on December 7, 1875, most of his leisure moments during the Christmas vacation of that year must have been spent on the first drafts of his masterpiece. These he presumably elaborated during the early months of 1876, culminating in the feast of Easter which is so unmistakably echoed in the final stanza of the poem.

Coming to the poem as he did with intensely religious and theological preoccupations, nourished on the *Spiritual Exercises* of St. Ignatius Loyola, the founder of his Order, it was natural for Hopkins to cast his poetical conceptions into the mold of a meditative poem—while including elements of the ode, the elegy, the lyric, and the ballad. From first to last he is addressing his words as much to God as to himself ("my heart") and his readers. In his opening words he declares his fundamental awareness of the divine presence and his personal relationship to God, as in the beginning of an Ignatian meditation: "Thou mastering me, God." Then at the end both of Part I and of the poem as a whole he brings his meditation to its climax in the form of an enthusiastic colloquy, or rather doxology of divine praise.

Given this form of an Ignatian meditation, according to the three powers of the soul: memory, understanding and will, where (we may ask) is the composition of place as its point of departure? Obviously, seeing that the poem as a whole is devoted to the subject of a shipwreck, one naturally identifies its composition of place with the site of the shipwreck—generally, the mouth of the Thames where it opens out into the North Sea (cf. stanza 21: "Thames would ruin them"), and more specifically, the sandbank called the Kentish Knock off the Essex coast near Harwich (as described in stanza 14). This is indeed where the wreck occurred, together with the incidents narrated in stanzas 14–28. But it is not the only, or even the principal composition of place. It may be the obvious one; but it is none the less a partial one. At the same time, it is juxtaposed, or rather counterpointed, with another which is not restricted to one part, or one series of stanzas, but subtly enters into the general structure of both parts.

This other composition of place is, needless to say, the actual place of the poem's composition. From here the poet contemplates the plight of the shipwrecked passengers, and openly contrasts his position with their position:

I was under a roof here, I was at rest,
And they the prey of the gales . . .

This is, to begin with, his main composition of place for the meditation he develops in Part I, where he makes precise reference to "the walls, altar and hour and night"—conceivably the chapel of St. Beuno's College, where he experienced in prayer as it were the finger of God, "and fled with a fling of the heart to the heart of the Host." From this point he goes on to draw a parallel between his interior state of soul and the situation of the college, whose wells are ever replenished "from the tall/Fells or flanks of the voel" rising behind it. Then, leaving the chapel and passing along the chapel gallery, he comes out onto the terraced garden and perhaps climbs what he calls in a letter the "flights of steps seemingly up to heaven lined with burning aspiration upon aspiration of scarlet geraniums" (L III, p. 125). Here he has the whole Vale of Clwyd spread out before him and the stars shining in the wide expanse of heaven above him.

In this meditative frame of mind he sees perhaps the silver line of the Clwyd threading its way through the darkness of the valley past the cathedral city of St. Asaph to the Irish Sea on the horizon—with eyes not only of sense, but also of spirit. He is thinking of the mystic stress and stroke implicit in stars and storms—or more generally, in the fair and foul weather with which the valley is so delightfully variegated. In both he finds the same divine presence, that "rides time like riding a river." No doubt, the river he has in mind is the Clwyd before and below him; but there is evidence he is also thinking of another river, the Jordan. This is indicated as well by the continual reference of the poem as a whole (as we shall see), as by certain remarks of the poet in his Long Retreat notes for November 8, 1881, under the heading "The Great Sacrifice":

> Time has 3 dimensions and one positive pitch or direction. It is therefore not so much like any river or any sea as like the Sea of Galilee, which has the Jordan running through it and giving a current to the whole (S, p. 196).

In other words, just as the River Jordan runs into and through the Sea of Galilee, so the river of time (under the stress and stroke of God) flows into and has its swelling in "the dense and the driven Passion" of Christ.

One might be tempted to apply all this to the Vale of Clwyd, comparing the Clwyd to the Jordan and the Irish Sea to the Sea of Galilee—as I myself used to do while meditating on the life of Christ during my three years' sojourn at St. Beuno's College (when Hopkins was yet little more than a name to me). But this is not quite the parallel he has in mind. His point is that the river of time does not merely flow into the sea and there lose itself, but that it flows through the sea, retaining its characteristic current "in high flood." Thus the Jordan flows not just into, but through the Sea of Galilee, before continuing its course southward along a sunken valley to the Dead Sea. Nevertheless, the comparison with the Clwyd is still in the poet's mind. Only he identifies the Sea of Galilee, not with the Irish Sea in the distance, but with the valley spread out beneath him.

This identification naturally occurs to one who, while regularly meditating on the gospels, often sees the valley beneath him filled with morning mist or cloud, and the hills rising out of the vapor on all sides (except the side toward the Irish Sea). Such is the sight described by Hopkins in his *Journal* for September 27, 1874—though on that occasion it was not so much a wide sea as "a long slender straight river of dull white cloud rolling down all the bed of Clwyd from as far as I could look up the valley to the sea" (J, p. 260). There are also times, though he makes no mention of them, when the river of cloud spreads out into a vast sea filling the valley from hill to hill. It was, no doubt, his memory of such times that prompted him to make a detailed comparison between the Sea of Galilee and the Vale of Clwyd in his "Dominical" sermon for mid-Lent Sunday, March 11, 1877 (that is, before his ordination to the priesthood later in the same year). To make the miracle of the loaves and fishes, as related in John 6, more vivid to his audience, Hopkins developed the theme—which he evidently cherished from the time of *The Wreck* a year earlier—of a parallel between the sea, beside which Christ had worked his miracle, and the vale, beside which he was now preaching his sermon. Just as the Jordan, he remarked, runs through that sea with a strong stream, so the Clwyd flows through the vale; while the measurements of the sea correspond more or less to the distance from Ruthin up the valley to St. Asaph lower down. Only, he added, "the Jordan runs from north to south, not like the Clwyd from south to north." He went on to identify the different places visited by Christ in terms of the valley, concluding that "the place of the miracle seems to have been at the north end of the lake, on the east side of the Jordan, as it might be at this very spot where we are now upon the slope of Maenefa" (S, p. 226).

The significance of this detailed comparison becomes evident as we pass from Part I to Part II of *The Wreck*. Here, as I have remarked, the ostensible composition of place is the mouth of the Thames and the sandbank on which the ship was wrecked. But even here the poet is all the time conscious of his "bower of bone" and his "heart in hiding," if only by way of contrast:

> **Away in the loveable west,**
> **On a pastoral forehead of Wales . . .**

His very use of the word "forehead" in this phrase, with its implication of a headland like the Great or the Little Orm, conjures up the scene of the Vale of Clwyd as a sea of clouds with the river of time running through. Maenefa (or Mynefyr), on whose slopes St. Beuno's is built, is not itself a headland jutting out into the sea; but it certainly juts out into the valley. Or insofar as the whole line of hills, of which it is a part, runs north to the Irish Sea and culminates in the steep Voel (which from inland may seem to be a headland), the poet may possibly be hinting at the historical association of that part of the Irish Sea with the drowning of Milton's college friend, Edward King, who thus became the subject of *Lycidas*. (Milton too, it may be remembered, speaks in his poem of "the Galilean lake" and its "pilot," St. Peter.)

In Part II of his poem Hopkins is less aware of the river flowing through the valley, or sea, than of the sea itself—considered specially as a place of storms, and consequently as a setting for shipwreck. The particular events he recalls in this part from the gospels are, accordingly, those associated rather with the sea than with its shore or the towns and villages ranged round it. The first event is that recorded in Matthew 8:

> And when he entered into the boat his disciples followed him. And, behold, a great tempest arose in the sea, so that the boat was covered with waves; but he was asleep. And they came to him and awaked him, saying: Lord, save us, we perish. And Jesus saith to them: Why are you fearful, O ye of little faith? Then rising up, he commanded the winds and the sea; and there came a great calm. But the men wondered, saying: What manner of man is this, for the winds and the sea obey him?

This is, of course, the event which is explicitly alluded to in stanza 25 of *The Wreck*, where the firm faith of the tall nun is contrasted with the weak faith of the disciples in the storm:

> **They were else-minded then, altogether, the men**
> **Woke thee with a *We are perishing* in the weather of Gennesareth.**

(Incidentally, this form "we are perishing" is used in none of the existing versions of the bible in Hopkins' time; though it was later adopted for the Revised Standard Version in 1946.) Maybe the contrast was itself suggested to the poet's mind by the similarity in tone and structure of the nun's "O Christ, Christ, come quickly!" to the disciples' urgent appeal, "Lord, save us, we perish!" One might add that their amazement at the way even the winds and sea obeyed him is further echoed both in the beginning of the poem, where God is addressed as "sway of the sea," and in the end, where he is said to quench the "ocean of a motionable mind."

The second event is that recorded a few chapters later in Matthew 14: it comes immediately after the miracle of loaves and fishes (also recorded in John 6).

> And forthwith Jesus obliged his disciples to go up into the boat and to go before him over the water till he dismissed the people. . . . But the boat in the midst of the sea was tossed with the waves; for the wind was contrary. And, in the fourth watch of the night, he came to them, walking upon the sea. And

they, seeing him walking upon the sea, were troubled, saying: It is an apparition. And they cried out for fear. And immediately Jesus spoke to them, saying: Be of good heart. It is I. Fear ye not. And Peter, making answer, said: Lord, if it be thou, bid me come to thee upon the waters. And he said: Come. And Peter going down out of the boat walked upon the water to come to Jesus. But, seeing the wind strong, he was afraid; and when he began to sink, he cried out, saying: Lord, save me. And immediately Jesus, stretching forth his hand, took hold of him and said to him: O thou of little faith, why didst thou doubt? And, when they were come up into the boat, the wind ceased.

Between this passage and the poem there are an impressive number of connecting links. The time and circumstances of the gospel incident may well be echoed in the feelings of the passengers in the poem, when "frightful a nightfall folded rueful a day" (stanza 15). Then, Christ's walking on the waters is verbally echoed in the phrase of stanza 33: "the storm of his strides." The effect this manifestation of power has on the minds of his disciples is one of combined astonishment and fear, as they cry out, "It is an apparition!" It is effectively applied by the poet to the nun's experience of it looming like a ghost over the waters and presenting itself, like the ghost in *Hamlet*, as a "thing." There he breaks off, as he identifies, or imagines her identifying, the "thing" with "the Master," namely, Christ—just as on another occasion in the gospels John identified Christ standing on the shore, "It is the Lord" (John 21). Lastly, Peter's attempt to come to Christ over the waters and his sinking for lack of faith are variously echoed in Part I, possibly in the words, "thy terror, O Christ," in stanza 2, and more probably in the remark, "the faithful waver," in stanza 6. As for Peter's exclamation, "Lord, save me!" it may also be seen as entering (like that of the disciples in Matthew 8) into the call of the nun, "O Christ, Christ, come quickly!"

This tangled skein of reference to the various occasions in the gospels dealing with Christ and his disciples on the Sea of Galilee is still incidental to the main burden of the poet. It all forms part of the undercurrent flowing through the river of his thought; but it only attains "high flood"—paradoxically speaking—as it leaves the Sea of Galilee and moves as it were upstream and northward to the sources of the Jordan near Caesarea Philippi. Here it was (as we read in Matthew 16) that Christ asked his disciples, "Who do you say that I am?" and Peter answering for them all declared, "Thou art Christ, the Son of the living God." These words of Peter's confession provide the pattern of the poet's own act of faith, from the very beginning of his poem:

> **I did say yes**
> **O at lightning and lashed rod;**
> **Thou heardst me truer than tongue confess**
> **Thy terror, O Christ, O God . . .**

Here it is precisely his confession of faith in Christ as God which proves to be the poet's "best word," enabling him to "flash from the flame to the flame" and to "tower from the grace to the grace." It is, in other words, his timely utterance of *yes* to Christ which raises him in spirit to where Christ sits enthroned at the right hand of the Father as the eternal word of God.

Here too we find an important parallel between the word of the poet in the first part, and that of the nun in the second. For the nun too in her simple call to Christ "rears herself to divine ears"—as Peter himself is said to do in making his confession of faith. Like Peter on that occasion, she was enabled by divine revelation to "read the unshapeable shock night" and to know "the how and the why." In these words the poet is evidently making a hidden connection between the previous exclamations of the disciples and of Peter amid the waves of the Sea of Galilee and the subsequent confession of Peter at Caesarea Philippi. It is with all this in his mind that he recognizes in the nun "the Simon Peter of a soul"—that is to say, a soul like Simon Peter, who confessed his faith in Christ despite the storm of appearances tending to intimidate his spirit. Hence she is said to be "to the blast/Tarpe͏̈ian-fast"—with the solidity and strength of the Tarpeian rock in Rome, at whose foot Peter was confined in the Mamertine prison before being taken out for his crucifixion on the Vatican hill. The odd use of "Tarpe͏̈ian" in this phrase seems to imply the noun it would normally accompany, "rock"—the name Peter himself received from Christ in reward for his confession: "Thou art Peter (that is, rock); and upon this rock I will build my Church." As for "the blast," it is that produced by the powers of hell to which Christ refers in his following words: "And the gates of hell shall not prevail against it." It may also include a suggestion of the floods and winds which Christ describes in his Sermon on the Mount (Matthew 7) beating upon the house built upon rock, but not prevailing against it.

Thus it is that through his own *yes* to Christ, and through the nun's call to him, the poet looks to the word of Peter which won for him his name and its meaning of "rock." This is, indeed, not only Peter's name, but also that of Christ (as St. Paul says in 1 Corinthians 10:4: "And the rock was Christ") and of God himself in many places in the Old Testament. Then from Peter's word he goes on to recall the previous word of Mary, when she uttered her *yes* or *fiat* in response to the angel and so merited to become Mother of the Incarnate Word. As St. Leo remarks, in his first *Sermon on the Nativity,* she conceived the Word first in her mind, then in her body. St. Gregory adds that in order to attain to the conception of the eternal Word, she raised (or "reared") herself to the very throne of the godhead (*In I Reg.* 1). The poet too following the direction indicated by the nun and "the one woman without stain," raises his mind to where God himself, as "ground of being, and granite of it," is "throned behind/Death with a sovereignty that heeds but hides, bodes but abides." Here is the permanent ground of the rocklike faith in which both Peter and Mary, both the poet and the nun, share according to their respective circumstances. Here is the eternal source of that river of time which flows through the lives of men, inevitably leading them "to hero of Calvary, Christ, 's feet," where they find their heart "at bay" and finally "come out with it."

We may now follow the movement of the poet's mind, according to the gospels, from the events recorded by Matthew in the public life of Christ to a final event recorded by John in his risen life, when he appeared to his disciples on the shore of the Sea of Galilee (or, as it is there named, "the Sea of Tiberias"). In this passage there is a striking contrast between the disciples who have been laboring in their boat all night (though there is no mention of a storm or heavy waves), and the silent figure of their Master on the shore. The contrast is traditionally compared to that between the Church in this world of time and the risen Christ on the shore of eternity. As St. Gregory remarks in his homily on this passage.

> What is signified by the sea, but the present world, which is tossed on the tumults of chance and the waves of corruption? What by the firmness of the shore, but the perpetuity of eternal rest? (*Hom. 24 in Evang.*)

It is also a contrast we find reaching from the beginning to the end of Hopkins' poem, where he admires God in stanza 1 as "world's strand, sway of the sea," and in stanza 32 as "master of the tides . . . stanching, quenching ocean of a motionable mind." It is, again, from this passage that John's perception, "It is the Lord!" is applied to the nun as, "in wind's burly and beat of endragonèd seas," she recognizes "the Master,/*Ipse,* the only one, Christ, King, Head." Finally, just as in the sequel of this passage Peter is required to make a confession, not now of faith, but of love, and is rewarded with the title, not now of rock, but of shepherd: so too the nun serves a pastoral function as she obeys the finger of God's "lovely-felicitous Providence" and so "startles the poor sheep back" to their true fold with Christ.

This mention of "sheep," with its implication of their shepherd, serves to bring us also back to where we began, "on a pastoral forehead of Wales." For grazing sheep form a notable feature of the landscape of Maenefa, together with their shepherd and his dog. Their association with rocks is no less evident in the same landscape, where the naked rock stands out from the surrounding meadow in numerous places. Moreover, upon one craggy eminence is actually built a tiny chapel or church, known as the Rock Chapel, which juts out into the valley below like a headland. From its vantage point one may well appreciate the continually changing cloud formations over the Vale of Clwyd and its no less continually changing weather. Such was the "fresh and delightful sight" Hopkins describes in his *Journal* for October 19, 1874:

The day was rainy and a rolling wind; parts of the landscape, as the Orms' Heads, were blotted out by rain. The clouds westwards were a pied piece— sail-coloured brown and milky blue; a dun yellow tent of rays opened upon the skyline far off (J, p. 261).

Similarly, he refers in his "Dominical" sermon—perhaps recalling this very scene of the *Journal*—to times "when here a sheet of white rain coming from the sea blots out first the Orms' Heads on Moel Hiraddug, then spreads mile after mile, from hill to hill, from square to square of the fields, along the Vale of Clwyd" (S, p. 231). It may well be this same scene he has in mind when in stanza 34 of *The Wreck* he characterizes the coming of Christ as "not a doomsday-dazzle," nor "a lightning of fire hard-hurled," but "a released shower, let flash to the shire."

The complex movement of the poet's creative imagination is thus from the image of rocks (or the Rock Chapel), with their connotation of resistance to blasts of storm or tempest, to that of sheep gently grazing under the eyes of their shepherd—while a shower of rain comes moving across the valley, bringing added richness to the pastures. The contrast implied in this movement (with all its gospel associations) is closely akin to that between "as once at a crash Paul" (as it were under the stroke of a storm) and "as Austin, a lingering-out sweet skill" (as it were under the stress of the stars) in stanza 10. Or again, that between the plight of the nuns as "the prey of the gales" and the safety of the poet "under a roof here" and "at rest" in stanza 24. It is, in short, the contrast between the mastery of God, so strongly emphasized at the beginning of the poem, and the merciful kindness of Christ at the end, where he is seen "royally reclaiming his own" as "our hearts' charity's hearth's fire, our thoughts' chivalry's throng's Lord."

Note

Quotations from the bible are all taken from the Douay version, as being the one Hopkins would have used from the time of his conversion to the Catholic Church. References to the Fathers are all from the Roman Breviary, which Hopkins may well have been accustomed to recite during his years at St. Beuno's even before his ordination (when the recitation would have become obligatory).

Wreck of the *Deutschland* as it appeared on the morning of Thursday Week

Chapter VII

"Thou Mastering Me, God"

Unity in *The Wreck*

by James F. Cotter

Despite the complexity of its poetical techniques and the density of its theological thought, Gerard Manley Hopkins' *The Wreck of the Deutschland* is a highly single-minded and unified poem. Ironically, its unity is the one quality which critics, after carefully weighing the poem, have found wanting. Swept up in the poet's confusion in Part I of the ode ("where, where was a, where was a place?") and the tumultuous wreck in Part II, readers do not know where the poem is heading until its symphonic close. But that experience should be true of any work of art; its unity is the last thing to emerge. We only see the whole in the beginning when we have perceived a pattern in all the subsequent parts.

In the opening lines of *The Wreck*, poet and reader make a confession of God ("Thou mastering me") that acts as the focal point or inscape of what follows. The deity who is invoked is not some vague supreme being or angry God of wrath, the distant Creator or absentee landlord that comes to many minds when the word *God* is employed. Hopkins' fondness for the precise meaning of words must be steadfastly heeded here, for on our understanding of "the who and the why" our knowledge of the poem's unity depends. In fact, the ode elaborates the nature of this opening confession, although we do not know the poet's intent until the confession has been made narratively and explained both negatively and positively in the last third of the poem.

In stanza 24, the poet describes himself in pastoral Wales "under a roof" and at rest while the five nuns lay "prey of the gales" as their ship foundered on the Kentish shore. Here for a moment the two worlds of the poem come together and Hopkins repeats the nun's cry "O Christ, Christ, come quickly," as reported in the *Times*. In the next stanza, he asks, "The majesty! what did she mean?" and immediately prays for inspiration from the Holy Spirit, "arch and original Breath." God is described in the first stanza as "giver of breath," bestower not only of life but of the Holy Spirit as well. In stanzas 25, 26, and 27 the poet attempts to answer his own question: "What did she mean?" He rejects a reference to the historical Jesus or to the Christ in glory, because neither meditation on the life of Jesus past nor hope for future reward would be likely or natural at a time of "danger, electrical horror." What Christ, then, is she calling upon? In stanza 28, the author bursts out with the answer, "the Master,/*Ipse*, the only one, Christ, King, Head." The Master is the "mastering me/God" who is invoked in the first line of the poem and to whom the ode is addressed. He is also called "master of the tides" and "past all/Grasp God" in stanza 32. Christ, as *God*, is the focal point whom even "the uttermost," those who are far from acknowledging him, "mark" in the sinking of the *Deutschland*. It is Christ here-and-now, the author and finisher of faith, who answers the tall nun's call and the poet's opening prayer.

Is the act of faith in Christ's divinity enough to sustain the intellectual and emotional intensity of the poem? Obviously Hopkins intended the confession, once grasped in its critical actuality, laid bare in the very moment of death and echoing as it does the prayer of the first Christians, *Marana tha* ("Come, Lord"), to be sufficiently important and compelling enough to warrant the writing of his ode. Before we dismiss or accept the significance of this act of faith, we owe it to the poet to find out why he believed the nun's cry to be historically noteworthy and what he interpreted it to mean both for himself and for his contemporaries. We must first examine the implications for him in calling on Christ as God.

In the spirit of St. Ignatius' Principle and Foundation, Hopkins begins with his personal experience of God. The divine offers tangible proof of its presence in the bones and sinews of man by creating him and then re-creating him in grace. The poet tells us he has physically experienced the Holy Spirit, the "finger" of God, and then, in the second stanza, gives us a specific instance of feeling overwhelmed by God while presumably making the *Spiritual Exercises* in a chapel at night. Again with the aid of the Spirit, the "dovewinged" heart of the poet reaches out to Christ its goal. The gift of grace still holds the author fast, moving through him like sand in an hourglass or water seeping into a well. This deeply existential presence of the divine nature in the poet's life is his share in Christ's life who, as a fellow human being, imparts to other men "the gospel proffer" of his godhead. Christ does this through his Spirit and through his eucharistic body the host. He is "giver of breath and bread" in the full sense, just as he is "World's strand, sway of the sea" since as sand and water his life runs through men.

Experience of Jesus from within leads the poet to discover him in the world,

> **Since, tho' he is under the world's splendour and wonder,**
> **His mystery must be instressed, stressed;**
> **For I greet him the days I meet him, and bless when I understand.**

The awareness of the cosmic Christ is twofold for Hopkins: from within ("instressed") and then from without ("stressed"). This personal contact corresponds to a twofold presence of Christ in the world: in beauty ("lovely-asunder/Starlight") and disaster ("glory in thunder"). The stress that "stars and storms deliver" derives not from man's direct knowledge of Christ's divinity in its heavenly state, but from the historical person of Jesus from his conception ("Warm-laid grave of a womb-life grey") to his death on the cross. The "womb-life" of the Word prefigures and enacts the inner presence of Christ in his faithful, just as "the dense and the driven Passion" occurs here like a storm, an overwhelming exterior event which carries the divine life also. Notice how all the images that make up Part II of the ode are already introduced:

strand and sea, sand and water, stars and storm, and how each is identified with Christ's working in and outside man.

Belief in God, then, comes to man not from above, but through time "like riding a river"; it is founded on personal and historical reality; it assents not to abstract doctrine but to an event, the death and resurrection of Jesus. The pierced heart of the crucified Lord is "out with it," and men go to Calvary not out of mere intellectual conviction but from a profoundly human need. The act of faith is an act of heart; it is recognition born in love. The reality of God makes itself manifest in defeat, humiliation, and resignation, as well as in peaceful contemplation and prayer.

Through the crucified Christ's death, the Holy Spirit is released and man returns to the Father. Hopkins ends this section of the ode with a petition to the Trinity: "Be adored among men,/God, three-numberèd form." Christian religion is not so much monotheistic, as triadic. The believer does not worship the "God of the philosophers," as Pascal observed, nor even a God whose existence he has proved rationally, but the Father, Son, and Spirit revealed to man in scripture. The poet addresses God who as "Father and fondler of heart" probes the soul, who has his "dark descending" as the Spirit, and who is adored as Christ the King. Man comes to the Trinity through experience of Jesus, whether "at a crash" like Paul or with "a lingering-out sweet skill" like Augustine. Hopkins can vouch for both experiences: "Thou art lightning and love, I found it, a winter and warm."

The narration of the shipwreck reenacts the sacred history which the poet has reviewed as the ground of each man's knowledge of God. The ship leaves the fatherland behind: "O Father, not under thy feathers nor ever as guessing/The goal was a shoal," as "Into the snows she sweeps,/Hurling the haven behind." Nevertheless she is still the *Deutschland* and this departure may yet result in a return to the Father through redemptive suffering. So the incarnate Word emptied himself, undergoing even death on a cross, that men might become his brothers and sons too of God. The tall nun's confession words "the who and the why," and the Word is born again in suffering by her expression of love: "wording it how but by him that present and past/Heaven and earth are word of, worded by?" Just as the Father generates the Son in eternity, so he sends the Son to re-create the world which was first created by and through him.

The idea of the creative and redemptive Word was introduced in the prologue of St. John's gospel. It was developed by the early fathers and received its fullest treatment before the Middle Ages in the writings of St. Augustine. Christology led naturally to a doctrine of the Trinity, and the two topics are intimately connected in Hopkins' spiritual commentaries and sermons. To see the importance of the nun's confession we need to know something of the doctrine. Briefly then: The first act or procession of the Father is the Son; the Father himself is the act of no one. Actor, begetter, generator, he fathers-forth the Son. Since his is a mind capable of thought, he thinks the Logos who is of his own nature, one with him as an idea belongs to the person who ponders it. But while human knowledge is ephemeral, the Father's thought of himself is eternal and generates a deity like himself. In knowing his Son, the Father loves him and the Word, who knows all things, acknowledges this love. The return of love for love is the second act or procession and it proceeds from both Father and Son. This ecstasy of love is a "spiration" or breathing of the same love in both and is the Holy Spirit, a person who also subsists in himself but exists only in unity with the Father and Son since he is their love.

This psychological explanation of the triune God developed from the study of man's own mind and will. Interestingly enough, the doctrine was used in turn to explain man's own nature as a reflection both through creation and grace of the divine image. The text of Genesis, "And God said: Let us make man to our image and likeness," provided the basis for a whole Christian anthropology that Hopkins still found relevant enough to employ in his poem. In his *Scale of Perfection,* Walter Hilton sums up the teachings of St. Augustine and St. Thomas Aquinas:

> The soul of man is a life with three powers—memory, understanding, and will—made in the image and likeness of the Blessed Trinity, whole, perfect, and righteous. The memory has the likeness of the Father, inasmuch as it was given power to retain His image, neither forgetting it nor being distracted by creatures. The understanding was made bright without error or darkness, as perfect as it might be in a body not glorified; and so it has the likeness of the Son, who is eternal Wisdom. The will was made pure, springing up to God without love of the flesh or of creatures, by the sovereign goodness of the Holy Ghost, who is divine love. So man's soul, which may be called a created trinity, was perfected in the memory, sight, and love of the uncreated Blessed Trinity, which is God.

This was man's state in Adam before the fall; through the grace of the Son man may again recover some of that divine likeness, becoming a new man in the second Adam, Christ, the perfect image of the Trinity.

In confessing Christ as God, the nun reveals the triune nature of God, her act being a divine activity revealed in an historical event. Remembering Jesus, she knows him in the crisis of the storm, speaks his name, and joins him in love. Her act is trinitarian, like that of Mary whose *fiat* to the Father caused the Son to be conceived in her womb through the overshadowing Spirit. The poet's activity is also exactly parallel. Through his memory, he first recalls a critical moment in his own life; then he reviews the sinking of the *Deutschland.* He next struggles to understand the meaning of the nun's cry, until he too acknowledges the "Lord of living and dead." Finally, he unites with the new knowledge a loving prayer for the other men and women who perished in the storm, that they may be one with the five sisters in eternal rest. He extends this hope to all of England and sees renewal already happening: Christ the light of the world is "new born to the world,/Double-naturèd name." The ode ends by again addressing Jesus as Lord of mind and heart, the source of man's restored image of God, and the goal of the one and many, of the inner and outer worlds of love and action: "Our hearts' charity's hearth's fire, our thoughts' chivalry's throng's Lord." By faith men know and love their maker and themselves.

What significance did Hopkins see in the shipwreck for his contemporaries? Whether or not they were aware of the meaning of the nun's cry and the central focus it gave to the event, the poet testifies that its reality as a revelation of Christ's mystery has already taken place and does not now depend on anyone's individual support. By God's mercy, one day others will also know the truth. Indeed, Christ has been present in men's minds and hearts revealing the triune God from the beginning of time, for he is the Lord of history. Hopkins was fond of finding unconscious traces of the doctrine of the Trinity in other religions. His devotion to the pre-Socratic philosophers bears special witness to this study. The writings of Parmenides on Being, of Heraclitus on the Logos, and of Anaximenes on the breath and air that embrace the universe contain the inspired teachings of the Word before his birth. These theophanies of Christ, as Justin Martyr called them, dominate Old Testament history. Christ is the creator in the six days of Genesis, the God of Abraham, Isaac, and Jacob, the savior of Noah and mankind, "I AM" to Moses, and David's shepherd and Lord. With Clement of Alexandria and other fathers of the Church, Hopkins did not confine these revelations to Hebraic religion; they are found in the philosophy of the Greeks, especially of Plato, in the Roman poets and Sibylline oracles, and in Welsh and Hindu texts.

Man's likeness to God in his reason, a point insisted on in the poet's correspondence, is clearly outlined in this passage from the pre-Socratic Epicharmus of Syracuse:

> The Logos steers men and ever preserves them on the right path. Men have the power of calculation, but there is also the divine Logos. Human reasoning is born from the divine Logos, which furnishes each man with the passageway both of life and of nourishment. The divine Logos is present in all the arts, ever teaching men what they must do to obtain good results. For it is not man, but God, who discovered the arts.

The Word, "giver of breath and bread" ("life and nourishment"), is born in the nun's mental grasp or inscape of the end and purpose of the storm; her "heart-throe, birth of a brain" becomes a bell to "startle the poor sheep back." "According to Heraclitus," notes Sextus Empiricus, "it is by inbreathing the divine Reason that we become intelligent." Memory, reason, and breathing are the trinity in man that expresses his natural likeness to God. *The Wreck* narrates the physical occurrence of this truth, in the nun's call and the poet's response.

The function of the Logos for the pre-Socratics was not only to order men's minds but to control the elements as they struggled with one another for supremacy. Heraclitus observed: "Fire lives in the death of earth, air in the death of fire, water in the death of air, and earth in the death of water." The Logos masters this movement by making it cyclical, upward and downward in perpetual motion. In Hopkins' ode, water lashes the shore, snow falls from the air, and wind buffets the sea. With the rising sun, a scene of carnage appeared, as reported in the *Times*, but the fiery sun, for Hopkins, brings calm and illumination. The Christic nature of the elements, already mentioned, comes together in the dawning image of Christ as sunlight and a "released shower, let flash to the shire." Empedocles, who replaced the Logos with Love, pictured the cosmic process as a spiral, with Strife separating the four elements and Love reuniting them in the One. Strife falls to the lowest depth of the vortex while Love spins to the center. Hopkins' detailed description of the "whirlwind-swivellèd snow," "the whorl and the wheel," "the burl of the fountains of air," and the swirling "inboard seas" demonstrates the purposeful motion at work in things, so that for Christ the Orion of light "Storm flakes were scroll-leaved flowers." Anaxagoras accepted the spiral as the cosmic principle but rejected the twofold source of Empedocles. For him rotary motion springs from "unlimited, autonomous, and unmixed Mind." He wrote: "Mind set in order all that was to be, all that *ever* was but no longer is, and all that is now or ever will be. This includes the revolving movement of the stars, of the sun and moon, and of the air and aether as they are being separated off." Whether as Logos or Spirit of Love or as "Stanching, quenching ocean of a motionable mind," Christ reconciles divine immanence with transcendence since he is both "Ground of being, and granite of it" and "past all/Grasp God, throned behind/Death. . . ." He rules the inner and outer worlds, sets the motion of stars and storms, and shines on mankind with his light.

If Christ is God, the universe is intelligible and loving, even in its most tragic moments. The calamity of December 7, 1875, was not just another disaster that—ever since the Lisbon earthquake the century before had shaken the faith of Europeans in "lovely-felicitous Providence"—confirmed the Victorians in the implacable inhumanity of nature, eloquently described by the English geologist Charles Lyell as a

chaotic destructiveness pitting oceans against seacoasts, floods and hur-
ricanes against land. Taking issue with the basic proof of a scientifically
disillusioned age, Hopkins brought to bear all his learning in the western
tradition and his singular gifts as a poet to show order and purpose in
the tragedy: "The goal was a shoal," for convergence inheres in the
cataclysm. His ode is not only unified, it is about that unity, creating it in
minute detail from the first to the last acclamation to Christ. The nun
perceived the truth, proclaimed it, and died, joining a long line of virgin
martyrs and witnesses. With "heart right" and "single eye," she "read
the unshapeable shock night" and christened "her wild-worst Best."
The reader's task is the same: to see Christ in the poem as the poet has
worded him.

A precedent for the young Hopkins in his ambitious undertaking
existed in Alfred Tennyson's ode, *In Memoriam*. Like *The Wreck of the
Deutschland,* his poem begins with an invocation to the "Strong Son of
God" who is Lord of life and death. Overwhelmed by a profound sense
of the undisguised hostility of nature, Tennyson sought in faith a reason
for resignation to the death of his close friend, Arthur Hallam. His faith
came only after struggle and wavering and it was hard won. He writes:

> I stretch lame hands of faith, and grope,
>   And gather dust and chaff, and call
>   To what I feel is Lord of all,
> And faintly trust the larger hope.

What Tennyson hesitantly reaches for, Hopkins has obviously
achieved:

> **I kiss my hand**
>   **To the stars, lovely-asunder**
> **Starlight, wafting him out of it, and**
>   **Glow, glory in thunder . . .**

But the aspiration of the older poet, his dream of a "fuller minstrel" to
"Ring in the Christ that is to be," must have stirred the Jesuit poet and
inspired him to set his sights on a masterpiece of poetry and a landmark
of creative thought. He was disappointed indeed when the editors of
The Month refused to publish his ode and when his friend Robert
Bridges dismissed it as nonsense. A hundred years later we have a
clearer perception of what Hopkins intended, but it may take another
century of religious and literary research before we can measure the
poem's greatness. In the meantime, what the nun announced in the
storm's tumult remains, not buried in newspaper accounts, but celebrated in song. The poet continues to challenge us to search for its
meaning, as he searched, with intelligence and good will. Her inscape
may then become ours, as he also made it his own.

Chapter VIII

"The Rarest-Veinèd Unraveller"

Hopkins as Best Guide to *The Wreck*

by Marcella M. Holloway

In Hopkins' defense of his ode he has given us significant clues on how to respond to the "Dragon." This defense we find in scattered letters to Bridges, Patmore, Dixon, and to Father Coleridge, editor of *The Month*, who ultimately refused to publish the poem. It is not only in the defense of his ode that we find Hopkins a reliable guide, but also in his penetrating observations on the nature of poetry itself, observations that have in some respects anticipated our "new criticism" by almost a century. Hopkins thought long and deeply on the nature of the sound structure and he was not unaware of the levels of meaning patterns in poetry. "What becomes of my verses I care little, but about things like this, what I write or could write on philosophical matters, I do," he wrote to Dixon in 1887. And his reason for this choice is significant: "the verses stand or fall by their simple selves . . . but if the other things are unsaid right they will be said by somebody else wrong, and that is what will not let me rest" (L II, p. 150).

And yet, ironically, how much has been said wrong about the meanings of Hopkins' poems, especially about this particular ode, because we did not have the right guide. It is not my intention here to review the many interpretations of Hopkins' *The Wreck of the Deutschland*. I simply want to indicate how Hopkins can be a most trustworthy guide in and through the labyrinthine ways. In outlining this approach to the ode I am aware of "the intentional fallacy" trap. But I align myself with T. S. Eliot who believed that the poets who are also critics—and what a distinguished group of poet-critics we can boast of—have in their criticism significant help for interpreting their own art. For such a poet who is also a critic is, according to Eliot, "always trying to defend the kind of poetry he is writing, or to formulate the kind he wants to write" ("The Music of Poetry," in *Poetry and Poets*, p. 26).

In letting Hopkins be our guide I would like to emphasize three areas in which he can be most helpful; namely, in prosody, especially for the insights he gives us into the oral nature of poetry; in the metaphorical or figurative meanings, for the light he throws on the underthought level of poetry and its antithetical parallel structure; and finally, in his own probing into the sense of mystery and sacrifice that underpins the entire meaning structure of this ode.

Hopkins' definition of poetry has become by now a classic one: "Poetry," he writes in his *Journal*, "is speech framed for contemplation of the mind by way of hearing or speech framed to be heard for its own sake and interest even over and above its interest in meaning. Some matter and meaning is essential to it but only as an element necessary to support and employ the shape which is contemplated for its own sake" (J, p. 289). Hopkins is here stressing the oral nature of poetry. He anticipates by almost a century the work that critics in our time are doing in attempting to bring us to an awareness of the true nature of poetry as "sound" patterns. Too long have we thought of poetry as "object" and used our eyes, not our ears, to experience it. Even today some of our leading critics discuss poetry as "object." Walter Ong, S. J., points out how unaware we are of its "radically acoustic quality" when we have poetic criticism presented under such titles as *The Well-Wrought Urn*, *The Verbal Icon*, or even Eliot's "objective correlative" or Rene Wellek's "stratified norms." Not that the critics, who have been preoccupied with poetry as objects, structure, skeleton, and stratified systems, have ignored the world of voice and sound, but according to Father Ong, they "have based their explanations perhaps too innocently on spatial analogies" (*The Barbarian Within*, p. 27).

Hopkins did not ignore the world of voice and sound. In fact, his defense of his ode rests on such a world as opposed to Bridges' approach to poetry. In his preface to the 1918 edition of Hopkins' poetry, Bridges acknowledged that he was "shamefully worsted in a brave frontal assault" on this poem because "both subject and treatment" were distasteful to him. This kind of approach to poetry is still with us. It is the kind that despoils the poem of its integrity, the kind that searches out "content" apart from "form," whereas Hopkins was aware of the poem as a unified structure of words. In fact, he describes his ode as having its origin in the irrevocable union of the event with the sound patterns. Dixon had asked if he wrote poetry and he tells him that though he had written poetry and burned it on entering the Society of Jesus, when the *Deutschland* was wrecked in the mouth of the Thames in the winter of 1875 and five Franciscan nuns exiled from Germany were drowned, he was so affected by the account and with a hint from the rector that someone write a poem on the subject, he set out to produce one. Then he adds these pertinent words: "I had long had haunting my ear the echo of a new rhythm which now I realized on paper" (L II, p. 14). What is significant here is that the poem is born out of sound patterns, out of living speech. It is event-melded to designed and patterned sound. Thus, if we focused our attention on approaching the poem where Hopkins would have it, we would not be looking for meanings divorced from those patterned sounds. We would not have the kind of bifurcating approach to the poem that Claude Abbott, for example, made when he marveled "at the technical strength" but saw as the subject of the poem the drowning of five nuns and forty-five other people. And this subject, says Abbott, "is unable to bear the stress of an ode so ambitious. The poet is handicapped by the academic religious subject and by his determination to make the poem safe as doctrine" (L I, p. xxvi).

But even more recently, critics continue to search out "content" divorced from the sound patterns and tell us what the poem is about. Elisabeth Schneider says: "The poem is an ode on conversion, conversion to the Catholic Church" (Schneider, p. 14). The main theme of Part I, she believes, is his own personal conversion and the main theme of Part II, the conversion of all England. And so fifty years after Bridges wrote his preface we still have the poem constricted in a narrow sectarian framework.

How would Hopkins want us to approach his poem? Certainly he would want us to delight in the word patterns, remembering that words by their nature have sound and meaning. He would want us especially to be aware of the particular genre he was using, namely, the ode. Some of his instructions to Bridges on how to read this poem are relevant here: "If it is obscure do not bother yourself with the meaning," he tells his friend, "but pay attention to the best and most intelligible stanzas as the two last stanzas of each part and the narrative of the Wreck" (L I, p. 46). Bridges would have preferred more narrative, but Hopkins calls his attention to the genre he is working through: "The Deutschland would be more interesting if there were more wreck and less discourse, but still it is an ode and not primarily a narrative. There is some narrative in Pindar, but the principal business is lyrical" (L I, p. 49). The poem must be grasped as "utterance," as "heightened speech." And to enter the world of the ode with Hopkins as guide is to experience this poem as personal utterance, as a cry. It is to enter a world of I-Thou relationships. And in this kind of world of art, fluid in sound, words are not reduced to objects or icons, but are basically what words are—utterances, cries.

Let us try then to discover the shape of the ode and contemplate it for its own sake. The easiest way, Hopkins tells us, to get at this fluid shape is through the culminating stanzas of both parts of the poem. If we let the sound patterns of these two culminating stanzas of each part penetrate our being, we experience the urgency of the voice asking that God "be adored among men," that God master, even though the mastery be through wrecking and storm, but most emphatically "out of us all/Mastery, but be adored, but be adored King." Part I ends with the implicit cry of yes which has penetrated the whole section from the explicit cry: "I did say yes/O at lightning and lashed rod" to complete obeisance to Christ, "To hero of Calvary, Christ,'s feet—/Never ask if meaning it, wanting it, warned of it—men go." The pattern is struggle, battling with God on the private level, in the secret of the poet's own heart. No wonder Hopkins could say to his friend Bridges: "I may add for your greater interest and edification that what refers to myself in the poem is all strictly and literally true and did all occur; nothing is added for poetical padding" (L I, p. 46). And Part II of the ode ends in the grand climax, with the resurrection motif, the upward surge after the battle and the storm. The closing lines that haunt our ears are those which show the prince and high priest, triumphant, at the end of his quest. Once again it is through wrecking and storm (literal ones this time) that the movement is completed.

I think within Hopkins' own theory we have what John Wain has pointed out as the two chief principles upon which his work is founded, "irreducibility and simultaneity" (*The Chatterton Lecture to the British Academy*, p. 177). Or to use McLuhan's terminology, we should respond to this ode not as a sequential and linear form but as a simultaneous and multidimensional structure. This kind of response was not, as we have seen, Bridges' experience of the ode. Hence John Wain's interest in what he calls "the Bridges-Hopkins dialectic," an historical, symbolic confrontation in which "the whole dilemma of the modern artist is there, perhaps the whole dilemma of modern man" (Ibid.).

To understand how far Hopkins prescinded from the nineteenth-century theory of poetry we cannot affirm too strongly his emphasis on the oral nature of poetry and, we might add, on its aural nature. The very reason he employed sprung rhythm is related intimately to this concept: "It is," he told Bridges, "the nearest to the rhythm of prose, that is, the native and natural rhythm of speech, the least forced, the most rhetorical and emphatic of all possible rhythms, combining, as it seems to me, opposite and one wd. have thought, incompatible excellences, markedness of rhythm—that is rhythm's self and naturalness of expression" (L I, p. 46). In fact, Hopkins had once thought of writing little prose pieces above his poems so that the logical meaning could be cleared, as it were, out of the way, and the poem then confronted as a poem should be—on its own.

Because Hopkins wanted the poem to be confronted on its own, wanted the sound patterns to be unmistakable, he marked accents throughout the ode. Father Coleridge, editor of *The Month*, was dismayed. This was something so very strange, this offended the eye. This was something a century ahead of its time, calling attention to the sound patterns. Hopkins desired to be read orally and to be read correctly. Father Coleridge asked him to do away with the marks. Hopkins wrote to his mother: "I would gladly have done without them if I thought my readers would scan right unaided but I am afraid they will not, and if the lines are not rightly scanned they are ruined" (L III, p. 138). He agreed, nevertheless, to eliminate the marks, that is, most of them. But the poem did not appear in *The Month*, or for that matter in any other publication during Hopkins' life. As theorist he was ahead of his time and his theory was necessary for the proper approach to this poem. His correspondence on the fate of the poem closes in an aside to his mother, "About the Deutschland 'sigh no more.' I am glad it has not appeared" (L III, p. 141).

There is a close relation between Hopkins' use of sprung rhythm and his theories of that rhythm. And those theories can provide an intelligent approach to the oral structure of the ode and alert the hearer to the many subtleties involved in this "marked figure of sound." This essay, however, cannot consider the many aspects of Hopkins' prosody. The purpose here is to indicate that Hopkins as critic and theorist is an indispensable guide to a rhythmic analysis of the ode.

During his life Hopkins was not to experience that sense of understanding which every artist needs. Canon Dixon was prepared to admire even when there was not the insight that should accompany admiration. He wrote to Hopkins about his reaction to this poem: "The Deutschland is enormously powerful; it has however such elements of deep distress in it that one reads it with less excited delight though not with less interest than the others" (L II, p. 32). Apparently Dixon did not experience through the patterns of sound the tremendous surge of joy under suffering, the great movement toward Christ, in lines like: "I fled with a fling of the heart to the heart of the Host" in Part I, or where the passion is only one part of the movement, the downward thrust, followed by the resurrection motif in Part II:

> **the uttermost mark**
> **Our passion-plungèd giant risen,**
> **The Christ of the Father compassionate, fetched in the storm**
> **of his strides.**

Coventry Patmore too was among Hopkins' contemporaries who broke poems apart into "content" and "form." He bifurcated the poem into style and matter, separating how a thing is done from what is done. Patmore conceived of style as a kind of decoration or clothing for the matter. And in this conception he reflects his own times. He writes to Hopkins of his first reaction to his poetry: "It seems to me that the thought and feeling of these poems, if expressed without any obscuring novelty of mode, are such as often to require the whole attention to apprehend and digest them; and are therefore of a kind to appeal to the few." Here we are worlds away from the modern conception of metaphor as essential meaning. Hopkins apparently attempted to explain to his friend his way of composition but it was a way that Patmore could not comprehend. Patmore replied: "What you say about your modes of composition disposes, at once, of some of what I thought were sound critical objections against writing upon theory . . . but how such modes, or at least some of them, as for example your alliteration, came to be the spontaneous expression of your poetical feelings, I cannot understand, and I do not think I ever shall" (L III, p. 353). As to his response to the great ode, Patmore writes in this same letter, "But I do not think that I could ever become sufficiently accustomed to your favourite Poem, 'The Wreck of the Deutschland' to reconcile me to its strangenesses." We are once again at the heart of the creative process itself. Patmore conceives of the art object as idea plus style; Hopkins conceives of the poem as a totally unified structure of sound patterns, a structure in which all is style, in which there are not two ways of saying what is being spoken in the poem. If we grasp Hopkins' concept of the unified nature of the poem, we realize then how feeble is the paraphrase in exploring meaning.

Now let us turn to some very enlightening theory on the ways Hopkins sees meanings embodied in the poem. He writes to his friend Baillie about what he considers a new principle of organization he has discovered:

> My thought is that in any lyric passage of the tragic poets (perhaps not so much in Euripides as in the others) there are—usually—I will not say always, it is not likely—two strains of thought running together and like counter-pointed; the overthought that which everybody, editors, see (when one does see anything—which in the great corruption of the text and original obscurity of the diction is not everywhere) and which might for instance be abridged or paraphrased in square marginal blocks as in some books carefully written; the other, the underthought, conveyed chiefly in the choice of metaphors etc used and often only half realized by the poet himself, not having a connection and suggested by some circumstance of the scene or of the story (L III, p. 252).

These two strains of thought, the overthought and the underthought are of invaluable help in penetrating his own ode. This concept of the underthought has become basic theory in twentieth-century literary theory. At this point I am not interested in proving that Hopkins is an unacknowledged legislator and that he anticipated this approach long before the nineteen-twenties. Francis Noel Lees has, I believe, success-fully taken that subject as far as it can go at present in his article, "Gerard Manley Hopkins, Scholar and the Matter of Imagery" (*British Journal of Aesthetics,* 1975). Hopkins, at least, thought he had discov-ered this principle, for in this same letter quoted above to Baillie he speaks of an intended book on the chorus and lyric parts of Greek plays, and adds, "I think what I should say would throw a new light and that if I did not perhaps no one else would . . . I do not anticipate being anticipated—so to say" (L III, p. 252).

What Hopkins calls the "overthought" we can readily dispose of, for it is the obvious paraphrasable parts of the ode, what we might call the literal meanings: the sailing of the *Deutschland* on a Saturday from Bremen, bound for America, with two hundred passengers, its running into a dreadful storm off the English coast, striking the combs of a smother of sand, the long waiting-out for help, the drowning of a fourth of the passengers, including five Franciscan nuns exiled from Germany because of their religion. All this is quite obvious narrative material and is of the kind Bridges wanted more of. But since, as Hopkins says, this poem is primarily an ode, then we must look for riches deeper than those in the narrative materials. The shipwreck provided Hopkins with an occasion, an event to which and out of which he could operate as artist. It is to the underthought, conveyed, as he says of the Greek lyrics, chiefly in the choice of metaphors, that we must look for the crucial meanings which hold the whole design together.

The storm images binding both parts of the ode are the most obvious images and these are part of the basic water and fire symbols. But what I would like to call attention to is Hopkins' insight into the relation of the metaphorical underthought to the overthought. He does not see these two levels as reinforcing or simply paralleling each other. These two strains of thought, he tells us, run together like "counterpointed." Only when we grasp this concept will the ode yield its full greatness. The relationship of the meaning (the narrative parts) and the metaphor (the figurative meanings) is counterpointed. The most striking counterpart to the death imagery, the actual drowning of the five nuns and the passengers, is the resurrection imagery on the figurative level. This insight into the nature of counterpoint is one that Hopkins carries through the entire artistic form. It is there first of all in the sound strata, in the counterpointed rhythmic patterns, and it is there not only in the large area of the narrative structure but even within basic image patterns. It is a theory Hopkins grappled with from his undergraduate days at Oxford and which he designated as "antithetical parallelism."

If as Lees says, "Hopkins the professor should be granted the status as innovator in criticism that Hopkins the poet already possesses in poetry" (*British Journal of Aesthetics*, p. 171), why should we not take the logical step and use Hopkins' critical theory to help us penetrate the ode? The counterpointed underthought has enough challenge for repeated returns to the ode and discoveries yet to be made that Hopkins the theorist acknowledged are "often only half realized by the poet himself."

Take the poem on any level, theme, character, setting, time—and the parallelisms are obvious, built into antithetical shapes. God is lord of "living and dead," he binds bones and fashions flesh, then almost unmakes his doing. His love is "a winter and warm," and he is a "Father and fondler of heart," but his is a "dark descending" yet he is most "merciful then." He is master of the tides but also "ground of being." He is throned behind "Death with a sovereignty that heeds but hides, bodes but abides." Death plays his dramatic role as villain who separates and as friend who unites, for he is either a sword or a flange and a rail. The storm flakes become "scroll-leaved flowers, lily showers." And the wild waters are "fall-gold mercies" in which the nuns bathe.

The setting is shaped into antithetical parallels too: the walls, altar, hour and night of the private battle, against the Kentish Knock of the public battle. In both there is a yielding to God: "I did say yes/O at lightning and lashed rod" is paralleled by the nun's cry: "The cross to her she calls Christ to her, christens her wild-worst Best." And how obvious is the design of utterance, of cry, in these random examples.

At the heart of the ode is the mystery of suffering resolved in the Christ figure, "Our passion-plungèd giant risen." The poem is filled with this kind of antithetical movement. There must be a going down into the depths of baptismal waters, a union with the passion before the Easter triumph. At the end of the poem the nun has finished her battle and has come from the "endragonèd seas" to the "heaven-haven of the re-ward."

The riches in the water and fire symbols are too vast to be explored individually in a paper of this length. However, using Hopkins' theory of counterpoint in the underthought and his insights into the nature of "antithetical parallelisms" gives one a technique for discovering the integral shape of the ode. The water symbol carries the great counter-pointed theme of Christ's incarnation, passion, death, and resurrection and the parallel situation of the nun in her death by drowning and ultimate arrival at the heaven-haven of her reward. Fire is a life symbol in the dramatic portrayal of the sacrificial act of putting off self to take on Christ, the saying yes at "lightning and lashed rod." It is the great energy symbol: "and with fire in him forge thy will." The fire symbol counterpoints the water symbol in such lines as those which describe the death of the nuns where they are "sealed in wild waters" and "bathe in his fall-gold mercies" and "breathe in his all-fire glances."

The total shape filled with antithetical tensions ultimately rests in harmony so that the final form is seen as one that moves from the beat of the seas of time to the heaven-haven of eternity, from time past and present to time future. Chaos resolves into courtly harmony where the prince and the high priest are one and the night will have given way to a crimson-cresseted east, where Christ the hero will rule all hearts and minds.

Hopkins' last line of this ode deserves long and serious contempla-tion, for in this line culminates the crucial theme of the ode. The line operates artistically in much the same way as the final line in *The Windhover*: "Fall, gall themselves, and gash gold-vermilion." Here the passion is caught in the trilogy of "fall, gall, and gash," and culminates in the resurrection of the "gold-vermilion" where the kingship and triumph is caught in "gold" and the suffering transfigured and linked to the gold in "vermilion." In the last line of *The Wreck of the Deutsch-land*, a line almost wholly neglected by the critics who probe to find meanings, is a world in microcosm reflecting the macrocosm projected in the total ode. Christ is a king: "Our hearts' charity's hearth's fire, our thoughts' chivalry's throng's Lord." Here the grammar structures with their bold piling up of genitives, reinforce the meaning of "mastery" and what Christ possesses is the total man, heart and mind. His burning dominion covers the private arena of home, the hearth's fire of being, the center of love; and the public domain of mind where he is seen as the Lord, coming back in triumph, followed by his throngs, but throngs of noble thoughts. It is a kingdom not of this world. Here in this line the battle imagery of the poem culminates in a dramatic climax of homecoming, and the Son comes back to the Father, "Kind, but royally reclaiming his own."

Hopkins can also be a helpful guide through the theological under-pinnings of the ode. His notes on the Long Retreat of 1881 are espe-cially significant in alerting us to his concept of time. And these insights into the nature of time help one discover new dimensions in the ode. "Time," he writes, "has 3 dimensions and one positive pitch or direc-tion" (S, p. 196). The dimensions are undoubtedly time past, present, and future. These aspects of time in the ode are easily recognized in the overthought or narrative parts. But the "pitch or direction" is a part of the underthought and even in this dimension the tug of counterpoint is felt. Highlighting the whole structure are the forward-thrust images of movement toward Christ. There are reinforcing forward-thrust move-ments on the subjective, personal level of the speaker in Part I, and public forward-thrust movements on the part of the nun in Part II. The emphatic design in the poet's experience is the thrust to the eucharist: "I fled with a fling of the heart to the heart of the Host." The nun's forward pitch is to utter Christ and even in that utterance is an explicit, overt counterpoint:

> 'O Christ, Christ, come quickly':
> **The cross to her she calls Christ to her, christens her wild-worst**
> **Best.**

The poem is a mine of haunting poetical phrases like the ones just quoted, but these isolated phrases must be grasped as an integral part of the dynamic whole, for "all's to one thing wrought." The movement is down (through suffering) but the ultimate direction spirals up toward God through identity with the "passion-plungèd giant risen."

In his Commentary on the *Spiritual Exercises,* Hopkins wrote: "God's utterance of himself is God the Word, outside himself is this world. This world then is word, expression, news of God. Therefore, its end, its purpose, its meaning, is God and its life or work to name and praise him" (S, p. 129). A passage like this can be a guide in directing one to a deeper awareness of this ode as "utterance" and as "cry," and within the time dimension the present, the now, becomes dynamic. The suffering, of course, culminates in a complete forward thrust when the nun has attained the "heaven-haven of the reward" and the poet raises his voice in supplication that for England this will be a new birth. The nun's cry is a giving birth to Christ anew: "But here was heart-throe, birth of a brain,/Word, that heard and kept thee and uttered thee outright." The reason for her cry is dramatized in stanza 28, in which she recognizes Christ as "*Ipse*, the only one." Here is a perfect act of self-sacrifice. The price paid for her recognition, her utterance, is the entering into the passion and resurrection: "What was the feast followed the night/Thou hadst glory of this nun?" And the answer comes through unmistakably: "Feast of the one woman without stain."

The nature of the mystery Hopkins is here embodying in the ode becomes clearer when we turn to his further theorizing on the nature of "time." We have seen how the forward thrust is embodied in the poem. But Hopkins says: "It [time] is therefore not so much like any river or any sea as like the Sea of Galilee, which has the Jordan running through it and giving a current to the whole" (S, p. 196). This concept of time giving a current to the whole identifies all acts in the time cycle of the incarnation. It also throws light on the meaning of such a line in the ode referring to the incarnation as "It rides time like riding a river." Thus the nun uttering Christ is identified with Mary giving birth to Christ. The act is identical but antithetical: for the nun there was "heart-throe, birth of a brain." But the feast following the suffering is Mary's: "Feast of the one woman without stain." We have embodied in these lines Hopkins' theory of poetry as "utterance," the identity within the incarnational world of the birth of Christ in historical time and his renewed birth through all subsequent time as "utterance" so that Mary and the nun play parallel but antithetical parts. The celebration of Mary's Immaculate Conception, the calendar date of December 8, is identified here with the historical event of the wreck of the *Deutschland*. And the poet reminds us of this in his dedication of the ode: "To the happy memory of five Franciscan nuns exiles by the Falk Laws, drowned between midnight and morning of Dec. 7th, 1875." The nun's feast and Mary's feast are the same. We have then a living embodiment of Hopkins' theory that time is like the Sea of Galilee, with the Jordan "running through it and giving a current to the whole."

Hopkins' thinking on the meaning of sacrifice, especially on what he calls "the great sacrifice," helps us to come to terms with the ode in its profoundest depths. Note in this passage from his Long Retreat of 1881 how key words from the ode reverberate through his writing, words like "glory" and "sacrifice." In this particular passage he is pondering the mystery of why Christ went forth from the Father:

> To give God glory and that by sacrifice, sacrifice offered in the barren wilderness outside of God, as the children of Israel were led into the wilderness to offer sacrifice. This sacrifice and this outward procession is a consequence and shadow of the procession of the Trinity, from which mystery sacrifice takes its rise (S, p. 197).

The thoughts embodied in this passage give one a deeper appreciation of those final lines of the ode. In these lines the ode culminates in the public triumphal procession of Christ leading his victorious army back to the Father, the ultimate thrust of all time dimension. Hopkins in his Long Retreat notes meditates on this upward thrust movement of all being. Of the Virgin Mary he says, she "was beyond others redeemed, because it was her more than all other creatures that Christ meant to win from nothingness and it was her that he meant to raise the highest" (S, p. 197). The ode is filled with echoes of this raising to higher and higher levels: "To tower from the grace to the grace." What we experience aesthetically in the ode is what Hopkins discovered through years and years of meditation and embodied in this art form: "God gave things a forward and perpetual motion" (S, pp. 197–98).

Perhaps we have had too many attempts to pin the ode down to specific meanings. Once we have grasped the nature of poetry, to use Hopkins' own phrase, as "speech heightened," we will be less apt to want to restrict it. He wrote to Bridges, "Granted that it needs study and is obscure, for indeed I was not overdesirous that the meaning of all should be quite clear, at least unmistakable" (L I, p. 50). Nevertheless, he has given us significant clues in his defense of the ode and in his meditations on "time" and the mystery of sacrifice. The great Dragon is verbal expression and, as Father Ong reminds us about the nature of verbal expression, "in its ineluctable interiority" all verbal expression, but "in particular all true literature, remains forever something mysterious" (The Barbarian Within, p. 29).

On this centenary anniversary of The Wreck of the Deutschland the kind of appreciative response to Hopkins' ode ought to be the kind he himself had to Wordsworth's Ode on the Intimations of Immortality. When derogatory or perhaps simply belittling remarks were made of Wordsworth's ode by Canon Dixon, Hopkins jumped to the defense. And the words he used in that defense could so aptly apply to his own ode. For Hopkins, this Wordsworth poem was one of a dozen or half dozen of the finest odes of the world. He says few men have had something happen to them that does not happen to other men; that is, they have, as he expresses it, "seen something." And human nature in these men who see something gets a shock. When Wordsworth wrote his ode, "human nature got another of those shocks, and the tremble from it is spreading." Of the ode itself Hopkins wrote: "Now the interest and importance of the matter were here of the highest, his insight was at its very deepest, and hence to my mind the extreme value of the poem. His powers rose, I hold, with the subject: the execution is so fine. The rhymes are so musically interlaced, the rhythms so happily succeed . . . the diction throughout is so charged and steeped in beauty and yearning." He then tells Dixon that "there is not a bit of good in my going on if, which is to me so strange in you and disconcerting, you do not feel anything of this." May he not have had in mind the kind of response his own ode suffered from those who ought to have understood, poets like Bridges, Dixon, and Patmore? Bridges had called it "presumptious [sic] jugglery." But Hopkins defends Wordsworth's ode to the hilt. To Dixon's derogations he cries out: "For my part I shd. think St. George and St. Thomas of Canterbury wore roses in heaven for England's sake on the day that ode, not without their intercession, was penned" (L II, p. 148).

Hopkins too saw something and that something is so deeply mysterious that the tremble from his insight ought to be spreading still. The actual wreck of the *Deutschland* provided him with the occasion. Certainly the interest and importance of the matter is of the highest—God's mastering man and man's response to that touch. Hopkins' powers rose with the subject. His is the execution of a highly wrought, severely disciplined artifact in the rhythms of vital speech, a rhythm which had long been haunting his ear (L II, p. 14).

What he says of Wordworth's ode we now say of his ode: "The execution is so fine. The rhymes are so musically interlaced, the rhythms so happily succeed."

The poem must be accepted and contemplated on its own terms. Any attempt to impose meanings on it, to separate content from form, dismembers the great dragon. Surely on the day his ode was penned St. George and St. Thomas of Canterbury ought to have worn roses in heaven not only for England's sake, but for the sake of the kingdom of God.

Rescue of the Survivors of the *Deutschland* by Harwich steam-tug *Liverpool*

Chapter IX

"Man Jack the Man Is"

The Wreck from the Perspective of *The Shepherd's Brow*

by Robert Boyle, S. J.

The shepherd's brow, fronting forked lightning, owns
The horror and the havoc and the glory
Of it. Angels fall, they are towers, from heaven—a story
Of just, majestical, and giant groans.
But man—we, scaffold of score brittle bones;
Who breathe, from ground long babyhood to hoary
Age gasp; whose breath is our *memento mori*—
What bass is *our* viol for tragic tones?
He! Hand to mouth he lives, and voids with shame;
And, blazoned in however bold the name,
Man Jack the man is, just; his mate a hussy.
And I that die these deaths, that feed this flame,
That . . . in smooth spoons spy life's masque mirrored: tame
My tempests there, my fire and fever fussy.

When, on a soft Dublin day in early April of 1889, Hopkins, brooding over his poetic products of the last fourteen years, cast his mind's eye on his once beloved firstborn, *The Wreck of the Deutschland*, I believe he experienced a feeling of disgust and revulsion. Not with the poem, exactly, but with the posing, shrill-voiced young poet whose categories were so narrow ("O world wide of its good!"), whose condemnations were so sweeping ("beast of the waste wood"), and whose egoism could challenge omnipotence ("Thóu mastering mé"). With Shelleyan semigrandeur bidding him too, like the voice of *Epipsychidion*, to "dare beacon the rocks on which high hearts are wrecked," and with pseudo-Pauline boasting bringing him to shout with humble pride to the world "I did say yes," he compared himself on his pastoral forehead of Wales, with safe shepherd's brow, to the tall German nun drowning in the Kentish waters, and found the two of them, quasi-martyrs for Christ, quite satisfactory. A decade and a half later, with the chill April mist invading his tiny room on the top floor of the building where James Joyce would discuss the language of the conqueror with another English Jesuit a few years later, that same poet spat out a disillusioned rejection of the inflated aspect of his younger self. The sonnet in which he did this, quoted above and the second-last he wrote, was despised and rejected by Bridges, but it has for me a special value, indicating, as I think it does, an underlying and particularly probing level operating below the deepest level I had previously found in Hopkins' powerful early ode.

In this light (or perhaps, this shadow), I propose to compare, in this anniversary tribute to Hopkins' beloved firstborn poem, the early ode and the almost final sonnet. Hopkins' heroism and profound theological grasp of his own and of the nun's situations have been plumbed often enough, by critics who, like Mariani, share a good deal of Hopkins' own vigor, insight, and expressiveness. But the ridiculous aspects of that somewhat fanatical little man's heroic challenging of divine power and of his faintly magnanimous free choice to assent instead of dissent, that Browningesque complacent bluster (without the partially chewed bread and cheese but not without the bravado) of his satisfaction in his victory over fear of cosmic threat, have received little sympathetic treatment, and this seems to me a good time to attempt some.

Hopkins, in the midst of his theological studies in drafty, rambling St. Beuno's in North Wales, took himself, in basic matters, very seriously. His humor was not Falstaffian but rather, insofar as it existed at all, Holofernian, expressing itself most obviously in whimsical letters, wry triolets, and in pedantic practical jokes. When it came to his relationship to Christ, he was not prepared to smile at all, but, like the Stephen Dedalus whose creator he came within a few years of teaching, he strained to see himself elevated (in Hopkins' case because of his real belief in the infinite power of his "opponent") to epic pinnacles, requiring for expression the imagery, diction, and rhythmic sweep of the poet he most admired, Milton.

Thus in the first stanza of his ode, God's finger searches him out and touches him at the division of body and spirit, in the center of his very heart, threatening his evidently significant existence. And the rod of infinite authority lashed out at him, the apparently destructive lightning came hurtling toward him, and he sees himself choosing to say the *yes* of acceptance rather than hurling back that *no* (which Stephen Dedalus chose), which, as Hopkins develops in those baroque retreat notes so closely allied to the retreat sermons in *Portrait of the Artist as a Young Man*, would have found the divine tempest a descending whirlwind of fiery torment. The young poet enjoys and dwells on his happy self through the next eight stanzas, celebrating the Word, indeed, but as a consequence presenting Christ also as a foil to the admirably affirmative poet. He concludes the first part of his Christmas ode as a tardy Magus bringing his valuable gift of adoration to the newborn king.

There is at least some justice in looking at the poem from this angle, especially since Hopkins himself did something like that, and even in wondering if the overingenious young Romantic is not at least tending to subordinate not only the cosmos but God too to his own almost frenetic "Serviam!" The bird image in stanza 3, with a glance at bird images in following poems, may give some perspective on this possible attitude. The dove image follows what I take to be the bird image in stanza 2, where I see a pentecostal hawk sweeping and hurling like the later windhover, and in this case treading the smaller bird, the swooning heart ("swooning" a word that Hopkins, like Joyce, knew from Skeat to be an Anglo-Saxon derivation quite at home in chivalric context). In stanza 3, although I am deeply interested in Eileen Kennedy's recent attractive suggestion, in *Victorian Poetry* (Vol. 11, 1973, pp. 247–51), that the dove is the symbol-bringing bird of Noah, I nevertheless still find the same bird who operates in *The Handsome Heart*:

> What the heart is! which, like carriers let fly—
> Doff darkness, homing nature knows the rest . . .

This one, in stanza 3, since its home is the heart of the Host, which leads into infinity, flashes and towers indefinitely.

When a divine rather than a created dove shows up a few months later, in *God's Grandeur*, it has achieved cosmic size and reveals its Miltonic genealogy. Here the pentecostal hawk of stanza 2 becomes the creative dove allied to Milton's epic dovelike Spirit brooding on the vast abyss to make it pregnant. Hopkins in *The Wreck* sees both himself and the nun, like Mary (in a special sense) and Peter, Paul, Augustine, and all successful humans, made pregnant with Christ, and that special Pauline insight—"My dear children, with whom I am in labor again, until Christ is formed in you" (Galatians 4:19)—adds considerable depth to Hopkins' echo of Milton. Doves scatter flakes in the farmyard of *The Starlight Night*, not unallied to the storm flakes of stanza 21, and thrushes strike the ear like loving lightning in *Spring*. The mothering wing of *In the Valley of the Elwy* contrasts with the absent wing of stanza 12. The soul as "a dare-gale skylark" is limited and suppressed by the body, a bone-cage, while the skylark of *The Sea and the Skylark* foreshadows the kingfisher and the great bell to come in No. 57, ringing out the pure self which speaks and spells the Word. Then, mastering the equine wind and buckled in his knightly pride, the great bird of literature, if the smallest of hawks, the windhover, glides in, and as an Ignatian knight with ride and jar echoes the triumphal march of *The Wreck's* final syllables—though the speaker of the sonnet, like St. Alphonsus and like Christ, achieves that victory in a realm beyond human natural sight, in contrast to the suffering and death which human eyes can note.

And the birds get bigger. The winged heart of *Hurrahing in Harvest* can hurl the whole earth behind him, and is rivaled only by the symbol of the artist Purcell, that great storm fowl which, like God in No. 69, scatters a colossal smile into the purple darkness, revealing that self which is the Word.

A diminution appears in *Peace*, where the dove is small and shy, and broods now over a much smaller cosmos, the war-torn heart—or, rather, it is small enough to enter the heart and coo again over fragile life that, the poem suggests, won't last long either. It will be destroyed by those winged gryphons, the "beakleaved boughs dragonish" of *Spelt from Sibyl's Leaves*. And in his final three poems, concerned like the Purcell sonnet with artistic production, the busy little birds, like the lovely star-eyed strawberry-breasted throstle of *The May Magnificat*, can build nests for new life, but the sterile speaker cannot build, he says. He manages to write three magnificent self-contemning sonnets (having for years had, as he tells Bridges on January 12, 1888, no jet of inspiration that will produce anything larger than a sonnet) to express his inability to write at all. The man who started out his mature career as a poet with the confident claim to be uttering prophetic truth, impelled to ring out from his own inspired breast, touched like the breast cavity of the nun by the finger of God and set into clangorous motion, the inexpressible reality of the Pauline "mystery hidden for ages in God" of Ephesians 3—now, in *The Shepherd's Brow*, that same man with altered view looks back at his efforts to be a hawklike Son of Thunder, gazing unblinking and unafraid at the blinding "glory bare" of the Word, a new and greater Milton justifying the ways of God to man, and sees all that activity as a mere "fussy" flutter of fretting wings. What brought about such a change?

Here I see the more mature and manly Hopkins condemning with a truly Browningesque honesty the measure of youthful pretentiousness of the earlier years with the contemptuous adjectives "tame" and, most detestable to a balanced and now more tolerant man, "fussy." But some do not find any change at all. Bridges did, and judging such cynicism unworthy and uncharacteristic, banished the penultimate sonnet to the fragments. Several recent critics, disagreeing with Bridges, have sought to rescue the sonnet. Some years ago, in *Renascence* (Spring 1963) Sister Mary Hugh Campbell objected to Bridges' judgment, and in a most intelligent and stimulating reading, brought out many of the sonnet's strong points. Two unfortunate readings, however, weaken her defense, as I see it. She finds the "voiding" image very ugly, and owing to not having seen the early drafts, she is able to take "tame" as a verb and to find Hopkins addressing a pious, patient prayer to the Holy Spirit in the final lines. She also takes the "He" of line 9 to be the shepherd, which strikes me as unlikely. She does read the spoon image with remarkable acuity, I judge: "On the surface his daily existence seems ordered and urbane and perfect, a life whose 'smooth spoons' symbolize the safe distance that keeps him from both the great trials of 'forked lightning' and the indignities of the shepherd's 'hand to mouth' existence." She further sees the effect on the speaker of seeing "his own distorted image reflected to him in upside-down fashion" and realizing that appearances deceive, that no person really comprehends another, that he is a subject only for amusing masque, not tragedy. But, I am afraid, her misreading of "tame" leads her to emasculate this most healthy and virile poem.

Robert B. Clark, S. J., does the same thing in his generally perceptive and occasionally brilliant "Hopkins's 'The Shepherd's Brow'," in *Victorian Newsletter* (Fall 1965). He sees the shepherd as Moses, because of "forked, horrifying, and glorious" lightning, a good possible reference to "that shepherd" of *Paradise Lost*, I, 8. He somehow arrives at the conclusion, however, that the poem is an endorsement of religious meditation.

Paul Mariani, with his usual insight, in "The Artistic and Tonal Integrity of Hopkins' 'The Shepherd's Brow'," in *Victorian Poetry* (Spring 1968), sees Hopkins' face or "masque" comic in comparison with the noble forehead of Moses or the ravaged visage of Milton's Satan, "... and he ends his meditation with a prayer of humility, chiding himself for having thought his 'tempests' were other than the 'fire and fever fussy' of a precisionist." Maybe, but I incline to see the "tempest" as an echo of Lear's "the tempest in my mind" and the fussy fever from Macbeth's murderously cynical "fretful fever," and these both contrasted to the winds and flames of the pentecostal Spirit. The final lines sound to me not like a prayer but like a deeply felt expectoration of disgust. I cannot find the "deeply instressed heroism in this self-chiding patience" that Mariani does, perhaps because I've been reading too much Joyce. But I must say that it seems rather a relief to hear the somewhat inflated poser of *The Wreck* saying at last, in effect, "This human stink-hole, including me, does smell." He admits that he smells of mortality, that he has a defecating body, and that his epic stance has its ridiculous aspects. Like Lear, and with similar bitter vulgarity, he perceives that he is, in contrast to the majestic threatening forked lightning, "a poor, bare, forked animal."

Mariani finds Hopkins' spoon image strikingly similar to one of George Eliot's in *Middlemarch*: "I am not sure that the greatest man of his age, if ever that solitary superlative existed, could escape these unfavourable reflections of himself in various small mirrors; and even Milton, looking for his portrait in a spoon, must submit to have the facial angle of a bumpkin" (Book I, Chapter x). The discussion of Eliot's commentator in the rest of the paragraph—"what fading of hopes, or what deeper fixity of self-delusion" and "Mr. Casaubon, too, was the center of his own world; if he was liable to think that others were providentially made for him . . . this trait is not quite alien to us . . ."— also has relevance to Hopkins' thinking in his sonnet, as he looks back at that would-be Catholic Milton who could so confidently picture and express himself as the center of God's providential interest. This mature sonnet I see as a reaction to that indeed orthodox yet somewhat adolescent egotism.

Mariani does not see it so. He sees the sonnet as a further expression of the heroism he finds throughout Hopkins' work, and, up to a point, I have no quarrel with that. A true hero, as I conceive him, is also a realist. Shakespeare's Bottom happens to be one of my heroes (and, to my mind, one of Shakespeare's). Hopkins is all the more a hero to me when he faces, with disgust for his past self-deceit, the fact that he is a jackass. But I must reluctantly quarrel (reluctant because of my respect for Mariani's insight and because I have on more than one occasion discovered him being right where I had long been wrong) with his notion that this poem is a colloquy between Hopkins and Christ: "The mention of Milton, of his 'bumpkin' reflection in a spoon, of the inner conflicts and of the growing uneasiness with what is or is not found within us when we submit to an earnest self-examination, and perhaps even the unflattering figure of Casaubon himself have been transformed in the alembic of Hopkins' poetic imagination into a deeply instressed, personal colloquy between Hopkins and his Lord. George Eliot's wittily probing scrutiny of Casaubon contrasts with Hopkins' searing flame of intense self-examination.'' As I can see it, Christ is nowhere present in this sonnet. Hopkins is looking at a pretentious fool who set out to be a Catholic Milton, not only a ''just'' man in the scriptural sense of No. 57, but a ''just'' poet as well, an inspired spokesman for God, a justifier of God's ways; and he sees an ineffectual sonneteer whose tragic bass is expressed in water-closet noises.

In No. 57, Hopkins echoes Paul's ''I live now, not I, but Christ lives in me'' (Galatians 2:20) when he says that the ''I,'' the divinized person, ''says'' a new self, a ''just'' self who is more than the righteous man of the Old Testament just man, more, for example, than Abraham and Joseph as ''just'' men. The ''I'' of whom Hopkins speaks is both the limited human person and the human-divine Christ, all at once in totally mysterious identity: ''I *am* all at once what he *is*, since he *was* what I *am*,'' as Hopkins puts it in *Heraclitean Fire*, far more aware than Joyce that ''I am'' is the sacred name of God. Thus when he says, ''I say more: the just man justices,'' it is evident that the Pauline insight into ''just'' has lifted the word beyond merely rational levels. So when we see the word twice used in *The Shepherd's Brow*, with its emphasis now not on the capacity for divinization but with the stress on the at least apparent unfitness of man for anything but animal functions, we get more of the force of Hopkins' realistic appraisal of his human situation. He is not cynically rejecting the divine; he is, like Bottom, though in more complex and somewhat bitter mood, ultimately still expressing the same wonder that God could embrace his human creature, but now an idealistic stress on the spirit with little attention to the body does not appear. In *The Shepherd's Brow* he is at the opposite horizon of faith, still believing but finding what he once accepted as an object of divine interest, the ''I'' of *The Wreck*, now as an asinine and self-deluded versifier. The ''just'' of line 4 of the sonnet refers to the effect of Milton's stern God's just punishments, but the ''just'' of line 11, while grammatically it conveys the sense of ''precisely that and nothing more,'' expresses the vast expanses within a human being of having potentiality to be both a divinized ''just man'' and ''just a man Jack.'' In a mood where he can concentrate on himself in that second class, in a background of having overstressed the first one, especially an authentic hero might well be bitterly disgusted.

If indeed Hopkins was recalling George Eliot's powerful passage— and I have no doubt of it—it would probably increase his bitterness, since he disapproved of her. His contempt, as well as his self-conscious effort to salvage Christian charity, appears in his remark to Bridges: "How admirable are Blackmore and Hardy! Their merits are much eclipsed by the overdone reputation of the Evans-Eliot-Lewis-Cross woman (poor creature! one ought not to speak slightingly, I know), half real power, half imposition" (L I, p. 239). A case cannot convincingly be made against Hopkins as antifeminist. His admiration for the Blessed Virgin might in some circles be considered irrelevant, but his praise and imitation of Christina Rossetti, even if misguided, would indicate that he could appreciate a woman's product. His admiration of the tall nun and of St. Winefred could, I suppose, be attributed to their Catholicism, and some, like whoever wrote the Hopkins material in *The Oxford Anthology of English Literature* in 1973, probably would consider that Hopkins was drawn by the masculinity of their wills. That writer, by the way, could find explanations for Hopkins' revulsion in *The Shepherd's Brow* that I do not find, since with what I consider critical irresponsibility he states as a fact that Hopkins was a homosexual—the "possibly homosexual" of his introduction modulates easily into "the latent homosexuality he shared with Whitman" in the notes—and goes so far as to find the "baffled or repressed sexual passion" breaking out in the suggestive coinage "gaygangs," referring to those evidently lustful clouds roystering in the heavens of *Heraclitean Fire*. Other more responsible critics have felt, indeed, often however without considering Hopkins' own efforts to be strictly faithful to a sacrificial celibacy, that Hopkins' observation of and fondness for some males and the infrequency of his expression of equal fondness for females might be based on homosexual attitudes. Obviously that may have been the case. But the perpetrator of the Hopkins section of the Oxford textbook, offered for sale to a generation or so of truth-seeking students, substitutes a firm act of subjective faith for objective certitude. He thus bridges the gap between possibility and fact, and makes clear to the unwary that Hopkins, like the Shakespeare of Wilde's *Portrait of Mr. W. H.*, shows forth his homosexuality in his gay adjectives. A difference to be noted is that Wilde was writing honest fiction.

I see no evidence that Hopkins disliked women. His dislike of Mary Anne Evans, although *Romola* he had in 1865 accepted as "great" (L III, p. 224), was no doubt prompted more by her offense to his own decidedly puritanical standards—how else could he have been led into the monstrous opinion that Shakespeare's Beatrice was not only vain but "impure minded" (L III, p. 309)—than by her femininity or her literary power. And the very fact that he was now deriving a Miltonic context and a specific crass image from the masterful work of a woman he had formerly condemned as pagan and lacking in understanding and personal morality might stress for him his own pedantic hypocrisy.

Since I see Hopkins' sonnet as concerned centrally with his own artistic aims and products, it may be useful to mention how I see this mirror image, so important to artists since St. Paul used it to express how darkly we in our present fallen state can barely distinguish shadowy realities; since Hamlet defined drama (and for many deceived critics literary art) as a mirror held up to nature (Shakespeare thus, according to Oscar Wilde, demonstrated Hamlet's madness, since, as Wilde well preached, art does not reflect but determines); and since the reputedly dull lecturer on mathematics, Charles Lutwidge Dodgson, had in the logical twistings of his imagination found it to be a measure of rationality and the deceptions therein. Before I ran into Mariani's happy perception of the Eliot passage (though I believe I saw the reference first in the note in the fourth edition of *The Poems*, and I am not clear who derived the discovery from whom), I had wondered whether or not Eliot had been influenced in her own image by the vivid reflections in Dickens' mirror in *Our Mutual Friend*, Chapter Two, where "The great looking-glass above the sideboard, reflects the table and the company." Among those reflected is "charming old Lady Tippins on Veneering's right; with an immense obtuse drab oblong face, like a face in a tablespoon . . ." The approaches of these three powerful Victorian artists to this same image strike me as expressive of characteristic attitudes: Dickens' vulgar but powerful spoon distorts faces which resemble the aristocratically distorted houyhnhnm face of Lady Tippins, a possibly implied emotional attitude of Dickens toward the forces operative in the ruling class; Eliot's spoon distorts the aristocratic and admirable face of Milton into the earthy, common features of a bumpkin, a comfortable acceptance of the superiority of the educated and talented; Hopkins' spoon reduces his fancied elegant masque-role to his own small bathroom wind and sickly fire, not Miltonic pentecost, implying an attitude of judgment reaching beneath social forces to the basic pretensions of a pitiable animal. I suspect that these three images point toward one reason why Hopkins seems to most critics in our time a more important artist than the first two, so famous and influential in their time.

I myself see the shepherd of the sonnet's line 1 as basically Hopkins himself, ironically conceived as an epic or elegiac creation of himself as the greatest of literary artists, just as Lycidas and Satan and Adam and Christ are basically Milton, who powerfully expresses their human experience out of his own. The sonnet is, as I read it, concerned with Hopkins' literary career, such as it was, and, from many of the things Hopkins said to Bridges and especially to Dixon about the loss to England's ear of the neglect accorded their poems, from Hopkins' own poetic complaints of being left with only a "lonely began," from his edifying but sometimes frustrating efforts to escape the dead letter office and reach, as the nun apparently did, the divine ears, I do gather that Hopkins could identify most readily with the frustrated Lycidas. Further,

Lycidas, like the nun of Hopkins' "firstborn," fronted lightning and tempest and drowned and, like her too, shared in some analogy with the beams that flamed in the forehead of the morning sky, the crimson-cresseted east. Although Moses does seem in many striking ways to fit better into that shepherd's role, I am attracted to Lycidas both because he does fit and principally because I figure that Hopkins needs an elegy to go with the following epic of fallen angels (towers like the tall nun who towered in the tumult); with the somber Grecian treatment of Samson's vast strength yet liable, like Caradoc, to fall; with the low viol solemn music of the great religious Miltonic sonnets; and with the relatively trivial masque—all the forms which Milton brought to the peak of per-fection and all of which Hopkins attempted, and most often, in the larger forms, failed. But not only Lycidas and Moses, but Adam and the Bethlehem shepherds will in some ways fit the background. And maybe the Good Shepherd would serve best, from his role both in Milton and in *The Wreck*, and from the fact that he can best be set off against the "He," the ephemeral man of bones and breath who follows, a species in which shepherds and poets both exist. But in any case I take Hopkins as once aspiring to create out of his own poetic being a heroic shepherd of a story, a superhuman angel, and music which would enclose all the tragic grief and transcendent glory that the human heart has known, and do it better even than Milton could.

Thomas K. Beyette sees things somewhat in that vein too, in his "Hopkins' Phenomenology of Art in 'The Shepherd's Brow'," in *Victo-rian Poetry* (Vol. 11, 1973, pp. 207–13). With fine insight he considers the last three sonnets as concerned with the writing of poetry, and adds perceptive and interesting points to the readings of his predecessors. He disagrees with them, as I do, in their finding the final lines Christlike and pious, and considers that Hopkins is speaking of the fact that, as he complained to Bridges, he had no inspiration greater than that which, like an ephemeral blowpipe flame, would produce merely a sonnet. The pentecostal fire so generously apparent in *The Wreck* and the flam-boyant vigor sweeping upward the soaring *Windhover* has in this sonnet dwindled to a flickering fever, a disease, which can produce only com-plaining poems which Beyette sees as smooth spoons. In this I am forced to leave him, since, among other difficulties, I cannot form any Hopkinsian notion of spying life through poems (in this Hopkins is not like Stephen Dedalus), and I would be forced also, as I can see it now, to wonder, if the sonnets were smooth spoons, whether or not the epics might be corrugated soup ladles. In other words, I find nothing to impel me to consider the smooth spoons as anything other than literal spoons and distorting mirrors, since they work perfectly as such. I recall my own experience in Jesuit dining halls, waiting with downcast eyes while the faculty and other head-table officials filed past my table, and watching their black forms reflected in the large and small spoons on the table.

Hopkins might have had some such experience in his own imagination, as well as his response to the practice of literary artists all around him using the image with power and genius. In Hopkins' sonnet the harmless and useful real spoons balance effectively with the opening threatening metaphorical forks, and the food they convey to him does quiet his mildly tempestuous appetites and sustain his fretful fever. They serve him as an animal, but distort and limit him as an artist, and reveal to him, as I see it, that he is no more fit to write sonnets than to create, as he attempted to do with Caradoc, another ravaged Satan.

The light, then, that *The Shepherd's Brow* throws on *The Wreck* is that in the sonnet Hopkins reveals his mature perception of some of those immaturities he was conscious of in his letter to Bridges in 1881: "I agree that the *Eurydice* shews more mastery in art, still I think the best lines in the *Deutschland* are better than the best in the other. One may be biased in favour of one's firstborn though. There are some immaturities in it I should never be guilty of now" (L I, p. 119). Those immaturities could be anything, extremes of rhythm or diction or imagery, but I suspect the principal one is the slightly paranoic willingness to accept himself—"I may add for your greater interest and edification that what refers to myself in the poem is all strictly and literally true and did all occur; nothing is added for poetical padding" (L I, p. 47)—as an object of heroic stature, a character, really, in the inspired epic of a Catholic Milton. He actually was of heroic stature, I myself believe, but I am only slightly less embarrassed at his own acceptance and expression of this notion than I am when a lesser hero like Shelley does the same thing. Had Shelley lived to be forty-four, he might too have revealed a ripening manliness in a *The Shepherd's Brow* of his own, to balance *Prometheus* and *Epipsychidion*.

And Hopkins' mature balance helps to make *The Wreck* look better, at least to me, because I find the experience expressed in it based on something not yet expressed and deeper and solider than the slightly hectic projection of faith the poem reveals. *The Shepherd's Brow* suggests to me a profound spiritual adjustment at work in Hopkins' "subnesciousness" (to use Joyce's expressive word, deeper than subconsciousness). I seem to find some qualification of his overly intense discipleship of Scotus, of Milton, and of the narrower aspects of the Catholicism he found operative in his islands (vivid in the experience of Stephen Dedalus) when, as in this second-last sonnet, he faces up finally and without qualification to the tyranny of the Prufrockian life-measuring spoon. This late reaction suggests beneath *The Wreck* a human honesty that will realize fully one day that faith is not a flight from nor a negation of human animality, an illusion that the young Hopkins, like the young Stephen Dedalus, at least approached. *The Shepherd's Brow* indicates no great love for animality, indeed, but it does show an acceptance of it. And the final and in many ways the greatest of Hopkins' poems, *To R. B.,* celebrates in a new and whole-some way the beauty and joy of sexual intercourse and the gestation of a new animal—not only a "Simon Peter of a soul," bound in by a cage of bones—as the perfect symbol of the conception and gestation of an immortal poem.

As I look back, then, toward *The Wreck* from the vantage point of *The Shepherd's Brow,* I realize better than I did before why I felt some slight discomfort with Hopkins' too self-conscious expression, especially in stanza 28, of his inability to put the nun's ineffable vision into human sentences. He did not admit, or perhaps realize, the whole reason for his necessary failure. Throughout *The Wreck,* I believe, his expression occasionally fell short of his powerful vision, owing to too romantic a reaction to the knightly imagery of the *Spiritual Exercises,* too narrow a view of the operation of Catholic faith, and above all an unwillingness to accept his own animality. He produced a powerful ode, but a flawed one. His success flowed from the power of his experience, his ability to listen to his heart beyond the limits of his brain, and his realization that the music, the counterpoint, of his responsive verse would best carry his feeling into the accepting, time-centered eardrums, as well as to the more objective, space-oriented retinas, of other humans. To the hearing, he could best express, better than eyes could see, the deepest mystery of the Word his brain could not comprehend but his heart could apprehend. He slipped into some measure of treachery to his heart and his poetic vision, I now judge, when he turned to the formulations of theology to express the cure for the nun's extremity. In *Heraclitean Fire* he would remain true to his heart by expressing what he believed and felt, not by expressing the obligation of all men to come to Christ's feet. In that overwhelming "sonnet" he remained a poet, not a theologian merely. But in *The Wreck,* as in a few other poems like *To What Serves Mortal Beauty?* we see him at climactic moments bowing to a dogma which may or may not be operative for every human, rather than expressing the movement and the multileveled counterpoint of the heart, to which every human can respond. He falters as a poet, I judge, when with the confidence of a dogmatist he tries, with the mere meanings of human words, to break through rational bounds to boundless mystery.

As in stanza 28 he approaches the statement which should clarify what the nun meant, he experiences, owing to his turning from his heart to his brain, from his intuition to his reason, the unaccustomed frustration of his fancy. He attributes the breakdown of his fancy wholly to the havoc and glory of what the nun experienced, and adverts not at all to his own human asininity in making a direct assault on the adamantine limits of reason. He attempts precisely what Shakespeare, his other great master along with Milton, attempted in *A Midsummer Night's Dream,* the treatment of the artist's role in expressing ineffable mystery, the "strange and admirable," but Hopkins misses one point that Shakespeare, through the admirable ass Bottom, hit exactly. Shakespeare shows Bottom's acceptance of his "dream" and the breakdown of his effort to express it in human sentences, his turning to St. Paul for some kind of analogy for the embrace of a fairy queen, and his final resolve to get the literary artist, Peter Quince, to bring about the miracle of expression of the experience in black ink. Hopkins, aiming directly at expression of the nun's experience, suffers the same breakdown as does Bottom, uses the same Pauline text as does Shakespeare, and by calling on the mere names which symbolize all of Catholic tradition on the Mystical Body, the union of Christ and Christian, acts as if he had achieved his direct artistic aim. He has stepped outside of her experience and his own in order to complete his effort to express what the nun meant by her mysterious Johannine cry, and thus while his response is satisfactorily theological, it tends to limit and diminish an actually ineffable human experience. Hopkins does not fail, certainly, but neither, as I can now judge the matter, does he succeed as fully as he does succeed in some later, and particularly his three final, poems. Shakespeare succeeds totally by maintaining the basic ambivalence of a "dream," experienced by a human ass under the influence of forces he cannot comprehend. He accepts and works with human animality throughout, the very element the young Hopkins neglected.

When Bottom awakes from his "dream" of having been embraced by the fairy queen, he paraphrases St. Paul in his own effort to find expression for the ineffable: "The eye of man hath not heard, the ear of man hath not seen, man's hand is not able to taste, his tongue to conceive, nor his heart to report, what my dream was" (IV, 1). Paul in 1 Corinthians 2:9 had turned to Isaiah to find some poetic effort to express the ineffable, quoted here in a translation, from the Geneva Bible of 1560, which Shakespeare may have followed: "But as it is written, The things which eye hathe not sene, nether eare hathe heard, nether came into mans heart, are, which God hathe prepared for them that love him." Shakespeare thus effects an analogy between the deepest Pauline insight into mystery and the strange and admirable human experience of honest and open Bottom. Shakespeare proceeds to do something of special interest to literary artists, including Hopkins and especially James Joyce. Bottom, unable to express, not his thought, but a strange experience which transcended his reason and left his fancy paralyzed, can only stammer: "Methought I was—there is no man can tell what. Methought I was—and methought I had—but man is but a patched fool if he will offer to say what methought I had." This is precisely what happens to Hopkins in stanza 28:

> But how shall I . . . make me room there:
> Reach me a . . . Fancy, come faster—
> Strike you the sight of it? look at it loom there,
> Thing that she . . . There then!

Joyce in his own mysterious effort to breach the limits of consciousness and to broach what visions may lie in and beyond the subnesciousness, maybe foul but certainly unknown, willing to risk an experience of hell as Hopkins strove to point toward an experience of heaven, turns to ineffectual puns and riddles (and pins and needles) as other mature artists turn to ass's heads and distorted spoon reflections: "Helldsdend, whelldselse! Lonedom's breach lay foulend up uncouth not be broached by punns and reedles" (*Finnegans Wake*, 239).

Bottom, having failed in his effort to express what he has apprehended (short of comprehension, or rather, far beyond that rational grasp so praised by Theseus at the opening of Act V), turns to the literary artist, his director, producer, and writer, the *alter ego* of Shakespeare himself: "I will get Peter Quince to write a ballad of this dream." The only chance for getting some expression of this suprarational mystery, lacking a prophet or an apostle, is to call on that creative imagination so contemned by the practical Theseus as lunacy. In *The Wreck* Hopkins gets the message from his heart, not from his brain, he does not comprehend it—"What can it be, this glee?"—and his faithful fancy breaks down in its effort to provide poetic expression to infinite mystery, and can only point with names at that most rare vision which escapes reason.

Hopkins does happily provide, with skillful indirection, a Pauline and Shakespearean base for Fancy's plight in *The Wreck*'s stanza 26, when he paraphrases the Pauline passage to which Bottom had turned:

> What by your measure is the heaven of desire,
> The treasure never eyesight got, nor was ever guessed what for the
> hearing?

Directly this is merely an expression of the heart's cheer in the coming of spring and the cuckoo's clear call, analogous to the heart's hurrah in harvest. But Hopkins, a profound meditator on the mysteries of Paul, was in a position better than Shakespeare's to know how perfectly this passage with its bottomless underthought would prepare the responsive hearer for another rare vision of a mystery that can find expression, if at all, only in the miracle of a poet's black ink.

Hopkins suggests further, at the close of stanza 27, that music must enter in to bolster and fill out the limited song of the mind, as he turns the tempest and ocean into a Wagnerian orchestra:

> Other, I gather, in measure her mind's
> Burden, in wind's burly and beat of endragonèd seas.

In this too Hopkins is close to the greatest expresser of mystery in our own century, one who emerged from the same tradition and milieu in which Hopkins achieved his marvelous art, and whose magnificent words I here apply as tribute to Hopkins' sublime achievement of a century ago. This Irish voice, like Hopkins in the tradition of the prowess and pride of the ancient *poeta*, even more than Hopkins like the hearty Gaelic fashioners of the Book of Kells, prepared for his own final expression of his most rare vision with many references to Paul and to Bottom, and in the following climactic passage which I choose for an echo and a companion to the music of Hopkins, he expresses in his own magnificently musical way that most rare vision of the ultimate Word, the suprarational reality which the mind cannot code but the heart, like the hearts of Hopkins and of the nun on the wrecked *Deutschland*, can chord and cord. In his own strange, admirable way, closer than first appears to the multileveled way of Hopkins, Joyce expresses the ineffable Word in musical counterpoint that rings out from that Bottom-like close mixture and intermingling of ear and eye that transforms the tragic tones of mortal experience, so deeply intuited by Hopkins in *The Shepherd's Brow*, into the vision that the eye, like the nun of the *Deutschland*, still yearns to see again, and quickly:

> The prouts who will invent a writing there ultimately is the poeta, still more learned, who discovered the raiding there originally. That's the point of eschatology our book of kills reaches for now in soandso many counterpoint words. What can't be coded can be decorded if an ear aye seize what no eye ere grieved for (*Finnegans Wake*, 482).

Wreckers at work in the saloon. The tall nun stood on this table to cry out through the broken skylight

Chapter X

"Strike You the Sight of It?"

Intimations of Myth and Tragedy in
The Wreck

by Alison D. Sulloway

G erard Manley Hopkins' great ode, *The Wreck of the Deutsch-land*, well deserves an anthology devoted to it. But the very diversity of legitimate explications that it has stimulated, in this anthology and elsewhere, suggests that no one study can be considered definitive, since the ode yields almost as many acceptable interpretations as *Hamlet*. It has been fashioned like some geological formation, with layer upon layer of alluvial material embedded in it. Once Hopkins had broken his seven years of poetic silence, a volcanic upheaval seems to have taken place, uncovering a series of deposits representing Hopkins' present and his past.

The top layer is a deliberate gloss upon the Ignatian *Spiritual Exercises*, and it has rightly elicited enormous attention. Such an explication does justice to the Ignatian paradoxes of frightened awe, serene comfort, and radiant joy, but it fails to duplicate a cryptic quality in the ode, a dreamy, mythical distancing, which restrains the immediate and shattering sense of agony and the hyperbolic joy as well. If one accepts the ode as a theophany, a description of a divine event, during which Christ's appearance upon the waters fulfills intimations of earlier theophanies in pagan myths and the bible, one can thus account for many embryonic elements in it that otherwise remain inexplicable.

Hopkins was immensely sensitive to several problems that may appear to require discrete solutions but that seemed to him to present baffling aspects of the same ontological mystery: where does Christian truth begin in time and space? Obviously Christian truth was always present in the world before the incarnation, but how present, how visible, and when there, what were its effects and who were its witnesses? As a Jesuit priest, a student of comparative myth, of philology, and of Greek literature, Hopkins became convinced that there were intimations of the incarnation in classical myth and tragedy, and in searching for these intimations, he was able to answer a double question about the past, the world's past and his own past. For just as there had been intimations of the incarnation in myths everywhere, and particularly in classical tragedy, with its emphasis on death and sacrifice, so in his own pre-Catholic past there had also been intimations of his coming conversion. Thus, in his scrupulous way, he was able to salvage, from his Protestant, Oxonian, and classical past, anything that prefigured his witness as a Catholic and a Jesuit. At Oxford, he had awaited his own conversion, and he had purposefully struggled to achieve it. He came to believe that all potentially salvageable men and women had also struggled throughout past time to be worthy of the incarnation when it should transpire. Since they did not yet have the model of the crucifixion before them, their efforts were largely subconscious; but the alluvial remnants of their subconscious attempts as pre-Christian witnesses were embedded in certain pagan myths and in Greek tragedies, where the element of sacrifice for the common weal was most prominent. For

Hopkins interpreted tragic illuminations that issued from human suffering as flawed paradigms of the incarnation, both before and after the fact of Christ's perfect self-sacrifice.

It is not surprising, then, that Hopkins' ode contains elements of myths that appear with great regularity in both eastern and western religions; these elements seem to correspond to some profound and cosmic intimations about the nature of human experience. Myths of violent death by fire or water are archetypal events celebrated by tribal and urban societies everywhere at all times. The myths may encompass catastrophes for individuals or for the entire human race, except for a saved and precious remnant; the myths may contain tales of ancient catastrophes or prophecies of catastrophes to come. Hopkins' symbolic metaphors of fire and water, his emphasis upon the sacred virginity of his tall nun, his deep love for Christ, the crucified and resurrected young God, his sense that the nun's purposeful suffering had all happened many times before December 7, 1875, and might happen often again, all create in his ode a startling sense of familiarity quite characteristic of archetypes.

Hopkins clearly could not have had in mind anything as elaborate as Jung's concept of the archetypes and the archetypal drama played out in every human soul, as the commands of one archetype conflict with the commands of another. But he discussed Greek and Indian mythologies with Robert Bridges and Canon Dixon, not always, it must be admitted, in a way complimentary to the Greek myths, despite his great respect for classical poetry and classical drama (cf. L I, p. 217; L II, pp. 146–47). And in 1877, nine years after he had entered the Jesuit novitiate, he began an extraordinary correspondence with Alexander Baillie, another Oxford graduate, who had gone out to Egypt. This correspondence, of which we have only Hopkins' letters, went on for eleven years, and during these years, Hopkins returned again and again, with obsessive force and frequency, to a theory not then usually acceptable, that Greek mythology and classical Greek civilization originated in the Near East and not in Greece at all. Letter after letter impetuously urges upon Baillie the theory that the alphabet and the myths and religion surrounding the Greek pantheon had their genesis in parts of the world considerably closer to Christ's birthplace than the Greek peninsula; in short that "Egyptian civilization may well have rocked the cradle of Greek," since "the history of heathen religions is the history of foreign worships introduced and adopted, sometimes with resistance at first" (L III, pp. 268, 260).

Now all this amateur investigation of the genesis of classical Greek civilization would seem utterly incongruous in a man whose letters to Canon Dixon had carried rebukes of the Greek gods' conduct, and who had sternly ordered Bridges to forget the Greek myths and the Greek pantheon, since they were neither aesthetically nor morally appropriate models for modern poetry—at least in the hands of agnostics or skeptics. These intransigent remarks about the immorality of much Greek mythology seem all the more incongruous when we consider that Hopkins was simultaneously carrying on his morally neutral controversy with Baillie about the geographical genesis of just those myths and important figures in just that pantheon. But the incongruity disappears when we assume that Hopkins was once again searching for evidence of pre-Christian theophanies in Greek myth and Greek drama, and trying to separate the pre-Christian intimations of Christ's passion from corrupt and positively immoral classical material. In comedy, particularly in Homeric comedy, he complained elliptically, there is too much impropriety—even immorality—to prefigure anything of importance to Christians (L II, p. 146). It would be found, of course, in the sacrificial elements, the religious elements in tragedy, rather than in comedy: and where he found it, he was comforted to believe that it originated in North Africa or Asia Minor, that is, somewhere near the place where Christ was later to undergo the perfect human sacrifice. Christ's passion was a divine completion of the plan glimpsed first, among other places, in the imperfect, yet impressive, sacrificial rituals of Greek tragedy. No wonder that Hopkins seriously considered writing "a treatise on the idea of sacrifice in ancient religions" (S, p. 213).

In a provocative discussion of *The Wreck of the Deutschland*, James Cotter remarked that for Hopkins, "Father, Word, and Spirit are revealed in pre-Christian myths, Greek, Egyptian, Welsh and even Hindu, as Hopkins carefully remarked." To bring some order into the mystery of "Christ's role in creation," Hopkins redefined "from the fathers and Duns Scotus the theory of the pre-existence of Christ's created nature." Christ is master "of all human history . . . Christ's presence in the midst of the disaster of December 7, 1875, is but one facet of his ubiquity and penetration in space and time, of which the Bible offers a full and compendious account." Cotter also believes that Hopkins may be recalling St. Augustine's "theory of cosmic time in history. [St. Augustine's] considerations of the Greek and Roman past . . . led him to see pagan history as submitting to the purposes and providence of God" (Cotter, pp. 16–17, 156–57). Certainly Hopkins agreed with Duns Scotus that even before the incarnation, "in the beginning of the world, Christ could have had a true temporal existence in a sacramental manner," as Hopkins himself paraphrased Scotus; as Father Devlin, editor of Hopkins' sermons, remarked: "[Hopkins'] final conclusion is that it is within God's power to make the Body of Christ really present *universaliter*, anywhere or everywhere in the universe" (S, pp. 115, 114). Thus, Christ could radiate outward, around the globe from the Near East, just as he could radiate backward into mythological time and forward into future time, since he could transcend both time and space. That is why Hopkins' insistence upon the ubiquity of the myth of moral sacrifice is so crucial; its ubiquity is its intimation to us of its necessity as part of God's purpose—in total time: past, present, and future, and in total space around the globe. Those who have been even subconsciously ready for intimations of Christ's passion, by means of their own imperfect submission to the mortal consummation required in tragedy, have been silent witnesses preparing the way for Christ's sinless life and sinless death.

Hopkins' abiding fascination with Greek mythology and Greek drama, especially Greek tragedy, is apparent in all of his correspondence. But we need to search for specific elements of the tragic pattern in *The Wreck of the Deutschland* beyond Bodkin's "distinctive tragic attitude" which characterizes its "poetic exaltation." Nor does Canon Dixon's description of the ode help us much; it "is enormously powerful: it has however . . . elements of deep distress in it" (L II, p. 32). For a satisfactory explanation of some cryptic, alluvial material in the ode, we need to look at a study of myth and tragic ritual. According to Gilbert Murray, in the myths of sacrificed young gods or demigods, the ritual death of Dionysus, Attis, Adonis, Pan, Thammuz, or Osiris takes place by distinct processional steps, and this processional pattern is later imitated by most Greek tragedians, and in the purest form by Aeschylus and Sophocles, and at times by Euripides. There is an "*Agon* or Contest, the Year against its enemy, Light against Darkness, Summer against Winter." A *Pathos* then takes place, "generally a ritual sacrificial death, in which Adonis or Attis is slain . . . Osiris, Dionysus, Pentheus, Orpheus, Hippolytus torn to pieces." A *Messenger* then appears to announce the *Pathos*, which has taken place—in tragedy's replication of the mythic mode—offstage. The announcement of the sacrificial death is followed by a *Threnos*, and then an *Anagnorisis*, a "discovery or recognition of the slain and mutilated" young god, "followed by his Resurrection or *Apotheosis* or, in some sense, his *Epiphany* in glory," a process which Murray calls "by the general name of *Theophany*." The theophany "naturally goes with a *Peripeteia*, or extreme change of feeling from grief to joy" (J. Harrison, *Themis*, pp. 343–44).

In Hopkins' tragic ode to the *Deutschland* and to the Franciscan nuns who were sacrificed in the waters of the Thames, one may easily observe all of the ritual events, and even some of the processional order that Murray identified as characteristic of myth and tragedy. Part I of the ode is a microcosmic tragedy of which Part II is the macrocosm; but the combined two parts of the ode form the microcosm of a yet larger macrocosm: Hopkins and the tall nun both imitate the sacrifice of Christ, accepting their own suffering as part of a divine plan. In so doing, they each undergo first an *Agon*, a contest between types of "Light against Darkness" (*Themis*, p. 343). Then they accept the suffering, and thus become the *Messengers* who discover or recognize the affinity between their own sufferings and the passion of Christ. But before they experience the *Anagnorisis*, the recognition, they both cry out against the sufferings that God's purposes entail for them, just as Christ cried out in "intolerable grief" (L II, p. 138) in the Garden of Gethsemani (S, p. 220). And W. H. Gardner suggests that the shipwreck itself,

> . . . with its dramatic episode of the "tall nun" (stanzas 12–28), becomes the node round which the poet harmonizes his faith in God and his painful feelings about the problem of suffering—the tragic aspect of human life. The wreck of the Deutschland is the symbol of the whole world's plight since the Fall of Man—symbol of man's inevitable shipwreck in this earthly existence. This inescapable tragic agony is at once symbolized, explained, and mitigated by the Passion of Christ (*Penguin*, pp. 221–22).

The Wreck of the Deutschland opens with the announcement that an *Agon*, or contest is taking place: "Thou mastering me God!" The mastery which the poet-*Messenger* both longs for and dreads—"Thou hast . . . almost unmade, what with dread, Thy doing"—is quickly consummated:

> **The frown of his face**
> **Before me, the hurtle of hell**
> **Behind, where, where was a, where was a place?**
> **I whirled out wings that spell**
> **And fled with a fling of the heart to the heart of the Host.**
> **My heart, but you were dovewinged, I can tell,**
> **Carrier-witted, I am bold to boast,**
> **To flash from the flame to the flame then, tower from the grace to the grace.**

Stanza 3 has created a compressed paradigm of Bodkin's "distinctive tragic attitude"; the self of the human contestant—the poet-*Messenger*—is clearly propelled "toward the surrender of personal claims and the merging of the self within a greater power," the power of the mastering God. This stanza has also compressed three steps in the ritual tragic process: the *Agon* or contest, the *Pathos* or ritual immolation, and the *Anagnorisis* or recognition of the meaning of this suffering.

The poet's *Agon* or contest with two figures, God and Satan, ends for the moment in God's protective sternness; the human contestant flees "with a fling of the heart to the heart of the Host." A miniature *Pathos* takes place. The "self of the imaginative aspiration," as Bodkin described the tragic contestant, "this self which is asserted is magnified by that same collective force to which submission is finally made" (*Archetypal Patterns*, p. 23). Hopkins' poet-contestant is "laced with fire of stress," and his "midriff" is "astrain" with "the tension of the two impulses" which Bodkin was later to identify as part of the tragic conflict between the "tendencies of self-assertion and submission" (Ibid.) The *Pathos* of the asserting self is not in itself tragic. The process may be tragic, but the outcome is not. For the self dies to itself only to be momentarily risen in grace. The aspiration is there, flashing "from the flame to the flame, then," but protected from its own raw, crude egotism: towering "from the grace to the grace." The *Anagnorisis*, the recognition, is elliptically suggested by the response of the contestant to the Host. The contestant's heart is "dovewinged," "Carrier-witted," behaving simultaneously like the dove, the messenger of God, and those who receive the messenger, a divinely inspired carrier pigeon. Hopkins himself is playing many roles in Part I. He is imitating the great sacrifice of Christ; he is announcing his own imitation, and he is playing witness to the role of suffering in Christ and those who suffer with him.

Hints of the *Anagnorisis* take place throughout Part I, although we do not yet know what it is that the poet-contestant has recognized. But the poet's asserting self sublimates his assertion by asserting that he has vigorously complied with what is being asked of him. The verbs and the verbals in the opening stanzas of Part I are active, energetic, as though he were saying, "I recognize you, and I dedicate my active, impetuous, energetic self to you"; "over again I *feel* thy finger and *find* thee"; "I did *say yes/O* at lightning and lashed rod;/Thou heardst me truer than tongue *confess*/Thy terror, O Christ, O God"; "I can tell . . . I am *bold* to *boast*"; "I *kiss my hand* . . . I *bless* when I *understand*."

Stanza 7 combines several ritual steps in the tragic procession. The poet serves both as *Messenger* and witness in future time of Christ's birth in the manger—"It dates from day of his going in Galilee . . . Manger, maiden's knee"—and Messenger of Christ's passion—"The dense and the driven Passion, and frightful sweat." Stanza 7 is also a *Threnos* for the young God who suffered for all humanity. Here the poet's heart is "hard at bay" for his Master, Christ, rather than for himself. Stanzas 9 and 10 accomplish "a *Peripeteia*, or extreme change of feeling from grief to joy," which Murray was later to insist is the natural tragic accompaniment of the young god's "Resurrection or Apotheosis or, in some sense his *Epiphany*," a ritual which Murray calls a "*Theophany*" (*Themis*, p. 344). One distinct *Theophany* appears in stanza 10. St. Paul's conversion on the road to Damascus is elliptically described: "once at a crash Paul!" was converted, whereas St. Augustine's conversion was not so dramatic or swift. But Part I concludes with a hyperbolic invocation to the risen Christ to "Make mercy in all of us, out of us all Mastery, but be adored, but be adored King."

In some ways stanza 6 is the most interesting of all. It attempts to justify Hopkins' theory about intimations of the incarnation, both before and after that event. Hopkins' comments upon human time and space as opposed to divine management of time and space are indeed cryptic:

> Time has 3 dimensions and one positive pitch or direction. It is therefore not so much like any river or any sea as like the Sea of Galilee, which has the Jordan running through it and giving a current to the whole (S, p. 196).

On this complex subject, Father Devlin says that Hopkins was struggling to understand "the evolution through many ups and downs of God's plan in history, a plan which may be said to be the incorporation of the universe into the Mystical Body of Christ. The '3 dimensions' would presumably be past, present, and future," or perhaps the manner in which "the influence of coming events . . . take shape in the minds and wills of men before they actually happen" (S, p. 306).

Stanza 6 introduces the problem of time both before and after the incarnation:

> Not out of his bliss
> Springs the stress felt
> Nor first from heaven (and few know this)
> Swings the stroke dealt—
> Stroke and a stress that stars and storms deliver,
> That guilt is hushed by, hearts are flushed by and melt—
> But it rides time like riding a river
> (And here the faithful waver, the faithless fable and miss).

Peter Milward suggests that stanzas 5 and 7 offer clues to Hopkins' intentions:

> Since, tho' he is under the world's splendour and wonder,
> His mystery must be instressed, stressed . . .

The poet's idea, Father Milward suggests, "is that God's presence in the world is somehow potential, at least with respect to the human intellect, until it is recognized in the act of praise." In stanza 6, the fabling could refer to specific fables, such as Plato's *Phaedrus* and *The Republic*, as Milward suggests, or to any pagan myth which attempts to unravel God's plan in history. In any case, the fables "express what has been 'felt before,' but inevitably they fall short of that reality which alone can satisfy the human heart." And Milward also seems to be suggesting that in stanza 6, Hopkins is attempting to account for the problem of cosmic human suffering, both before and after the incarnation, as such suffering is depicted by the Israelites' sacrifices in the wilderness ·(Milward, pp. 39–43).

Since Part II functions as a macrocosm of Part I, we will encounter the same tragic processional pattern as we see in Part I. And since in Part I Hopkins is the contestant, the witness, and the *Messenger*, in Part II the tall nun, "the prophetess," plays the same triple role. Thus out of the cryptic vision of Part II emerges another Christian tragedy, the duplication of the tragedy in Part I, complete with *Agon* (contest), *Pathos* (death of the self), *Threnos* (lament), *Apotheosis* or *Theophany* (appearance of the sacrificed God in support of the human *Pathos* taking place), and a distinct *Peripeteia* (a sharp reversal from fear, awe, and anguish, to radiant joy), which accompanies the *Anagnorisis* (the acceptance by the nun and the poet that these imitations of Christ's *Pathos* are part of God's purpose).

Stanza 11 accomplishes something like the tragic or mythic "*Agon* or Contest, the Year against its enemy, Light against Darkness, Summer against Winter" (*Themis*, p. 343), or in this case, fragile, mutable humanity against death:

> "Some find me a sword; some
>   The flange and the rail; flame,
> Fang, or flood" goes Death on drum,
>   And storms bugle his fame.
> But we dream we are rooted in earth—Dust!
> Flesh falls within sight of us, we, though our flower the same,
>   Wave with the meadow, forget that there must
> The sour scythe cringe, and the blear share come.

Stanzas 12-17 describe, in human terms, the *Agon* of which stanza 11 was the symbolic representative. We are told that the *Deutschland* had left Germany with two hundred souls aboard and that she foundered on the Kentish Knock, driven there by the "infinite air," while many of her desperate passengers and crew "fought with God's cold," only to drown or be crushed as "they fell to the deck." Stanzas 17-23 indicate that now the tall nun is undergoing a spiritual *Agon* and *Pathos* of her own, before she surrenders her body to the waters. The magnitude of her sufferings is only matched by the magnitude of her comprehension (*Anagnorisis*) that all this anguish is there for some divine purpose: she is a "lioness," a "prophetess," a "virginal tongue" telling what she knows as *Messenger*. She "sees one thing, one"; in her recognition, "she rears herself to divine Ears." Stanzas 20-23 describe her fitness for the role of tragic contestant, sufferer, and *Messenger*. "She was first of a five . . . Of a coifèd sisterhood." The five Franciscan nuns symbolize both by their own faith and martyrdom, not only "Christ's five wounds," but the five wounds "reproduced in the stigmata received by St. Francis" (*Poems* 4, p. 261).

Gardner interprets the first two lines of stanza 22 in such a way as to suggest clearly that some process of *Anagnorisis* is going on—a "discovery or recognition of the slain and mutilated" young god (*Themis*, p. 344), in this case the martyred Christ:

> Five! the finding and sake
> And cipher of suffering Christ.

Finding, says Gardner, means "discovery" of the significance that the "emblematic figure" of the stigmatized Christ entails. And "finding" seems to mean the way in which suffering humans find Christ (*Poems* 4, p. 261).

Stanzas 24-28 represent the *Theophany*. The prophetic nun calls
"O Christ, Christ, come quickly"; the poet asks: "what did she mean?"
Stanzas 26-27 muse upon what the nun's own *Pathos* may mean for
her own salvation. They also suggest that there are other forms of
Pathos or self-sacrifice than actual death, for example, the performance
of secular and sacred duties under unbearable stress and privation: "the
sodden-with-its-sorrowing heart." Stanza 28 describes the actual
Theophany. At first, the poet is not sure what the nun has seen. He
stutters, stumbles, calls her vision—which is his vision—a "Fancy," and
an "it" which looms there in the darkness. But suddenly, "Strike you
the sight of it?" becomes "There then! the Master,/*Ipse,* the only one,
Christ, King, Head."

Stanzas 29-30 offer a *Peripeteia* (reversal of feeling) on the nun's
account. Stanza 29 alludes to the problem of time and eternity and what
it was that the nun had accepted. She was not fooled by mere human
time and space; she was a "single eye!" and a "heart right" and her
heart and eye

> **Read the unshapeable shock night**
> **And knew the who and the why;**
> **Wording it how but by him that present and past,**
> **Heaven and earth are word of, worded by?**

Despite the question mark that suggests an unresolved mystery, these
two stanzas are fully celebratory. But stanza 31 is a *Threnos*, a lament
for the pitiful "rest of them." The poet begs his heart to "go bleed at a
bitterer vein for the/Comfortless unconfessed of them," until he suddenly remembers that "lovely-felicitous Providence" may find means of
saving them from eternal damnation. The poet had anticipated this
moment, and this lament, earlier in Part II when he asked whether or
not the "dark . . . bay" of Christ's "blessing," "the million of rounds of
[his] mercy" might possibly "not reeve even them in?"

Stanzas 32-35 complete the *Peripeteia*, but now the poet has himself turned prophet. He undergoes a "Fancy," a vision of his own as to
the radiant joy that would sweep over all England, a joy that would
cancel the national horror over the *Deutschland*'s catastrophe—if, if
only England would read this prophetic tragedy aright with her own
"heart right" and "single eye." If this were to happen, her citizens
would all acclaim Hopkins' Christ and the nun's Christ. Cotter thinks
that stanzas 32 and 33 symbolize a type of new birth, perhaps, one
might add, a prophecy of souls saved from purgatory by the nun's
intercession, as Gardner suggests (*Poems* 4, p. 262), or perhaps a
prophecy of English souls saved from hell or purgatory, if, thanks to the
nun's intercession, England's conversion should take place. In any case,
as Cotter remarks,

Traditionally, Christ is often pictured in Byzantine and medieval art as calling the world into being, walking in the Garden of Eden, directing Noah to build his ark. He is master of the "Yore-flood" and of all human history since he predates it and since it leads up to and follows from his place in time. Hopkins' use of these theophanies is nowhere more graphic than in this section [stanzas 32 and 33] of the *Deutschland*.

Cotter's claim seems undeniable that "Christ's presence in the midst of the disaster of December 7, 1875, is but one facet of his ubiquity and penetration in space and time" (Cotter, p. 157); but the last four stanzas do not describe an accomplished *Theophany*, only a *Theophany* to be hoped for and prayed for. In stanza 32, Hopkins praises God for his capacity to leave his creatures both free and directed. God's "sovereignty" represents a custodianship which "heeds but hides, bodes but abides"; and his power and compassion are such that he can reach "Lower than death and the dark" to save all souls "pent in prison" whenever mercy is called for. Stanzas 34 and 35 invoke the paradoxical God, stern and compassionate, who, the poet hopes, will come to England as a "released shower, . . . not a lightning of fire hard-hurled," not "a dooms-day dazzle in his coming nor dark as he came." This time, the poet hopes that the tragic process of *Agon* and *Pathos* will not have to be repeated: Christ shall be "Kind, but royally reclaiming his own."

In stanza 35, the final stanza of the ode, the *Peripeteia* is even more ecstatic, as the poet contemplates the joy that would accompany Christ's conversion of England, if the nun should intercede for England, and her intercession be granted. "Our King back, oh, upon English souls!" the poet cries out, and he begs Christ to "easter" in the souls of English citizens, to "be a dayspring to the dimness" now in their souls. Once they have accepted Christ, almost as an entire people, he will be their "Pride, rose, prince, hero, high-priest," their "hearts' charity's hearth's fire," their "thoughts' chivalry's throng's Lord."

The tone of *The Wreck of the Deutschland* does not slavishly imitate the tone in Greek tragedies, even the tone in the tragedies of Hopkins' favorite, Aeschylus (L I, p. 256). In the first place, Hopkins knew and loved Renaissance tragedy as well. Moments in his own tragic ode are as grim as the vision in *Lear* or as horrible as Dr. Faustus' anguished cry for just one drop of Christ's blood. And then we must remember that Hopkins was temperamentally an evangelical Jesuit and a hyperbolic Victorian. In fact, his two *Peripeteiai* (in Parts I and II) remind us quite forcibly of the shift from rebellious anguish to joy in Tennyson's *In Memoriam*.

For Hopkins, the tension between rebellion and acceptance is far sharper than the tension, let us say, in Sophocles' Theban tragedies, the Orestes trilogy, or Euripides' *Suppliants*. Inevitably Hopkins believed the issues to be far more stark, more consequential, even, than the grave issues in Greek tragedy: they are nothing less than eternal damnation or eternal salvation. Nonetheless, Hopkins' quiet use of the ritual procession of tragedy suggests that he hoped God might find some way to save these pre-Christian dramatists from damnation, that he might in his infinite mercy "reeve even them in," because in their tragedies they intuitively foreshadowed the great human and divine event—the passion and resurrection of Christ.

Notes

a   Obviously I do not misrepresent Hopkins by teaching *The Wreck of the Deutschland* as mere myth or as a mere Victorian adaptation of the tragic mode. But it is a Christian tragedy that ends in joyous reconciliation of its creator to the extreme fear and suffering it describes; and in so doing, it is designed to purge its readers of rebellious anguish, as tragedy is designed to reconcile the audience to the ritual death of significant characters. And Greek tragedy, as we know, embodies patterned, ritualistic performances of communal myths.

b   Hopkins despised Greek mythology wherever the Greek gods were immoral, cowardly, lazy, or ill-bred. His comments to Robert Bridges and Canon Dixon on Greek mythology are exceedingly angry in tone, but, as always, his search for intimations of moral excellence reasserted itself; and he admitted to Dixon that "the Greek mythology is very susceptible of fine allegorical treatment . . . and so treated gives rise to the most beautiful results. No wonder: the moral evil is got rid of and the pure art, morally neutral and artistically so rich, remains and can even be turned to moral use" (L I, p. 217).

Chapter XI

"Never-Eldering Revel"

The Wreck and the Ode Tradition

by Warren Anderson

The purpose of this essay is to place *The Wreck of the Deutschland* in the development of the ode tradition. Its main divisions will be a survey of the Renaissance and post-Renaissance ode, especially in England, and a discussion of classical elements that figure in Hopkins' poem or have some relevance to it. For the second topic Pindar has central importance; it will involve Aeschylus, Timotheus, and Horace as well. Besides the victory ode and the choral lyric of tragedy, other types of Greek lyric poetry will be mentioned. To say this much already indicates the likelihood that the classical origins of *The Wreck* will prove to be varied and complex, with no exclusive claim or incontestably real existence. Given the problematical and diverse nature of previous studies devoted to the poem, any other conclusion would be suspect.

As a form of expression in western literature, the vernacular ode first took on an individual, identifiable nature during the later decades of the sixteenth century. In the year 1550 Pierre de Ronsard had published four books of odes, markedly though not exclusively Pindaric. "Le premier de France/J'ay pindarizé," he asserted (*Odes*, ii.2.36–37); unfortunately his pindarizing was pedestrian and unheroic.

The ode took its place in English poetry a generation later, when John Southern imitated Ronsard in the Pindaric lyrics of his *Pandore* (1584). The imitation was notably unskillful: it did not even embody the triadic structure of strophe, matching antistrophe, and differing epode. This arrangement characterizes the great majority of Pindar's odes, although a few repeat the same strophic pattern (as Hopkins did in *The Wreck*), and it had been reproduced by Ronsard. Southern's failure was not for lack of effort; it came rather from lack of understanding. Yet he did try, in however derivative and befuddled a manner, to write English pindarics. Moreover, his claim that he was the first to do so was essentially just, despite the fact that two years previously Thomas Watson had included a few imitations of Ronsardian odes in his *Passionate Century of Love*.

It is clear, nevertheless, that the spirit of Pindar which had thus been brought into England was a sadly insubstantial wraith. Ronsard's honest but misleading versions were being treated as representative of the original text by minor poets. These men did not adequately comprehend the merits of his versions, and they knew no Greek. They did have Latin, of course. The elegant conciseness of the Horatian ode had long been familiar, with Horace's vastly influential misinterpretation of Pindar's verse. For the Roman, it was a "measureless" torrent that swept away every obstacle, a force heedless of the laws of meter (*Odes*, iv.2).

The corrective needed was an edition of Pindar that would show the untruth of this well-intentioned claim. Unfortunately, the greater part of three centuries would pass before such a work appeared. The necessary minimum, an edition of the Greek text of Pindar in whatever form, had become available to English readers as early as 1513. At that time the study of Greek in England was just beginning. Unlike the precocious Hellenists of sixteenth-century Italy, Englishmen made slow headway with Pindar: there is no evidence that any of them read him in Greek before the early years of the following century. Few Elizabethans could have done so, although the tiny minority included Marlowe and probably the queen herself. For Shakespeare, "ode" meant nothing more than "love-song."

During the period after the death of Elizabeth, Jonson brought to ode writing a sound knowledge of Greek and the fervor of one who believed in classical learning—but not pedantry—as the spirit which ought to inform his native literature. He tried, not always successfully, to re-create not only the triadic structure favored by Pindar but the enjambment between lines and strophes, so striking a feature of *The Wreck*, and beyond this the terseness and spiritual exaltation of the victory odes. Among his longer poems, the *Ode to Sir William Sidney, on His Birth-Day* deserves more notice than it has received. Its manner has Pindaric dignity as well as Horatian blitheness. The third stanza will show the tone:

> This day says, then, the number of glad years
>   Are justly summ'd, that make you man;
>   Your vow
>   Must now
>   Strive all right ways it can,
>   To outstrip your peers:
>   Since he doth lack
>   Of going back
>   Little, whose will
>   Doth urge him to run wrong, or to stand still.

More famous is the second *Ode to Himself* (1629). Three of its lines encompass the list of classical poets thought to have been the progenitors of the ode:

>   . . . take the *Alcaic* lute [that of Alcaeus];
>   Or thine own *Horace*, or *Anacreon's* lyre;
>   Warm thee, by *Pindar's* fire . . .

Most celebrated of all is the *Ode to Sir Lucius Cary and Sir H. Morison.* The other two poems are monostrophic in the manner of Greek solo lyric; this noble and beautiful work uses the strophe-antistrophe-epode sequence, far more characteristic of Pindar. One stanza of the epode has become famous. Only a few lines need be recalled:

> It is not growing like a tree
> In bulk, doth make man better be . . .

A Lily of a day
Is fairer far, in May
Although it fall and die that night . . .

In small proportions we just beauties see;
And in short measures, life may perfect be.

The view that the spirit of this work is Roman seems open to argument; yet none can deny the importance of the Horatian strain in Jonson's lyrics or the strength of its presence in the writings of his followers, especially Herrick. It must likewise be granted that he usually fell short of realizing any distinctively Pindaric qualities. This realization was the achievement of his younger contemporary Milton, who wrote at Cambridge the most astonishing of all undergraduate poems, the "Prelude" and "Hymn" called *On the Morning of Christ's Nativity*. It was, as Gilbert Highet has said (*The Classical Tradition*, p. 237), the first truly Pindaric poem in English.

Professor Highet bases his statement on the mastery of asymmetrical meter and the vivid handling of imagery and myth. For students of *The Wreck of the Deutschland*, Milton's meter and rhyme scheme have a particular interest. The prelude, consisting of four stanzas, has the pattern $a^5b^5a^5b^5b^5c^5c^6$; the hymn has twenty-seven stanzas, arranged $a^3a^3b^5c^3c^3b^5d^4d^6$. Since Hopkins praised Milton as the supreme metrist, it seems more than coincidence that for his own poem he should have chosen a scheme ($a^{2/3}b^3a^4b^3c^5b^5c^4a^6$) that duplicated the first half of the prelude's rhyme sequence and much of the stress sequence employed in the hymn. Although one or two commentators have noted a general resemblance in passing, the parallel has received less than its due.

Milton's contrast of pagan gods put to flight by the coming of the true God was of no use to Hopkins, who personified only death in *The Wreck*. More helpful by far was his imagery of light, a heritage (however diminished) from Pindar. The principal examples are well-known: Christ deigned to lay aside "That glorious form, that light unsufferable,/And that far-beaming blaze of majesty" of his heavenly being; "the spangled host keep watch in squadrons bright" while the young Milton writes during that starlight night before Christmas morning, 1629; "A globe of circular light" shows "The helmèd Cherubim/and sworded Seraphim/ . . . in glittering ranks," those "Bright-harnessed angels . . . in order serviceable" with whose radiant presence the poem comes to a close. The staggering classical attainments of its author cannot be questioned; nor can we doubt his close and responsive reading of Pindar, with the evidence of the annotations that crowd the margins of his copy of the odes in their original Greek. That Milton thought of the Nativity poem as an ode is clear from his text: after the *topos* of feigned uncertainty (itself manifest in Pindar, and echoed sardonically by Ezra Pound)— "Heavenly Muse, . . . Hast thou no verse, no hymn, or solemn strain?"—comes the modest yet confident phrase "the humble ode."

To attempt any discussion of the choral lyrics of *Samson Agonistes*, which Hopkins held to be the chief foreshadowing of his own theory and practice of sprung rhythm (cf. Gardner, II, pp. 113-15, and the references given there), would take us beyond the bounds of this essay. One other work, however, must be noticed. *At a Solemn Musick* has tentatively been called an experiment in classical metrics (Shuster, p. 67, n. 15) and even a Pindaric ode with triadic structure (Nicolson, *Heath-Stubbs*, p. 36). Of the first twenty-eight lines eleven, including the first five, begin with a choriamb (-u u-) instead of two iambs. The strategy of rhythmic mimesis is admirably executed: after lines 1-5, the phrase used to make clear the iambic base of the poem is "That undisturbèd Song of pure concent [*concentus*, 'harmony']." As for strophic responsion, the stresses of lines 9-16 certainly answer those of lines 1-8 as antistrophe answers strophe, and lines 17-28 have the marked stress difference that an epode is supposed to embody. The rhyme patterns are not in question; they do not match.

What may have caught Hopkins' attention was something other than the larger structure, namely, the circularity of rhyme sequence in the "antistrophe." This begins with "Jubily" and offers no matching rhyme until it closes with "everlastingly." Seemingly a small matter, the point has significance for *The Wreck of the Deutschland*. Granted that the number of odes written before 1875 is beyond knowing, one negative characteristic readily becomes apparent in a great many of them (including those to which Hopkins refers): they lack any circular pattern in which an initial rhyme returns at last upon itself. The "antistrophe" of *At a Solemn Musick* must be judged a likely source for Hopkins' choice of the scheme *ababcbca*. Less evidently, the Miltonic counterpointing of amphimacers against an iambic base, especially at the beginning of a poem, may have influenced that fateful decision to use "Thou mastering me" as an initial line—arguable style indeed. One point that tells against this possibility is the complaint in the author's preface (*Poems* 4, p. 47) that the Milton of *Samson Agonistes* "does not let the reader clearly know what the ground-rhythm is meant to be."

The English ode had a long and honorable history beyond Milton. If nothing more than a brief summary is offered here, the reason can be simply stated: this later history does not appear to bear any significant relation to the impulses that in 1875 were moving Hopkins to write poetry again. A generation after Milton's Nativity poem, Abraham Cowley published several free translations and imitations of Pindar in his *Miscellanies* (1656). Never in any danger of greatness, Cowley was neither a fool nor a hack, and the supposition that he misunderstood Pindaric stanza structure merely discredits a succession of modern critics. His misdeed was to perpetuate Horace's view of Pindar as wild and ungovernable; untranslateable as well, Cowley added, unless literalness is abandoned.

The acceptance of his innovations by those who imitated him set the tone for the Augustan ode. Dryden, with far greater powers, produced brilliant examples of the form. *Alexander's Feast,* in which he makes the poet and lyre player Timotheus display the gamut of music's ethical powers, represents the height of mannered virtuosity. When in 1882 Hopkins wrote to Bridges about his intended ode on the martyrdom of Edmund Campion, he described it as "dithyrambic or what they used to call Pindaric (which as we have Pindar now is un-Pindaric), I mean in variable stanzas and not antistrophic; like *Alexander's Feast* or *Lycidas*" (L I, p. 147). Of Dryden's poem even the most sincere admirer must say that such a display of skill, and of sly wit as well, can only take place at an immense remove from Pindar.

It is difficult to feel that one comes any closer to him through the odes of Collins, Gray, and Cowper. All of them poets whom Hopkins loved and honored, they could not serve his special needs for *The Wreck of the Deutschland*. A muted, tender melancholy they had, and uncommon powers of natural description; they lacked force. The next possibility, an obvious one, is represented by the great odes of the Romantic period. To a Victorian reader these works did not seem so evident an improvement on eighteenth-century efforts as they do to many of us. All the same, it might be thought that in Wordsworth's *Intimations of Immortality*, if anywhere, Hopkins could have discerned an exaltation and generosity of spirit capable of speaking to his condition. Any such conjecture ignores the unbridgeable gulf that separated the views of God and nature held by these two poets. Considered technically, Wordsworth's poem was a wonderfully skilled transmutation of the free Pindaric inaugurated by Cowley and continued by Dryden. It had no novelty of form to offer a Victorian, especially one who could not profit from its content.

Supposing that Hopkins turned to other poets of his own time, the earlier works of Browning and Swinburne offered examples of counterpointed rhythms, heavy anapaests, bizarre rhyming; but there is no evidence of anything more than isolated instances of influence. The reservations that he expressed about both men reveal a temperamental aversion such that it must have been difficult for him to accept anything from their poetry knowingly. With Arnold he felt more at ease, but it was mainly Arnold the critic whom he admired. Neither the free lyrics of *The Strayed Reveller* nor the more constrained rhythms of *Empedocles on Etna* had any perceptible effect upon his writing. Tennyson can hardly be called a candidate, since he almost never used the ode form, and his experiments in lyric form were dismissed by Hopkins as "logaeodic dignified-doggrel" (L I, p. 71). His commemoration of the death and burial of Wellington (1852) shifts rhythms with great virtuosity but continues past any justifiable limit, weighed down by the solemnities of the laureateship. So far as *The Wreck* was concerned, the area of Tennyson's poetry that provoked a response from Hopkins was a different one altogether, as we shall see.

Three centuries of ode writing, beginning with the Pindarics of Ronsard, had failed to produce any unified conception of the ode as a literary form. During the nineteenth century it passed almost wholly out of use; modern criticism can deal with it only by noting recurring characteristics. We may say, then, that an ode was a composition either sacred or secular, with lines of varying length (usually rhymed) and not infrequently composed of matching stanzas or even triads, employing exalted diction and ideas of broader than individual significance, sometimes celebrating a joyous or mournful event, and likely to embody references to its classical origins, most of all through an emphasis on myth.

This list contains little that would be unacceptable in a definition of the classical ode, more particularly the work of Greek poets generally and of Pindar in particular. It misleads not so much through error as through partiality. The task remains of trying to get a sense of Pindar's lyrics—to "catch" them, Hopkins would have said—as they might have appeared to classically educated Englishmen a century ago.

One fact must be faced at the outset: the rhythmic structures of those lyrics had not been understood. Renaissance editors thought them incomprehensible and so printed them in lines of widely and arbitrarily varying length. This constitutes one historical explanation for comparable practices by one writer in England and on the Continent. It is reflected, for example, in the early "Storm and Stress" lyrics of Goethe, who avoided the ode form. The modern study of Greek metrics was begun by nineteenth-century German scholars such as August Boeckh, who in 1821 had published an influential work, *De metris Pindari*. By 1875, had the opportunity been given him, Hopkins could have found the metrical theories of another German, J. H. H. Schmidt (*Griechische Metrik*, Leipzig, 1872). Later he did encounter them, but apparently not until November of 1886 (L I, p. 233).

The errors contained in this doctrine can be discerned from a close reading of Father Bonn's trenchant essay in *Immortal Diamond*. One, which misled Hopkins along with a great many others, was the equating of dactyls with trochees. Schmidt's teaching beguiled even Richard Jebb: their essentials are set forth in the introduction to his edition of the *Oedipus Tyrannus* (1883), and Jebb continued to base his metrical analyses on them throughout his editing of the other Sophoclean tragedies. This edition ranks among the supreme achievements of classical scholarship: with Hopkins in such company, it would be a bold critic who ventured to write him off as dull-witted. Only during the present century have classicists begun to rescue the study of Greek metrics from anarchy, and thus to recognize the complexity of Pindar's rhythmic sequences, which are not a mere matter of individual lines but wind throughout the entire length of the strophe. Faced with such virtuosity, one must do something more than talk of combinations of metrical feet—for example, the supposed "logaoedic" ("speech-song") rhythm—as Hopkins and Jebb did.

To turn from theory to practice, W. H. Gardner suggests rhythmic parallels between the lyrics of Pindar and lines from *The Wreck*, "which was," he maintains, "to some extent modelled on Pindar" (Gardner, II, p. 118). If these represent deliberate borrowings (and it is unlikely that the possibility can ever be disproved), Hopkins needed no theoretical warrant. It sufficed that he was, at the same time, one of the best-trained classical scholars in England and also a poet with a singular awareness of rhythm.

On another and more elusive point of practice, Todd K. Bender has argued that Hopkins unified *The Wreck* by the use of a controlling symbol, namely, water, and that in so doing he anticipated a similar theory concerning Pindar's epinicians (Bender, pp. 86 ff.). This "catch-word" explanation of the odes was first brought forward in 1880, by the German scholar F. Metzger. J. B. Bury took it up enthusiastically in his 1890 edition of the *Nemeans*, and it has become widely known to classicists through the extreme presentation given in Gilbert Norwood's *Pindar* (1945). "Norwood's view," as F. N. Lees says in a recent article, "is that Pindar unifies seemingly discontinuous elements in a poem by evoking through metaphor and choice of vocabulary some 'sensible' object . . . to be a governing symbol; some object emblematically regarded, that is, the lyre or the bee and so on." This theory has not won any great measure of acceptance. The whole question of symbolic usage in Pindar and Hopkins calls for greater precision and more awareness of the nature of symbology than has yet been demonstrated.

Broad questions of terminology once again illustrate the tendency of theory and practice to drift out of alignment. In 1878, Hopkins said of *The Wreck*, "It is an ode and not primarily a narrative. There is some narrative in Pindar but the principal business is lyrical" (L I, p. 49). More than that, our survey of the English ode has shown the recurrence of characteristics which his poem clearly reflects. He cannot have doubted in 1875 that what he had undertaken was a part of the ode tradition.

The tradition itself, however, embodies a surprising degree of diversity; and this constitutes the paradigm, sometimes conscious but more often coincidental, of a still greater diversity that marked the practice of

Greek lyric poetry. Pindar's choral odes exemplify this very clearly. Of all the types included within his wide range, only the *epinikion*, the epinician or "victory-song," has survived intact and in any considerable quantity. Yet he himself never used the noun *epinikion* to describe his triumphal odes; normally he referred to them as *hymnoi*. (*Hymnos* often denoted a secular poem.) Moreover, they were sometimes regarded as examples of the *enkômion*, or encomium; in its most precise usage, this involved the praise of some eminent living person, such as a king or hero or athletic victor. The second *Isthmian* was even called a *thrênos*, or dirge, because the victor had died before it could be performed.

Pindar did write *thrênoi*, though only a few fragments have survived. The most substantial of these describes the joys of the blessed dead, who pass their days in the serene sunlight of an Elysian Hades, and also the gloomy fate of those who must suffer punishment. This fragment, together with a great many others, was at least theoretically accessible to Hopkins; one of his early journal entries shows that he had consulted a collection of them (J, p. 11). The lines are stamped with the gravity and beauty of Pindar's religious thought, which here is thought to show the influence of Orphism. H. W. Smyth seems to have had them strongly in mind when, a decade after the death of Hopkins, he wrote: "Pindar alone [*sc.* among the writers of dirges] did not attempt to offer consolation or awaken commiseration by [lamenting] the wretchedness of existence. . . . [He] alone grasped the full meaning of the relation of death to life. The soul is to him immortal because divine, and its destiny is endless felicity or endless pain" (*Greek Melic Poets,* p. cxxviii). The larger subject of the ethical and religious exaltation found in the epinicians remains for our later consideration.

Neither Pindar nor any other specific author can usually be associated with classical analogues or possible sources for *The Wreck*. This is only to be expected, since Hopkins was forthright about his loathing of allusiveness. In the final months of his life, he wrote to Bridges that "the effect of studying masterpieces is to make me admire and do otherwise" (L I, p. 291). It may nevertheless be useful to include here an account of some instances in which the classical background appears relevant to the thought and phrasing of the poem.

One extended account of a disaster at sea was familiar to Hopkins from his long study of Greek tragedy: the messenger's speeches (lines 353–514) in the *Persians* of Aeschylus, telling how the invading fleet had been destroyed at Salamis. Near the end of the fifth century, the radical poet Timotheus celebrated the same event—a crucial victory for the Greek cause—in wild lyric measures counterpointed on basic schemes and in even wilder diction, with every kind of obscure "kenning" and general extravagance. Only one or two lines of his poem, also called the *Persians*, were known until the beginning of the present century. Now that a large part of the text is available, classically trained students of Hopkins might not find a comparative study altogether pointless. The obvious case of Vergil's storm description in the *Aeneid* will be noted below.

The epigraph of *The Wreck* takes us by surprise: "*To the happy memory of five Franciscan nuns, exiles . . . drowned. . . .*" Behind these words can be heard the Christian formulaic phrase *in beatam memoriam*—the *beati* are the blessed dead—and behind this in turn the likelihood of a late Greek *eis makarian mnêmên.* The oxymoron set up between *happy* and *drowned* is utterly deliberate. Aware of the difficulty and the seeming cruelty of his paradoxical theme, Hopkins has grasped the nettle; and he has done so without a moment's hesitation. Before a word of the poem can reach our thoughts, he presents the *mysterium tremendum.* On a contemporary level, any thought of *in memoriam* would readily have called to mind Tennyson's poem, seemingly an earlier parallel but profoundly dissimilar.

The Wreck begins; and one can only wonder, sometimes perplexedly, at the intricate interlacing of rhymes and stresses. The circularity of the rhyme scheme has already been noted. A device for tension and balance, it functions in a manner comparable with that of the thematic
pattern called "ring-composition"—a sequence of themes building to a central unit, which is followed by a restatement in reversed order, for example, *abcdedcba.* This structural principle, evident in pre-Hellenic
art, has been strongly argued for the *Iliad.* During recent years its presence in Pindar's epinicians has become increasingly evident, thanks to continuing studies. To some this last point remains a matter of debate; what does seem certain, to anyone who has surveyed schemes of rhyme and stress in the earlier ode tradition, is that none of them can match the achievement of Hopkins.

For the content of "Thou mastering me" and the following line, Gardner cites an unidentified phrase from Pindar, *theos ho panta teuchôn brotois*, "god, the all-things-creating for mortals" (Fragment 130). This, he claims, was "almost certainly the inspiration" (Gardner, II, p. 122). But "creating" does not help us with either "mastering" or "giver" (here *zeidôros* is the closest Greek parallel). The three opening words may, however, owe something to a still more famous vocative phrase, also placed at the beginning of an ode. This is the *anaxiphormingges hymnoi* of Pindar's second *Olympian*; Hopkins had been moved to set the two words as plainchant at some time before January 1881 (L I, p. 123). The adjective applied to "hymns" means "ruling the lyre," and the verb embodied here is *anassein*, "to be lord or master" (*anax*). *Anassein* and *anax* could be used of men as well as gods; *anaxiphorminx* normally was limited to a god or a muse.

Once we go beyond the opening phrase of stanza 1, we find no striking resemblances in the epinicians. The real parallels and contrasts are with hymnal diction, the modes of address to a god employed in oral literature or in literature which closely represents the oral tradition, such as the Homeric poems. The earliest example we have is the prayer of Apollo's priest Chryses to his god, asking that the plague be checked, in the first book of the *Iliad* (451–56). The broad pattern, not fully represented there, is comprised of the following elements: the god's name (or names), lineage, attributes, and cult centers; then deeds accomplished by the god; finally the worshipper's request, often preceded by a reminder of past acts of piety or of divine aid granted. Hymnal diction has become deeply embedded in our poetic forms, and not least in the ode. The *Iliad* and *Odyssey* had early become a part of Hopkins' thinking, and by 1875 he had come to know a great deal of classical poetry in which these conventions of ritual prayer were continued. As always, he used them distinctively. In *The Wreck* he did so somewhat diffusedly, but with a notable concentration to be found in the initial stanza.

The content of the remainder of the poem owes little to classical precedent, but some possibilities seem worth mentioning. Stanza 14 describes the ship running aground, striking "not a reef or a rock/But the combs of a smother of sand," then rolling helplessly broadside to the waves. The details are reminiscent of the only comparable storm scene in classical literature, the wrecking of Aeneas' ships on the sandbanks near the coast of Africa. In the *Aeneid*, specific parallels are *undis dat latus, saxa, dorsum,* and *furit aestus harenis* (i, 104–10).

Again, the use of "revel" in stanza 18 must have puzzled many readers. The clue lies in its position between references to two types of song, the madrigal and the glee. (Both words have at least two meanings, since "madrigal" can also denote the poetic text used as libretto.) For Victorian poets and scholars, "revel" was the standard rendering of *kômos*. Usually this Greek term meant a wild carouse, but it could also refer to the triumphal procession honoring a victor in the games. It is, in fact, the root concept in *enkômion*, which was often difficult to distinguish from the *epinikion*. What matters here is that beyond these two meanings another was possible, "revel-song." Pindar uses the word four times with this sense, and it is certainly the one that "revel" demands in stanza 18. Conceivably, the unusual accompanying epithet "never-eldering" may owe something to Greek terms for "not growing old." Pindar's *agêraos* describes heaven-bestowed glory in the *Pythians* (ii, 52) and the blessed dead in a fragment (131, ed. Bowra); Euripides' terms are *agêratos* and *agêrôs*, the latter in his *Suppliant Maidens* (line 1178; see below, on Aeschylus). A never-aging, joyous triumph-song: this is what *The Wreck* has meant to so many, and as a characterization it is supported by the progress of the poem. An exalted mood of celebration, first evident only in the opening phrase of the epigraph, finally overwhelms all that had been elegiac; death is swallowed up in victory.

"O world wide of its good" in stanza 20 for a moment presents the Christian concept of sin as the pre-Christian Greek world had conceived of blameworthy error—that is, as missing the mark (*hamartanein*, originally a spearman's term). Later, two compound adjectives fail of complete success, "fall-gold" because of the reminiscence of Danaë and "Tarpeïan-fast" because Tarpeia betrayed Rome. In the former case the inadvertence (as one must surely suppose it) seems especially regrettable, since the term would otherwise constitute a strong parallel to the dominant imagery of light employed by Pindar, who spoke untiringly of gold and fire, of flare and dazzle and gleam. By contrast, the use of *Ipse* as a name of Christ is successful, not merely because of its prominence in the Latin of the Mass—though this undoubtedly constitutes one valid reason—but also because it was used during the classical period to refer to the emperor. Here Hopkins is more concerned with Christ the King than with Christ the Sacrifice; he anticipates the "sovereignty" of stanza 32, the "thunder-throne" and "royally reclaiming" of stanza 34, and (most important of all) the climactic "King" and "Lord" of stanza 35.

To speak further of the final stanza, it is possible that the first word, "Dame," has not been given full value in our readings. As a derivative of *domina*, it contains an echo of (*ma*) *donna*, and it is balanced off in a hint of ring-composition against the final "Lord" (*Dominus*). The relationships that Hopkins establishes in our conscious or subconscious minds between the drowned nun and the Virgin have often been commented on; their presence as a factor in the poem warrants placing a heavy stress of meaning on "Dame." The two sequences of interlocking genitives in the final line of *The Wreck* have always posed a problem. This difficulty can be partly accounted for by the fact that all of the genitive nouns modify nouns which are themselves parallel to the possessive genitive in line 6. The equation of "his" with "of him," a strained usage in English, reflects a normal feature of classical style. This fact emphasizes the complexity of the construction that Hopkins chose to employ for his climax.

Early in November 1885, he wrote to his brother Everard that "the Greeks carried lyric to its highest perfection in Pindar and the tragic choruses" ("Three Uncollected Letters"). The entire body of evidence from the journals, letters, and notebooks indicates that ten years earlier his view had been the same. We may reasonably ask why, in that case,

The Wreck of the Deutschland shows so little obvious indebtedness to either the Pindaric or the tragic choral ode.

Part of the answer lies in the fact that Pindar's thought could make no contribution to the paradox of mastery and mercy. For this, Hopkins could have drawn strength from the choruses of Aeschylus. Then as now, the most famous and imposing of the seven extant plays is the *Agamemnon*. In the third strophe of the opening chorus (176-83), Aeschylus asserts that men learn through suffering, despite their unwillingness to accept wisdom, and he adds that the grace (*charis*) which comes from the gods enthroned in majesty is "somehow violent" (*biaios*).The anticipation of Hopkins'paradox is astonishing.Its meaning is corroborated, and its force intensified, by many other passages elsewhere in the *Agamemnon* and in the other plays, notably the *Suppliant Maidens* (which may prefigure *The Wreck* in a number of respects, as Lees has noted). These reverent searchings of the dark and difficult mystery that is the mind of Zeus are heights of Greek religious thought.

The Aeschylean element in Hopkins has not gone entirely unnoticed by scholars. The single remaining question is whether any significant Pindaric element exists; and the answer must be that it does. It is that ethical and religious high-mindedness noted earlier. Among the most remarkable qualities of Pindar as a lyric poet is his ability to sustain this exaltation without seeming to tire. The occasion of a victory in the national games provided a point of departure for mythical and gnomic wisdom through which Pindar sought to show that, while the gods might touch a man's life with radiance, he was still only a shadow of a dream and must walk in humility. Of all the poets who had formed the ode tradition, only Pindar could have given Hopkins the example of sustained lyric flight that he needed; and of all the attempts to achieve a Pindaric magnificence and a Pindaric intensity of religious thought, no poem in that splendid tradition surpasses *The Wreck of the Deutschland*.

Note

In *The Ode* (London, 1969), John Heath-Stubbs has provided a brief summary of the origins of this literary type and its development in English poetry. The commentary of C. A. P. Ruck and W. H. Matheson, *Pindar: Selected Odes* (Ann Arbor, 1968), provides a detailed treatment of ring-composition for the general reader. Smyth's *Greek Melic Poets* of 1904 (London and New York) was reprinted in 1963 (New York). From the same turn-of-the-century period come the remarks of B. L. Gildersleeve in his edition of Pindar. These inform an article by Leo Hines, "Pindaric Imagery in G. M. Hopkins," *The Month*, xxix (1963), 294-307. For the most recent examination of Hopkins' concern with Aeschylus, see F. N. Lees, "Gerard Manley Hopkins, Scholar, and the Matter of Imagery,"

British Journal of Aesthetics, xv, 2 (1975), 159–71. Gilbert Highet's comment on Milton's Nativity ode is from The Classical Tradition. "Three Uncollected Letters" appeared in The Hopkins Research Bulletin, No. 4 (1973), pp. 3–14. Two of these letters, including the one from which I have quoted, were originally published by Father D. A. Bischoff in the Times Literary Supplement for December 8, 1972.

Chapter XII

"Speech Framed To Be Heard"

The Function and Value of Sound Effects
in *The Wreck*

by Kunio Shimane

But take breath and read it with the ears, as I always wish to be read, and my verse becomes all right," wrote G. M. Hopkins to Robert Bridges (L I, p. 79). There is almost a painful cry from Hopkins in the letter as to how he wanted his poetry to be read. He had to repeat the same wish to his friend and was compelled to do so by the nature and definition of his poetry:

> Poetry is speech framed for contemplation of the mind by the way of hearing or speech framed to be heard for its own sake and interest even over and above its interest of meaning. Some matter and meaning is essential to it but only as an element necessary to support and employ the shape which is contemplated for its own sake (J, p. 288).

In his mature poetry the "meaning" is not merely "an element necessary to support and employ the shape." The profoundness of his thoughts is by itself the source of one type of difficulty; and the "shape" framed in "speech" or language renders another type of difficulty. Their fusion, as I take it, is "the dragon folded in the gate" of his poetry.

What is noteworthy in the definition is the predominance of "speech" over content. This fact conceals the key to open the gate of his poetry.

In the context of the quoted letter and the concept of poetry, Hopkins distinguished spoken language from written language and placed an overdue stress on the former. He had to do it, for he knew well the limitation of letters automatically appealing to the eye rather than the ear. But both spoken and written languages are forms of speech. Writing by no means expresses fully what is spoken, but it is more than a mere record. It often reveals characteristics of a writer's speech which are usually overlooked by ordinary readers. Hopkins' readers are not requested so much to perceive the peculiarities of his speech through the written word; they are only asked to read it aloud. It would be ideal, if they were able to read the poems in his own accent.

For a serious student of Hopkins it is necessary to be conscious of his pronunciation, since he wrote his poetry in it. He should be sensitive to the historical and regional differences of the poet's pronunciation. Hopkins did not compose his poetry either in Shakespeare's pronunciation or that of Robert Burns or in American English. Try to read the following in the northern accent or with American pronunciation:

> No worst, there is none. Pitched *past* pitch of grief.

In either pronunciation the vowel in "past" is [ae], while in Hopkins' it would have been [a], which introduces a sharp contrast between the front vowels [i] in "grief" and [I] in "Pitched" and "pitch." This contrast implies a sense of conflict which intensifies the context of this surprising sonnet. It utterly disappears when one pronounces the vowel in "past" [ae]. On the other hand, recite a line from Tennyson in Hopkins' pronunciation or in what Daniel Jones called "Received Pronunciation" (abbreviation RP):

> "Tirra lirra," by the river
> Sang Sir *Lancelot.*

The first vowel in "Lancelot" in RP is a long, back vowel. In Tennyson's accent reflecting clearly his native Lincolnshire accent it would have been pronounced as a front and abrupt [ae]. This vowel in combination with the short, front [I] in "Tirra," "lirra," and "river" and with the same vowel in "Sang," and by the support of the trochaic meter, helps to convey the light movement of Sir Lancelot riding. But if the vowel in "Lancelot" is pronounced [a], it will be hampered.

Even in Hopkins' *The Wreck of the Deutschland* there is an instance where we should not follow the present-day RP:

Hope had grown grey hairs . . .

Today, the vowel in "Hope" and "grown" is commonly pronounced [əu], which makes a contrast between the front diphthongs in "grey" and "hairs" obscure. It would have been pronounced [ou] in Hopkins' day.

Considering his family, class, educational backgrounds, I think that Hopkins' pronunciation would have been one type of RP. Daniel Jones' *English Pronouncing Dictionary,* up to the twelfth edition (1963), is the representation of his own pronunciation. Born in 1881, he was eight when Hopkins died in 1889. The accent he heard and acquired would have been similar to that of the latter. If one's language acquisition were fairly well-established, as is commonly said, by one's early teens and the pronunciation remained throughout one's life, Jones' pronunciation may well be regarded as essentially that of the late nineteenth century and it would have had much in common with Hopkins' pronunciation. But the pronouncing dictionary is regarded as representative of the RP of the Edwardian era by English phoneticians. In spite of this, I will venture to analyze the sound effects in *The Wreck* based on the dictionary and the pronunciations of my English informants spoken in RP modified according to it, as it provides organic material presenting the pronunciation approximate to that of Hopkins.

Now, it is necessary to consider the general role of sounds in *The Wreck*. It is obvious that the starting point of the creative process of this long poem is the tall nun's words: "O Christ, come quickly," as reported in the *Times.* They excited Hopkins' "fancy"—imagination. In other words, they commenced the whole cycle of creation. He was able to see and hear and feel in his mind the storm, the wreck, and the "tumult" on board the ship. He tried to see what the tall nun had seen at the critical moment:

> **Fancy come faster—**
> **Strike you the sight of it?**

Inviting "Fancy" at the climax of the poem implies Hopkins' habit as a Jesuit and a poet. He was thoroughly trained to use his imagination properly by Ignatian contemplation. Everyday throughout his life he practiced the contemplation which was the heart of the Jesuit training, by first employing his imagination and then his intellect. The vividness in his poetry by means of images pertaining to the five senses had its root in a poetic sensitivity regulated by such discipline. In *The Wreck* and most of his sonnets, he makes use of this method, probably instinctively. It seems to me that this feature is more explicit in Hopkins than in, say, the holy sonnets of Donne. Reading Hopkins, therefore, requires the reader to follow the same procedure of total activity leading to a deeper understanding and fuller appreciation. He should begin by listening to the sounds of his poetry, as they have the important function to start this activity. We should interpret the poet's concern about being read aloud in this way.

The language of Hopkins' mature poetry has a distinctive characteristic: *consonant-rich*, with a superiority of the consonants over the vowels. *The Wreck of the Deutschland* has this more distinctively than most other poems. To sense this we only need to glance at:

> **They fought with God's cold—**
> **And they could not and fell to the deck**
> **(Crushed them) or water (and drowned them) or rolled**
> **With the sea-romp over the wreck.**

About half of the content words are ones which survive from OE. This shows Hopkins' preference for "Anglo-Saxon" words. But that all the words, except "water" and "over," are monosyllables, when pronounced, is more notable. In English most words begin and end in consonants; and this characteristic appears typically in monosyllables with their phonemic structure: CVC. That is to say, strong consonants surround a soft vowel, demonstrating the superiority of the former. Knowing this, the poet did not hesitate to use monosyllables of other origins. It is not enough to say that he preferred "Anglo-Saxon" monosyllables.

Simply because the majority of English words begin with a consonant or consonant cluster, alliteration in consonants is an innate technique in English poetry. This was the sole technique in the Old English alliterative poetry, combined with rhythm. As an able linguist and a phonetician, Hopkins applied them in his poetry as a matter of course, whether he was conscious of it or not. In fact he studied "Anglo-Saxon" poetry.

Roughly speaking, the wave forms of most consonants are irregular and unstable. When pronounced they are checked and hindered in the articulatory organs and muscles. They are nonresonant sounds with less sonority but not necessarily less strength than the vowels. In fact at their best they—that is, voiceless plosives, voiceless fricatives, and voiceless affricates—are very sharp and strong.

From these characteristics of consonants derive various connotations. Masculinity and dynamism are the greatest phonetic qualities of the language of *The Wreck*. Hopkins' unique use of consonants realized it. Look at and listen to:

> **And the sea flint-flake, black-backed in the regular blow,**
> **Sitting Eastnortheast, in cursed quarter, the wind;**
> **Wiry and white-fiery and whirlwind-swivellèd snow**
> **Spins to the widow-making unchilding unfathering deeps.**

This is an astonishingly forcible description of the storm. When one compares it with the newspaper accounts, one will be utterly impressed by the vast difference existing between poetry and prose. The description is the cream of the language of *The Wreck* and can stand examination from various points of view to yield its true value.

Hopkins belongs to the tradition of poetry written in masculine English. Rather, he is its champion in modern times. The contrasting poet, I think, is Milton who belongs to the tradition of poetry composed in *vowel-rich*, feminine English. The vowels are regular resonant sounds with greater sonority, implying softness, stability, vastness, heaviness, or other similar qualities. They are the phonetic qualities which enabled Milton to achieve his grand style in *Paradise Lost*. The foundation was his Latinism not only in syntax but also in vocabulary. The vowels are popularly called "musical tones," and the epic is a grand symphony to the accompaniment of the vowels. It is even sublime but at times heavy and static. Some similarity is found in Tennyson. The English language has a tremendous receptivity and potentiality to nurture these two traditions in poetry.

It is precisely because Hopkins' language is masculine and even rugged, when he employs vowels well, that their effect indeed becomes conspicuous:

> Earnest, earthless, equal, attuneable, vaulty, voluminous, . . . stupendous.

This is, in his poetry, a special, Miltonic line, whose vowels signify the "evening" which is to be "time's vast," overwhelming the poet. At the same time they suggest the heaviness of the poet's heart, since he must envisage such a night comparable to a "rack." The majority of the English words end in a consonant or consonant cluster; and it gives a sense of closedness or termination. On the contrary, very few of them end in a vowel. These open-syllabic words hint at a sense of openness and continuity. The poet makes use of it masterfully in *The Leaden Echo and the Golden Echo*. Especially the transition from "the leaden echo" to "the golden echo" is so striking in

Despair, despair, despair, despair.
THE GOLDEN ECHO

Spare!

that it must be read making the vowels prominent, long, and fading. Otherwise the poet's purpose cannot be achieved. By using open-syllabic words he tried to produce the effect of the echo relating to the theme: the transition from mortal beauty to the immortal beauty. This is the main technique in this great poem.

The very beginning of *The Wreck* underwent a great emendation. The original read in both MSS A and B:

> God mastering me;
> Giver of breath and bread . . .

The lines were changed to those we know in the printed text. The original had no less Hopkins-like techniques. The main one was the use of three alliterations. The rhythm was fixed as the places of the stresses were unquestionable. I think that Hopkins was satisfied with it and hesitated to correct it, since in MS A he clearly cancelled his emendation. It was in MS B that he decided on it. The actual change was the introduction of the word "Thou" which took the place of "God"; and which in turn changed the beginning of the second line. This correction brought forth dramatic improvements. The rhythm became subtle and allowed for a different stress. But it is the introduction of the open-syllabic "Thou" that is really far-reaching. Because of its implication of openness and continuity, it is *as if* the word extends to the very end of the poem, "Lord," both of which are the key words in it. It may be a little farfetched but at least it is undoubtedly a most suitable beginning for *The Wreck*.

There are three main usages of consonants in the poem relating to the theme, the descriptions both of the poet's spiritual crisis and the actual wreck, and that of the tall nun. Firstly, for both descriptions sharp fricative sounds are mainly employed. Secondly, for the depiction of the tall nun, plosives have a vital function. Thirdly, to express the mastery of God the poet consciously used liquid sounds. They are interrelated in the structure of the poem. The descriptions of both crises and the nun point to the theme expressed in the liquid sounds. But I do not mean that for the description of the nun, for example, only plosives are used and none other; what I am saying is that they are the most important and effective sounds in the description.

All this can be said of the other two consonant groups.

> *The swoon of a heart that the sweep and the hurl of thee trod*
> *Hard down with a horror of height:*
> And *the midriff astrain with leaning of, laced with fire of stress.*

Almost every word contains one or other of the fricative sounds. I have included an affricate [t] which is characteristic of a good pronunciation in RP. The affricate has both explosion and friction; that is, the former is followed by the latter. The frictions in the quoted stanza continue:

> *The frown of his face*
> *Before me, the hurtle of hell*
> *Behind, where, where was a, where was a place?*

Like [t], [p] also tends to be pronounced in RP as an affricate. In American English these consonant clusters are often pronounced separately. In the same accent, the word "where" is pronounced with an *h* sound in it when stressed, whereas in RP it does not seem to be a common practice. To the end the frictions persist in the stanza.

In these stanzas a strong sense of speedy fricative movement and urgency is produced by the fricatives and the rhythm; the repetition of "where" reinforces it. "Hurl," "sweep," "flash," "fling" are some of the pivotal words in *The Wreck* and their initial fricatives, supported by meaning, reinforce their common basic implication: fricative movement. As for the connotation of spiritual conflict, we should recall the last line of *Spelt from Sibyl's Leaves*:

> Where, selfwrung, selfstrung, sheathe- and shelterless,
>   thóughts agàinst thoughts ín groans grínd.

Without considering the role of the fricatives, we cannot feel the extraordinary friction caused by bare selves grating against each other. This sense of deep agony is prolonged in another "Terrible Sonnet":

> We hear our hearts grate on themselves: it kills
> To bruise them dearer.

The friction of an agonizing self has its root in Part I of *The Wreck*.

The zenith of the description of the storm is found in the thirteenth stanza:

> Into *the snows she sweeps,*
> *Hurling the haven behind,*
> *The Deutschland, on Sunday; and so the sky keeps,*
> *For the infinite air is unkind,*
> And *the sea flint-flake, black-backed in the regular blow,*
> Sitting Eastnortheast, in cursed qua*rter, the wind;*
> Wiry and white-fiery, and whirlwind-swivellèd snow
> Spins to *the widow-making unchilding unfathering deeps.*

I scarcely need to analyze the role of the fricatives and affricates here. A reader with a good ear, without knowing the rest of the poem or the background, would surmise that the *Deutschland* would be wrecked. This is a rare and incomparable description of a storm in English poetry. The initiation to a full appreciation of it is to listen to the ominous fricative movements and sounds of the waves, the winds, and the snow. Then it would be easy to imagine the scene. If one could do this, one could enter into the world of *The Wreck* without much difficulty.

When I was studying the B MS of the poem at the Bodleian Library, Oxford, I was eager to see the original version of the eighth stanza. In the B MS a new piece of paper was pasted in, on which Hopkins had written the revised version. I instantly suspected that a drastic change had been made. I believe it is worthwhile to print here the original stanza, as it is not recorded in *The Poems*:

> Is out with it: so
> We lash with the best or the worst
> Last; or a lush-kept plush-capped sloe
> We mouth, & the blue flesh burst
> Gushes—it flushes—the being with sour & sweet,
> At a flásh, fúll.—Hither then, lást or fírst,
> To Christ's to hero of Calvary's, feet,
> Never ask whether wishing it méaning it, wárned of it, mén gó.

This is impressive enough, except for the awkward seventh line, but the revised stanza is much more impressive and truly Hopkinsian. Among others, one notable emendation is the arrangement of the fricative [sh] at the end of words: "lash," "plush," "flesh," "Gush," "flush," and "flash." In the original, "Gushes" and "flushes" impede the continuation of the fricative sound. The continuation suggesting the spreading-out of the taste of the sloe in the mouth analogous to the effect of the divine word on men driving them to the "hero of Calvary, Christ's feet." In the distinctive RP, the fricative is pronounced so as to give a strong, rich sound.

The central figure in Part II of *The Wreck* is the tall Franciscan nun soon to be drowned with her colleagues and other passengers. She is the central figure owing to the metaphor of the bell. The poet gave a special mission to the plosives which describe her. To introduce her words, the poet carefully organized a scheme:

> Till a lioness arose breasting the babble,
> A prophetess towered in the tumult, a virginal tongue told.
>   . . . and the call of the tall nun
> To the men in the tops and the tackle rode over the storm's
>   brawling.
>   She to the black-about air, to the breaker, the thickly
>   Falling flakes, to the throng that catches and quails
>   Was calling 'O Christ, Christ, come quickly':
> The cross to her she calls Christ to her, christens her wild-worst
>   Best.
>   Or is it that she cried for the crown then,
> The keener to come at the comfort for feeling the combating
>   keen?

> . . . the breast of the
> Maiden could obey so, be a bell to, ring of it, and
> Startle the poor sheep back!

I have marked only those that have enough force and audibility when read aloud and that are mostly used as alliterations. I have included affricates, since they have explosion. The plosives and affricates are the ringing of the "bell" to "startle the poor sheep back." In this sense, the correction of the original phrasing, ". . . the breast of the/Maiden could swing with, be musical of it" to the above quoted in the thirty-first stanza is appropriate. Those plosives and affricates must be as sharp and strong as the sound of bells "to ride over the storm's brawling."

In relation to those sounds, I should point out that the Latin *Ipse* was selected in the twenty-eighth stanza because of its acoustic feature, especially that of [ps]. Hopkins had a choice between this word and "self," and preferred the first. In this case an examination only of the semantics of these words would not be enough.

In the initiation poem *Inversnaid*, Hopkins depicts a mountain brook by means of liquid sounds:

> This darksome burn, horseback brown,
> His rollrock highroad roaring down,
> In coop and in comb the fleece of his foam
> Flutes and low to the lake falls home.

Both *r* and *l* are liquid sounds and their phonetic significance has long since been established. They insinuate the flow of water and other liquids. In *The Wreck* they are employed to express the motion of ocean tides as well as the running of the river compared to the passing of time:

> But it rides time like riding a river.

The theme of this poem is condensed in this short line. The stresses are those found in MS A. It is not uncommon to compare time to a river. In Matthew Arnold's *Future* we find a typical example. In the quoted line, "it" means the mastery of Christ over human history which he "rides like riding a river" like a competent oarsman. Human history has one definite direction over which God reigns. In his devotional writing Hopkins explains it (S, p. 196).

In *The Wreck*, "ride," "royal," and "roll" are words signifying God's mastery. There is no doubt about the word "ride," and it appears as "outride" in the following:

> With mercy that outrides
> The all of water . . .

The other two are used in:

> Kind, but royally reclaiming his own . . .
> . . . rare-dear Britain, as his reign rolls . . .

In stanzas 32, 33, and 34, there is the imagery of "the all of water." It is natural that liquid sounds should be applied to express it. These stanzas correspond in significance and mood to stanzas 9 and 10 in Part I. In Part I God directs the "ocean of a motionable mind" of man whose malice he wrings "with wrecking and storm"; and in Part II he masters "the tides" of the sea which caused the storm and the wreck. All this is but a part of his rule over human history progressing toward the omega point. Indeed, the imagery of "the all of water" not only insinuates the theme but also gives unity to the poem. The metaphor consisting of the "ocean of a motionable mind" and the actual ocean tides is a most important one in *The Wreck*.

The structure of the poem is not very complicated. It comprises only two elements: the descriptions both of the poet's spiritual crisis and of the actual wreck including that of the tall nun, and their theological expositions. The fricatives, plosives, and liquids are key sounds in them.

What I have been treating is, in short, the *presence* of sound. Pause, on the other hand, signifies the *absence* of sound and is indicated by punctuation in written language. Although sounds do not exist in it, this does not necessarily mean the absence of meaning. In a sentence, a paragraph, a chapter, or even a book, punctuation is applied and, in spite of this, the meaning or intention of the author continues to the very end. The function of pause in terms of punctuation is probably greater in poetry than prose, as poetry is the direct echo of the poet's voice. Silence is often more effective than sound in speech. In poetry, I think that there are three kinds of pause: grammatical, sense, and breath. I make a distinction between the former two, since though they are in most cases in agreement, in some cases they contradict each other.

We may begin with a famous but fundamental instance in English poetry:

> Break, break, break,
> On thy cold gray stones, O sea!

The commas in the lines not only suggest but clearly mean the rhythm of the rolling and dashing tides. By placing commas between "break," which begins and ends in plosive sounds, Tennyson succeeded in conveying the perpetual rhythm of the ancient and never-ending motion in contrast to the shortness of his dear friend's life. The punctuation here is grammatical and, at the same time, pertains to both sense and breath.

There are, of course, several excellent cases in *The Wreck*. The A version of the eighteenth stanza reads:

> Ah, touched in your bower of bone,
> Are you! turned, for an exquisite smart,
> Have you! make words break from me here all alone.
> Do you!—mother of being in me, heart.
> O unteachably after evil but uttering truth,
>
> Why, tears! is it? tears such a melting, a madrigal start!

In three places the punctuation differs from the printed text based on the B MS. It seems strange to place a comma after "turned" in the second line, but it is parallel to the one after "Ah" in the first line. In the text a comma is put after "evil" in the fifth line and this is more grammatical. There is no mark between "tears" and "such" in the last line above. The original phrase was "what are there?" in both MSS and Hopkins deleted it for "is it? tears" leaving "tears" unpunctuated. However, I do not think that this is his oversight, as it occurred in the same manner in both MSS. On the whole the punctuation in the quotation is basically that of sense and breath mixed. When one reads it in the tempo, rhythm, and intonation guided by the punctuation, one can ascertain that it is emotional and emphatic.

Such use of punctuation leads inevitably to *no* use of it when it would normally be employed. If its use could produce effective instances as we have seen, the opposite could have the possibility of bringing about no less conspicuous examples. Here is one:

> Sitting Eastnortheast, in cursed quarter, the wind;
> Wiry and white-fiery and whirlwind-swivellèd snow
> Spins to the widow-making unchilding unfathering deeps.

Compare the first line with deliberate punctuation with the following two lines with no mark at all to the end. They thus realize a contrast in punctuation. No pause in the two lines suggests the speedy, incessant fury of the winds, the breakers, and the snow hammering at the *Deutschland*. By the contrast the force of their blows becomes greater still. The use and nonuse of pause here combining with other elements of sound effects is calculated to yield the exact effect the poet aimed at. A similar result of no punctuation is also found in the following:

> They fought with God's cold—
> And they could not and fell to the deck
> (Crushed them) or water (and drowned them) or rolled
> With the sea-romp over the wreck.

In the A MS a comma is found after "not" in the second line, while in the B it is not used. The latter case is preferable.

Pause has, therefore, an indispensable part in poetry. It is also one of the most important aspects of speech. We should not ignore the value and meaning of silence, while paying too much attention to sound.

Poetry is a form of art by means of articulate sounds in time, as Lessing mentions in his *Laocoön*. This statement contains a crucial point for considering poetry as speech as Hopkins defines it. To read and study his poetry necessitates the work of transcribing his poetry from written language to that of spoken language. This transformation means that we place his poetry in a revitalized oral tradition. One way to make this possible is that we pay greater attention to the original manuscripts.

I have referred to the MSS of *The Wreck of the Deutschland* whenever necessary. They, within the limits of writing, reflect the poet's own voice more faithfully than the printed text. When one sees the stresses in such lines in the A MS as:

> Dáme, at óur dóor
> Drówned & among óur shóals.

One cannot help feeling the sense of guilt and responsibility that Hopkins felt as an Englishman. He obviously read the *Times* editorial criticizing the delay in rescue at Harwich (December 13, 1875). The meaning of the stresses repeated on the two "our"s is unmistakable.

Moreover I am interested in the emendations in the MSS. They reveal the hidden process of the formation of sound effects, as shown in the several instances I have cited and examined above and manifest the development of creativity in Hopkins' poetry which is not similar to "prose fantastically written to rule."

Hopkins' poetic language is no doubt odd, as he confessed in a letter. The cause of the oddity could be referred to his disregard of conventional grammar. Alternatively, he had elaborated his "grammar of sounds" by which he contrived his sound effects. Without paying sufficient attention to them or trying to unravel the relationship between sound and sense, his poetry remains as formidable as ever. One should begin by reading according to his advice and "read it so that lines and stanzas should be left in the memory and superficial impressions" (L I, p. 50) deepen, and let the sounds ring in one's ears so that the auditory impressions may take some form in harmony with the meaning.

Jesuit training provided Hopkins' view of the world with decisive scope and depth. Strangely enough, during seven years' silence something happened within the walls of the Jesuit house to change his language drastically. Contrary to his obsession that writing poetry would contradict his vocation, the latter continued to supply the former with a poetic "pressure, a principle, Christ's gift."

Notes

a   When I say that the closed-syllabic word gives a sense of termination, and the open-syllabic word that of continuation, the effect is explained as literary and psychological rather than phonetical. The final consonants, especially the voiceless fricatives and affricates are very long. Most final vowels damp quickly in RP. But I have taken their sonority into consideration, and it is possible, when pronouncing, to prolong them.

b   Of course, I do not mean literally that the diphthong continues to the end of the poem. What I emphasize here is that the introduction of the open-syllabic word is extremely effective and impressive.

c   See my studies on: "The Manuscript of G. M. Hopkins' *The Wreck of the Deutschland:* The Bodleian MS. Eng. Poet. d. 149" (*Kiyo: Studies in English Literature*, X. Notre Dame Seishin University, Okayama, Japan, 1975); "The Sound of the Bell: A Scientific and Literary Analysis of G. M. Hopkins' *The Wreck of the Deutschland*" (*Kiyo*, VIII, 1973); "Restoration of the Tradition of Reciting Poetry" (*Kiyo*, VI, 1970).

Chapter XIII

"A Continuous Structural Parallelism"

Stanzaic Pattern in *The Wreck*

by John E. Keating

W hy do poets write long poems in fixed stanza forms, especially odes and elegies? In narratives, from *The Faerie Queene* to *The Earthly Paradise,* they may expect some indulgence if there is occasional discrepancy between form and thought, or a certain monotony; the subject matter and the sheer magnitude of the project make less than complete success tolerable to the reader. But in lyrical and reflective poetry, the reader is likely to require a richer development of the thought and a more exquisite matching of the rhythm of the stanzas to it. One need only mention the name of Swinburne to conjure up the perils of the fixed stanza.

If the poet, then, chooses to give up the freedom supremely exercised in pieces like *Lycidas* and *Intimations of Immortality,* he has indeed the opportunity of creating his own stanza, the perfect vessel for his thought. Yet it is a vessel that may turn earthen unless he can manipulate it so that each repetition will come out fresh in idea and movement. Wordsworth's *Ode to Duty* and Shelley's *Cloud,* for example, seem to me weakened by sameness, by a kind of singsong. On the other hand, in the odes of 1819, Keats evinces his consummate mastery in the dramatic treatment of subject matter and in modulating the stanzaic form to its presentation. *The Nightingale,* for example, shows intense and complex development of a theme and perfect accommodation of sound to sense. Through subtle accommodation of diction and rhythm, the same stanza form expresses the opening languor—"My heart aches, and a drowsy numbness pains/My sense . . . "; the excited escape in imagination—"Away! away! for I will fly to thee . . . "; the solemn asseveration of the nightingale's deathlessness—"Thou wast not born for death, immortal Bird!"; the returning bewilderment of the conclusion—"Forlorn! the very word is like a bell . . . " Keats had to contend with his problem for only eight stanzas; the poet of *The Wreck* undertook thirty-five.

Most poets have probably given full and conscious attention to their choice of stanzaic forms and the effects they hoped to produce by them. It is clear that Hopkins had devoted considerable thought to the aesthetics of the stanza. Ten years before the composition of *The Wreck of the Deutschland,* he had worked out the basic principles in his undergraduate paper, "On the Origin of Beauty: A Platonic Dialogue." The dialogue is an attempt to show that the beautiful is not a matter of mere taste, but of ascertainable law. "Complex beauty," the unnamed professor of aesthetics argues, arises from a conjunction of "regularity and irregularity":

> the beauty of the oak and the chestnut-fan and the sky is a mixture of likeness and difference or agreement and disagreement or consistency and variety or symmetry and change. . . . And if we did not feel the likeness we should not think them so beautiful, or if we did not feel the difference we should not think them so beautiful (J, p. 90).

Rhyme, he says, is "a short and valuable instance" of this principle, since the appeal of rhyme is that the sounds are partly alike, partly different. Further, "each stanza being considered as a work of art," rhyme indicates the points "where the principle of beauty is to be strongly marked," and also the structural proportions (J, pp. 101–02). The professor finally works out the view that the distinguishing characteristic of verse as opposed to prose is "a continuous structural parallelism, ranging from the technically so-called parallelism of the Psalms to the intricate structure of Greek or Italian or English verse" (J, p. 108). This view he applies to both the parts and the totality of literary works: "The two terms of a parallelism make a whole of beauty, but these wholes again may be the terms of a higher whole . . . " (J, p. 114).

The critical positions developed in "On the Origin of Beauty," whether or not we accept them as entirely convincing, furnish clues as to what may be looked for in a structural analysis of *The Wreck*. Within individual stanzas and in the poem as a whole, we may expect Hopkins to be concerned with symmetry, but to be equally concerned with all the variations that relieve it. At the start, I should like to emphasize the point that in examining the metrics and thought of *The Wreck*, I have no intention of arriving at a rigorous and comprehensive analysis. The poetry of Hopkins is really not a field for Procrustean prosodists. I am looking for general patterns, not simplistic formulas, and much of what I propose is tentative and exploratory.

More than once Hopkins insisted that his poetry is to be read aloud. Other poets too have favored spoken rendering of their work, and many have set an example of what they wanted done with it: they gave readings. Yet Hopkins' insistence that his poems were written for the ear furnishes special reason for turning from the neatly blocked divisions of the printed page to the pulsation of the lines as a listener experiences them.

Since each stanza of *The Wreck of the Deutschland* begins with a quatrain rhymed *abab,* there is commonly at the end of the fourth line a certain break, pause, or arrest. This line is end-stopped in all but three of the stanzas (8, 19, 21). In all but four it is followed by punctuation. In ten stanzas, this is terminal; in fifteen, it consists of the colon, semicolon, or dash. Hopkins did not always follow normal punctuation and even indulged in some eccentricities; still, the proportion of punctuated lines offers some indication of how he expected most stanzas to be read. What is more important, the break arises from the rhyme scheme, and is emphasized by the drop from the four stresses in the third line to the three-stress brevity of the fourth. The force of the break varies; where it is marked by terminal punctuation or an adversative word, it is of course strongest.

If we can put aside for a few moments our understandable prejudices in favor of *The Wreck* as Hopkins wrote it, let us consider what would happen if we removed the last four lines from a number of stanzas and so produced a new poem in quatrains. Let us begin at stanza 9.

> Be adored among men,
>   God, three-numberèd form;
> Wring thy rebel, dogged in den,
>   Man's malice, with wrecking and storm.

> With an anvil-ding
>   And with fire in him forge thy will
> Or rather, rather then, stealing as Spring
>   Through him, melt him but master him still . . .

> "Some find me a sword; some
>   The flange and the rail; flame,
> Fang, or flood" goes Death on drum,
>   And storms bugle his fame.

> On Saturday sailed from Bremen,
>   American-outward-bound,
> Take settler and seamen, tell men with women,
>   Two hundred souls in the round . . .

> Into the snows she sweeps,
>   Hurling the haven behind,
> The Deutschland, on Sunday; and so the sky keeps,
>   For the infinite air is unkind . . .

> She drove in the dark to leeward,
>   She struck—not a reef or a rock
> But the combs or a smother of sand: night drew her
>   Dead to the Kentish Knock . . .

Now although my surgery has weakened the linkage between stanzas, the amputated version might even do for *The Student's Cram Manual* or *The Busy Reader's Treasury of Condensed Masterpieces.* What I am suggesting is that the opening quatrains of many stranzas possess a unity and cohesiveness of their own that makes it possible to separate them from what follows. The process may also be reversed with some of the stanzas, though, for syntactic and other reasons, less readily; but the last four lines of stanzas 9, 10, and 11, for example, can be disengaged from the opening lines and read by themselves. Thus a conspicuous structural feature of the stanzas is that many begin with a quatrain set off both in metrics and thought from what is to follow. The break somewhat resembles the use of the volta in the Petrarchan sonnet, but there seems to be no further resemblance between it and the stanzas of *The Wreck.*

Then in line 5, a new surge of movement arises. It is marked by a new rhyme, c. But in line 6, the b rhyme recurs, echoing lines 2 and 4. Lines 5 and 6, each of five stresses, are longer than the first four; they thus stand out and counterpoise one another. The new c rhyme, contrasted with the echoing of the earlier b rhyme, sets up a kind of metrical countermovement or ambivalence, suggesting a transition to complication or imbroglio. This is maintained by use of the c rhyme again in line 7. The first seven lines of a stanza, then, are made up of two rhyme systems linked by the b rhyme, abab, cbc—a quatrain and a tercet, at once distinguishable and united. The hovering metrical effect leaves the ear expectant as to what rhyme will finally dominate. The function of the countermovement cbc in the tercet may be brought out by removing the b line from one of the stanzas where removal is syntactically feasible:

> **She was first of a five and came**
> **Of a coifèd sisterhood.**
> **(O Deutschland, double a desperate name!**
> **O world wide of its good!**
> **But Gertrude, lily, and Luther are two of a town,**
>
> **From life's dawn it is drawn down,**
> **Abel is Cain's brother and breasts they have sucked the same.)**

With the loss of the countermovement set up by the b rhyme, the stanza has lost the vibrant rhythm of the original and develops a singsong ending.

The tercet prepares the way for the conclusion. Line 7, shortened to four stresses, provides anticipatory contrast for the concluding six-stress line. With its length and sweep thus emphasized, the final line typically brings a stanza to its final asseveration or question. (Only two stanzas, 7 and 32, are connected with the following one; all the others have terminal punctuation.) Of equal importance to length is the reassertion of the a rhyme of lines 1 and 3, now somewhat evanescent in the hearer's memory. Thus at the end, the b and c rhymes, dominant for four lines, give way, and the stanza comes full circle with the recurrence of the opening rhyme, a. In length and in rhyme, then, line 8 effects a resolution of the metrical countermovement set up in the tercet, and serves as a powerful unifying force both for the metrics and the thought of a stanza.

In eight stanzas there are variations in the handling of the bipartite structure thus far described through varied placing of the midstanzaic break. In stanza 28, the break occurs within line 4; in stanzas 19, 21, 23, within line 5; in stanzas 3, 16, 34, at the end of line 5; and in stanza 8, within line 6. These variations do not seem to me to be violations of the typical structure, but rather the kind of departures from it which Hopkins considered safeguards against too great regularity.

Other variations from perfect symmetry or regularity are pervasive in *The Wreck.* One is to be found in the very proportions of the stanza which Hopkins devised. The quatrain is markedly shorter than the tercet and conclusion. In Part I, the ratio of stresses is 12 to 20; in Part II, 13 to 20. The juxtaposition of the unequal masses in the two segments thus serves as a basic structural provision against excessive balance. Then there is constant provision in various matters of detail which affect the entire texture of the poem. The use of sprung rhythm makes possible rich and abundant flexibility. The constant modulation of rhetorical structure and diction operates similarly. Consider, for example, the contrast between the sinuous and pictorial treatment in stanza 26, heightened by five feminine rhymes, and the terse, staccato handling of stanza 30; or again, the contrast between the anacolutha and colloquialism of stanza 31 and the directness and solemnity of stanza 32. Since, however, even the severest critics of *The Wreck* have never faulted it for excessive regularity, it will be enough to have mentioned these features without detailed consideration of them.

I should like now to consider the ways in which Hopkins utilizes his bipartite stanza for the presentation of his thought. Without examination of the overall unity of the poem at this point, it may be said that most stanzas tend to maintain a unity of their own, a characteristic suggested by Hopkins' remark, already quoted, "each stanza being considered as a work of art." It might be in order to recall a remark of Hopkins in another connection which should perhaps have stopped me earlier: "it is dreadful to explain these things in cold blood . . . " (L I, p. 164). But misguided by his own probings into the source of literary effects, I shall continue.

Within the unity of each stanza, the break in structure tends to signal a break in thought. Without attempting a rigorous division of the ways in which the break functions, or insisting on a definitive classification of all stanzas, I may comment on four typical developments. (By the way, these to some degree resemble the four main types of parallelism which scholars distinguish in the poetry of the bible.)

In about a third of the stanzas, the development is contrastive, antithetic, counterthematic. In many of these, the antithesis is marked by an adversative word, *but, not, no.* Stanzas 19, 20, 21, 22, for example, form an antithetical sequence. In the quatrain, a fact or idea is presented; after the break, another aspect of it is explored:

Blinds her; but she that weather sees one thing, one . . .

But Gertrude, lily, and Luther, are two of a town . . .

Gnashed; but thou art above, thou Orion of light . . .

But he scores it in scarlet himself on his own bespoken . . .

Without the adversative word, the antithesis may be present, but less obvious. In stanza 1, the contrast is between God as giver and God as destroyer, a contrast indicated by parallel use of "thou" at the beginning of lines 1 and 5. In stanza 24, it is between "I was under a roof here" and "She to the black-about air"; in stanza 25, it is marked by "else-minded": "They were else-minded then, altogether, the men . . . "

Antithesis is the most readily observable form of treatment in the bipartite stanzas, but they are no less effective for treatments which may be distinguished as 1) particularizing, 2) incremental, and 3) reflective.

Stanzas 13 and 14 are fairly clear examples of particularization. In stanza 13, the departure of the ship is given in relatively general terms in the quatrain: "Into the snows she sweeps . . . the infinite air is unkind . . . " Then come four lines of vivid details: "the sea flintflake . . . in cursed quarter, the wind;/Wiry and white-fiery and whirlwind-swivellèd snow . . . " In stanza 14, the grounding of the vessel is similarly treated; after what is mainly a statement of the facts in the quatrain, specific description follows: "And she beat the bank down with her bows and the ride of her keel:/The breakers rolled on her beam with ruinous shock . . . "

The development in stanzas like 17 may be called incremental. The narrative builds up through the break to the emergence of the tall nun as lioness and prophetess. Similarly in stanza 23, the poet moves from the salutation to St. Francis to the triumph in death of the five Franciscans, "sisterly sealed in wild waters."

Stanzas 5 and 6 illustrate a treatment that may be termed reflective. In both, words first employed in the quatrain are repeated and their implications brought out. Thus in stanza 5, the repeated "kiss my hand" leads into the poet's fuller understanding of how and why he may worship nature; in stanza 6, the repeated "stroke," "stress" introduce reflection on the way in which God's stroke and stress continue to influence mankind.

The stanzaic pattern of *The Wreck of the Deutschland,* then, is basically antiphonal. The latter part of each stanza typically provides some kind of response to the opening lines. Moreover, the two major divisions are themselves frequently divided so as to produce a minor antiphony.

What is the effect of the antiphonal development of the poem? It results, I believe, in what may be called in Arnold's phrase, a "dialogue of the mind with itself." For *The Wreck,* we must add, "and with its God." Hopkins is pondering the mysteries of religious faith in themselves and in relation to the world about him. In a letter to Bridges in 1883, he commented at length on the mysteries which he is instressing in *The Wreck.* For Bridges, he contended, a mystery is "an interesting uncertainty: the uncertainty ceasing, interest ceases also." But for Catholics, a mystery is "an incomprehensible certainty," not "an equation in theology, the dull algebra of schoolmen . . . but news of their dearest friend or friends . . . their knowledge leaves their minds swinging; poised, but on the quiver" (L I, pp. 187-88).

Hopkins, then is pondering these incomprehensible certainties, his mind on the quiver as it is confronted by the mysteries of faith and the mysteries that arise in relating faith to actual experience. God himself appears paradoxical; all-merciful yet all-just, he both promises heaven and threatens hellfire. God's creation is paradoxical; on the one hand, it brings forth "the dappled-with-damson west" and "pied and peeled May," and on the other, "the sea flint-flake" and "the black-about air." The Church is paradoxical; Hopkins trusts that she can convert Victorian England, and yet he knows that, facing the Kulturkampf, she cannot protect even five nuns in their homeland. Man himself is paradoxical; his race produced Abel and Cain, Gertrude and Luther, St. Francis and Herr von Falk, the nuns with their supreme faith and their despairing fellow passengers.

To consider these baffling contrarieties in one way and another, and to bring them to a resolution, the antiphonal stanza which Hopkins devised furnishes an admirable medium. The quatrains sharply introduce one phase of the thought, and the rest of the stanza alternates with development of it. Since the quatrains are the markedly shorter portion, the greater length of the last four lines provides for the needed elaboration and resolution.

Finally, a word should be said about the unifying effect of the stanzaic pattern in the structure of the poem as a whole. The point may be made by comparing it with another masterpiece, *Dover Beach.* In *Dover Beach,* the carefully managed indeterminacy of the rhythms throughout perfectly matches the concept of a meaningless universe which Arnold felt that he was forced to accept. In *The Wreck,* on the other hand, the ordered procession of stanzas paralleling one another constantly suggests metrically the possibility of a meaningful framework for man's thought and experience. Yet it is not an order effortlessly or artificially imposed. The variations which Hopkins insisted on in theory and employed in practice are exquisitely adapted not only to guard against monotony and facility but also to convey the complexity and intensity of the thinking. In total effect, then, the stanzaic pattern of *The Wreck of the Deutschland* serves as a consummate medium for a poem of troubled, yet living and persevering faith.

Chapter XIV

"Throned Behind Death"

A Memoir of *The Wreck*

by Ruth Seelhammer

There may be other Jesuits somewhere who have *The Wreck of the Deutschland* without book. The one I knew who had it died in Belfast last week. Among the books left behind in his room was a copy of the Penguin Poets edition of Hopkins, both covers off and well-worn. It was brought to me at my desk in the library and in taking it I discovered a postcard in it. The Jane Austen portrait done by her sister Cassandra, from the National Portrait Gallery, was on the card and it had been sent to him because if Gerard Manley Hopkins was this Jesuit's poet, Jane Austen was his novelist.

The card had been mailed to Father Charles Keenan from London and written to him on the day I had visited Roehampton and Stratford. I wanted him to know, as well, that on the previous day I had taken the train from Paddington Station to Oxford and had seen Balliol and St. Aloysius Church. Father Keenan had given me, before I left for London, his own map of Oxford which dated back to his Oxford days and degrees of thirty years before.

Although death came in Belfast, Father Keenan is buried in Dublin, in Glasnevin Cemetery, near Hopkins' own grave. The Jane Austen display commemorating the anniversary of her birth two hundred years ago, which I had arranged in the lobby display case in the library to welcome Father when he arrived home, is not in the right place to welcome him home. When gathering the books and pictures for the display I had spent some time looking for the Jane Austen postcard portrait which I knew I had had in my possession. I was taken by surprise when it appeared as it did. The display is still in the case as I write and sooner or later it must be dismantled and all those Jane Austen books he loved must then be returned to the impersonal library stacks.

The reason Father Keenan came to know Hopkins as he did is partly my fault although I suppose I cannot take credit for his managing to get himself buried so near to him. After Father's retirement from the English department of Gonzaga University a few years ago, he brought his questing mind to the reference department of the library where he spent the last three of his seventy-one years. In the month of April of this year he celebrated, with his friends and Jesuit family, his anniversary of fifty years as a Jesuit. Shortly afterward he left for the visit to his sister in Belfast, with ostensible plans to return to the university and to the library for the summer session beginning in the middle of June.

Having known him as English professor, library patron, and reference librarian, our acquaintance was intensified during his first summer here at the library when he and I were catapulted, at hardly a moment's notice, into a Hopkins' association by the death of Father John Keating, author of the Kent State University Bulletin issue of 1963 on *The Wreck of the Deutschland*. Father Robert Boyle, whose book on Hopkins opens many doors to metaphor, had expected to be free to come to

Gonzaga University in the summer of 1972 to teach a course on Hopkins. The final plans were delayed and when Father Boyle was unable to accept them, he suggested Father John Keating, who had been on the faculty with him at Kent State University, instead.

My first encounter with Father Keating, arranged through Father Boyle, took place during the 1971 Christmastime meeting of the Modern Language Association. In that winter world of Chicago, Father Keating gave witness to the special meaning the sonnet *To R. B.* had for him. In listening to the words of the sonnet in his voice, the "auditory imagination" which T. S. Eliot attributes to a poet's mind was given force. Father Keating told me that he had planned to use the summer for work on a new edition of his commentary on *The Wreck of the Deutschland* and that he felt it a startling piece of good fortune to have the opportunity to teach Hopkins while doing so and, moreover, to have access to the material in the Hopkins collection kept at Gonzaga University at the same time.

Summer came then and with it Father Keating's arrival. The substitution had worked itself out and details were arranged. He signed the guest register in the Hopkins Room on June 15. Enrollment in the Hopkins class was small, as had been expected. It included Father Keenan whose special field, before he came to the reference department of the library, had been Middle English studies. He said he had never really had the opportunity to study Hopkins and that since this one had presented itself he was certainly not going to miss it.

After the first class session had been held Father Keating came to the library and, during our conversation, said that he wondered if, since the class was of limited size, there might not be a room in the library itself where the sessions could be held. I knew what he had in mind and of course he was sure that I would know. We talked with Father Clifford Carroll, the director of libraries at that time, and he said, without hesitation, "Why don't you use the Hopkins Room?" A table was moved into the room and the space held the seven of us comfortably encompassed in the special Hopkins atmosphere that the room engenders.

We had four days in that room of Father Keating's enthusiasm, as he "spoke of Hopkins' poems, and prose, and life, with overflowing joy." The phrase comes from a poem one of the students in the class wrote after he was gone. When the second Monday came, everything changed. Father Keating ordinarily arrived at the library rather early, before the class, to spend some time in the Hopkins Room before the students came in. The key to the room was kept in a small, round, black, leather box on my desk and he would take the key from it and return it to me when the class was over.

That Monday I had been away from my desk for some time and when I returned I opened the black box to see if Father Keating had the key. It was still in the box. Since it was very near the time for the class to begin, I was somewhat surprised, but I remember no feeling of apprehension. I stood there wondering if I should call his room. Perhaps he had become engrossed in something and had not noticed the time. Just then Father Keenan came into the library office in an agitated state. He said that word had just come to him that Father Keating had been found, minutes previously, dead in his room at Jesuit House, where he was to have lived for the summer. The Hopkins class was not held on that day.

In the afternoon the head of the English department phoned the library to ask if I would take the class for the remaining five weeks of the summer session. Father Keating had spent the first week setting the scene, not as a map but as a garden, and the garden was ready for the placing of the poetry itself. We had the plan in his own words, that after introductory notes on Victorian literature and a review of Hopkins' background in the social and literary history of the Victorian period, he planned to take some time for the chronology of Hopkins' life and writing. The outline given to the students read "After this introduction, the principal work of the course will be taken up—detailed discussion of the poems, mainly the finished pieces of Hopkins' maturity, but with some attention to the early poems, fragments, and translations." This is where we had arrived and this was the point from which we had to continue. If I had not been so stunned, I might not have been so acquiescent but Father Keenan was there, as Jesuit, to give the help one would need. I knew I would need him especially when we talked of Scotism and when we did eventually discuss *Duns Scotus's Oxford*, Father's exposition of the differences between Scotism and Thomism as applied to Hopkins was as memorable as the "Towery city and branchy between towers" that started it off. With his Oxon degrees, his Jesuit training, and his erudite mind he was an anchor for us all.

Well, there was the evening to plan the course. I'm not at all sure that I knew, the next day, what we were going to do or how we were going to do it. To make the transition, in that Tuesday class, from Father Keating's presence, we began with the sonnet he loved most, *To R. B.* which presents clearly its particular roots in *The Wreck of the Deutschland* in the first line. "The fine delight that fathers thought" is a reminder of stanza 27 where "Time's tasking, it is fathers that asking for ease." The second line with "the blowpipe flame" returns us to the third stanza where we "flash from the flame to the flame then." "Breathes once" of the third line intimates the line of stanza 10, "Whether at once, as once at a crash Paul." "Quenched faster than it came" of the same line has its affinity with stanza 28, "Fancy, come faster." Line 6, "Within her wears, bears, cares and combs the same" takes us back to stanza 15, "carved with cares" or back to stanza 4, "And it crowds and it combs to the fall."

From *To R. B.* we moved to the other poems in more or less chronological order, leaving *The Wreck of the Deutschland* for the last. There is nothing new in the idea that Hopkins' later poetry has its roots in *The Wreck of the Deutschland* but how, specifically, so much if not everything, comes out of that beautiful dragon was what we came to know in the course of the summer. The connections, the fusion, the "holding together in a single field of force" of which Elizabeth Drew writes in her book on T. S. Eliot (p. 21) was so clear that when we reached those last days, going backward in time to end with *The Wreck of the Deutschland*, an unexpected gift was ours. The whole body of Hopkins' poetry seemed to become one to us and when we talked about Bridges' phrase of the dragon folded at the gate and of the others who had difficulty with the poem, such as the editor of *The Month* who refused to print it, we found ourselves in a completely converse position. One of the students commented that not everyone had been as fortunate as we in the class, to go from the last sonnet Hopkins wrote, through the other poetry, dipping back with each poem to its roots in *The Wreck of the Deutschland* and then, finally, going to *The Wreck of the Deutschland* itself which, in a sense, was already comprehensible to us. Its familiarity, from the understructure we had sought for the other poems, deflated the dragon myth effectively and brought us at the end to an understanding of the integrality of the body of the poet's work.

Father Keating did that for us by dying, by giving to us *To R. B.* as the link, and by giving me, imperceptibly, ineffably, the certain knowledge that in no way could I begin *The Wreck of the Deutschland* with merely overnight preparation. By the time the class was ready for it, I was ready, and we were together able to recognize "the roll, the rise, the carol, the creation" of that very last sonnet, set forth in that early, first work of Hopkins' renewal of his poetry-writing life.

In the introduction to *The Wheel of Fire*, by G. Wilson Knight (an exploration of Shakespeare's poetic symbols and imagery), T. S. Eliot writes that "Our impulse to interpret a work of art (by 'work of art' I mean here rather the work of one artist as a whole) is exactly as imperative and fundamental as our impulse to interpret the universe by metaphysics . . . " (p. xvii). What we sought in the class, and our finding of it, was a legacy from Father Keating, a legacy that brought a shining brightness to those morning hours in that room where Hopkins' works are not only lodged, but live.

The tracing of the effect of *The Wreck of the Deutschland* on Hopkins' other poems has been ably done in three commentaries on the poetry, one by Paul Mariani, one by Donald McChesney, and the third by Father Peter Milward, S. J. An approach from the opposite direction, a pursuit from *The Wreck of the Deutschland* forward into the other poetry, brings equal opulence and gives attestation to there being not one stanza which does not furnish substance for later poems.

If one were to start with the last stanza first, for instance, one would see that "Dame, at our door" is a forerunner of the thought in the last line of *St. Alphonsus Rodriguez* where "Alfonso watched the door." "Drowned, and among our shoals" brings to mind *Inversnaid* with "It rounds and rounds Despair to drowning." The third line, beginning "Remember us in the roads" takes us to *Felix Randal* with "Ah well, God rest him all road ever he offended!" Line 4 has "Our King back" to parallel "back to God" of *The Golden Echo* and, possibly, "Bid joy back" of the fragment beginning "Strike, churl." In line 5 the "crimson-cresseted east," while not appearing in a later poem, brings to mind the early lines on *The Nightingale* and its "crimson East, that bids for rain."

One could go on, *ad infinitum,* backward or forward. One could begin with the first, or any of the stanzas in between, from 2 to 34, and find them equally rich in their contribution to and their significance for the later works of Hopkins. The compression is such, the texture is such, that all the magnificence of his later work is latent in this structure of the year 1876.

When Father Boyle wrote, after the summer was over, saying that he had heard at the English Institute in September that Father Keating had died at Gonzaga University but knew nothing of the details, I wanted to tell him what this experience of death had been for the rest of us. "Could you fill me in on this," he asked, "when you get the time? Since my recommendation turned out so sadly . . . "

No, not sadly. One could not carry sadness for that death. To go back to that winter world of Chicago for a moment again, I had asked Father Keating there whether he really wanted, as the situation was still uncertain, to spend the summer in Spokane. His answer, and I do not remember all the exact words, was to the effect that to spend the summer teaching Hopkins, writing about Hopkins, working with the Hopkins Collection—(and these words I remember well), "A man can dream, can't he?" He died, it seems to me, where and when he would have wanted to die, could he have chosen. Perhaps he did choose.

I must ask, is it possible for certain people to choose? Surely Father Keenan died where and when he would have chosen. I sometimes think he knew all the time, during our discussions on Hopkins, that he would have that closeness to him in death, coming to him by what seemed accident, that he had in life. Now that we are in the first week of the summer session of this anniversary year of *The Wreck of the Deutschland* I must bring myself to thinking of dismantling the Jane Austen display in the lobby and replacing it with material on Hopkins' anniversary. Father Keenan was to have returned to the library on Monday. That Monday will never come. It will be, instead, the Monday of the anniversary of the death of Father Keating.

Although it was impossible to restrain the tears during the memorial Mass held for Father Keenan in the Jesuit Chapel here last week, I should not be sad. As one of the Jesuit family pointed out to me, while I waited afterward in the dark wondering how to move, I have lost a good friend here but he is where he will "Remember us in the roads, the heaven-haven of the reward" and I should not be sad.

Bibliographical Abbreviations

Primary

Poems 3   Poems of Gerard Manley Hopkins, third edition by W. H. Gardner. London, 1948.

Poems 4   The Poems of Gerard Manley Hopkins, fourth edition by W. H. Gardner and N. H. MacKenzie. London, 1967.

Penguin   Poems and Prose of Gerard Manley Hopkins, selected with an introduction and notes by W. H. Gardner, Penguin Poets edition. London, 1953.

J   The Journals and Papers of Gerard Manley Hopkins, edited by Humphrey House, completed by Graham Storey. London, 1959.

L I   The Letters of Gerard Manley Hopkins to Robert Bridges, edited with notes and an introduction by C. C. Abbott. London, 1935; revised, 1955.

L II   The Correspondence of Gerard Manley Hopkins and Richard Watson Dixon, edited with notes and an introduction by C. C. Abbott. London, 1935; revised, 1955.

L III   Further Letters of Gerard Manley Hopkins Including His Correspondence with Coventry Patmore, edited with notes and an introduction by C. C. Abbott. London, 1938; revised and enlarged, 1956.

S   The Sermons and Devotional Writings of Gerard Manley Hopkins, edited by Christopher Devlin, S.J. London, 1959.

Secondary

Bender   Gerard Manley Hopkins: The Classical Background and Critical Reception of His Work, by Todd K. Bender. Baltimore, 1966.

Boyle   Metaphor in Hopkins, by Robert Boyle, S.J. Chapel Hill, North Carolina, 1961.

Cotter   Inscape: The Christology and Poetry of Gerard Manley Hopkins, by James Finn Cotter. Pittsburgh, 1972.

Gardner   Gerard Manley Hopkins (1844-1889): A Study of Poetic Idiosyncrasy in Relation to Poetic Tradition, by W. H. Gardner. 2 vols. London, 1944, 1949.

Holloway   The Prosodic Theory of Gerard Manley Hopkins, by Marcella Holloway. Washington, D. C., 1947.

Keating   The Wreck of the Deutschland: An Essay and Commentary, by John E. Keating, Kent State University Bulletin, Research Series VI, 1963 (the entire issue).

Lees   *Gerard Manley Hopkins,* by Francis Noel Lees, Columbia
            Essays on Modern Writers No. 21. New York, 1966.

McChesney   *A Hopkins Commentary: An Explanatory Commentary on the
            Main Poems, 1876–89,* by Donald McChesney. London,
            1968.

MacKenzie   *Hopkins,* by Norman H. MacKenzie, Writers and Critics.
            London, 1968.

Mariani   *A Commentary on the Complete Poems of Gerard Manley
            Hopkins,* by Paul L. Mariani. Ithaca and London, 1970.

Martin   *Mastery and Mercy: A Study of Two Religious Poems: 'The
            Wreck of the Deutschland' by G. M. Hopkins and 'Ash
            Wednesday' by T. S Eliot,* by Philip Martin. London, 1957.

Milward   *A Commentary on G. M. Hopkins' The Wreck of the Deutsch-
            land,* by Peter Milward. Tokyo, 1968.

Pick   *Gerard Manley Hopkins: Priest and Poet,* by John Pick.
            London, 1942.

Schneider   *The Dragon in the Gate: Studies in the Poetry of G. M.
            Hopkins,* by Elisabeth W. Schneider. Berkeley, 1968.

Sulloway   *Gerard Manley Hopkins and the Victorian Temper,* by Alison
            G. Sulloway, London, 1972.

Thomas   *Hopkins the Jesuit: The Years of Training,* by Alfred Thomas,
            S.J. London, 1969.

Weyand   *Immortal Diamond: Studies in Gerard Manley Hopkins,* edited
            by Norman Weyand, S.J., with the assistance of Raymond V.
            Schoder, S.J. New York, 1949.

Notes on Contributors

Warren Anderson, professor of comparative literature at the University of Massachusetts, Amherst; has written on Victorian as well as classical literature, and is currently engaged on a book on Hopkins' classicism.

Robert Boyle, S.J., professor of English at Marquette University, Milwaukee; contributor to *Immortal Diamond* (1949), author of *Metaphor in Hopkins* (1961), and article on "Hopkins" in the New Catholic Encyclopedia (1967); currently working on a book on Joyce.

James Finn Cotter, professor of English at Mount Saint Mary College, Newburgh, New York; author of *Inscape: The Christology and Poetry of Gerard Manley Hopkins* (1972).

Marcella M. Holloway, professor of English at Fontbonne College, St. Louis; author of *The Prosodic Theory of Gerard Manley Hopkins* (1947, 1964).

John E. Keating, professor of English at Kent State University before his death in 1972; author of *The Wreck of the Deutschland: An Essay and Commentary* (1963).

Francis Noel Lees, reader in English literature at the University of Manchester, England; author of *Gerard Manley Hopkins* (1966) and contributor to *The Windhover: A Casebook* (1969).

Norman H. MacKenzie, professor of English at Queen's University, Kingston, Canada; editor of *Poems of Gerard Manley Hopkins,* fourth edition (1967), and *Poems by Gerard Manley Hopkins* (1974); author of *Hopkins* (Writers and Critics: 1968); currently preparing an Oxford English texts edition for the press.

Paul L. Mariani, professor of English at the University of Massachusetts, Amherst; author of *A Commentary on the Complete Poems of Gerard Manley Hopkins* (1970), as well as a recent study of William Carlos Williams.

Philip Martin, chancellor and canon of Wells Cathedral; author of *Mastery and Mercy* (1957).

Peter Milward, S.J., professor of English at Sophia University, Tokyo; helped to found the Hopkins Society of Japan; author of *A Commentary on Hopkins' The Wreck of the Deutschland* (1968), *A Commentary on the Sonnets of Hopkins* (1969), and *Landscape and Inscape* (1975).

Raymond V. Schoder, S.J., professor of classics at Loyola University of Chicago; coeditor and contributor to *Immortal Diamond* (1949), and photographer for *Landscape and Inscape* (1975).

Ruth Seelhammer, assistant librarian at Gonzaga University, Spokane, and custodian of the Hopkins Collection; compiler of *Hopkins Collected at Gonzaga* (1970); currently working on a Hopkins volume for the "Thesis Bibliography Series."

Kunio Shimane, assistant professor at Notre Dame University, Okayama, Japan; author of *The Poetry of Hopkins: The Fusing Point of Sound and Sense* (awaiting publication).

Alison G. Sulloway, associate professor in Victorian literature at Virginia Polytechnic; author of *Gerard Manley Hopkins and the Victorian Temper* (1972).